Origami Chicken

Origami Chicken

David Mitchell

BARNES & NOBLE BOOKS
NEW YORK

This edition published by Barnes and Noble Inc.,
by arrangement with PRC Publishing.

2005 Barnes and Noble Books

An imprint of Chrysalis Books Group plc

M 10 9 8 7 6 5 4 3 2 1

ISBN 0 7607 5964 2

Printed in Malaysia

Contents

Introduction

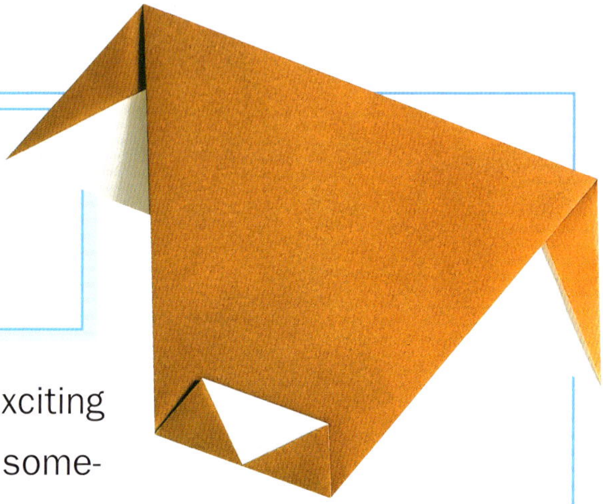

To many people, animal origami is the most exciting and interesting type of paperfolding. There is something almost magical about turning a blank sheet of paper into a swan, a pig or even a jumping frog, using only a few simple and easily learned folds.

Animal origami designs can be as realistic or complicated as you care to make them. Modern advances in paperfolding techniques mean that if you wanted, for instance, to design a sea urchin with the correct number of spines, or a snake complete with every individual scale, you very probably could (though you might need to learn some mathematics to help you). The designs in this book, however, are of a less difficult nature. Simple animal origami designs provide just enough information so that you can recognize the animal for what it is. The mouse in this book, for example, is clearly a mouse; it has a pointed nose, large ears and a long tail, though it does not have eyes, a mouth, or even legs! You have to imagine these details for yourself.

All the designs in this book are easy to fold and understand. They have been organized so that the most basic designs, suitable for absolute beginners, are at the beginning, and those that require slightly more experience are toward the end. You will find that many designs use similar motifs (or folding sequences) that are part of the vocabulary of origami design. The tail of the Pointer and of the Mouse are, for instance, made in similar ways, as are the ears of the Mouse and the horns of the Grazing Buffalo. The Rooster and the Woodpecker start in an identical way.

Some of the designs were created especially for this book, while others are traditional. Many traditional paperfolds come from Japan because that is where the idea of folding paper into representations of animals, birds, fish, and flowers first originated. There are independent paperfolding traditions in other cultures but they are almost completely geometric in nature, the notable exception being the "Little Bird" design, known as the Cocotte in France and the Pajarita in Spain (though it is so little like a bird to look at that it is known as the Hobby Horse in England).

The word traditional is often misunderstood. A traditional design is not necessarily ancient. Traditional simply means that we do not know who created the design or when it was first used. Sometimes there may be some kind of solid historical evidence, a picture of the finished fold or even, very occasionally, diagrams, to show that the design was in existence a hundred or more years ago, but usually the design just exists in the memory of paperfolders, and is passed on from person to person, teacher to pupil, parent to child, or friend to friend.

It is the aim of this book to appeal to the beginner as well as the adept paperfolder. Once you've grasped the basics, perhaps you too will be able to pass on your origami knowledge to others, or even develop some of your own projects. Either way, I am sure you'll enjoy making the origami animals on the following pages.

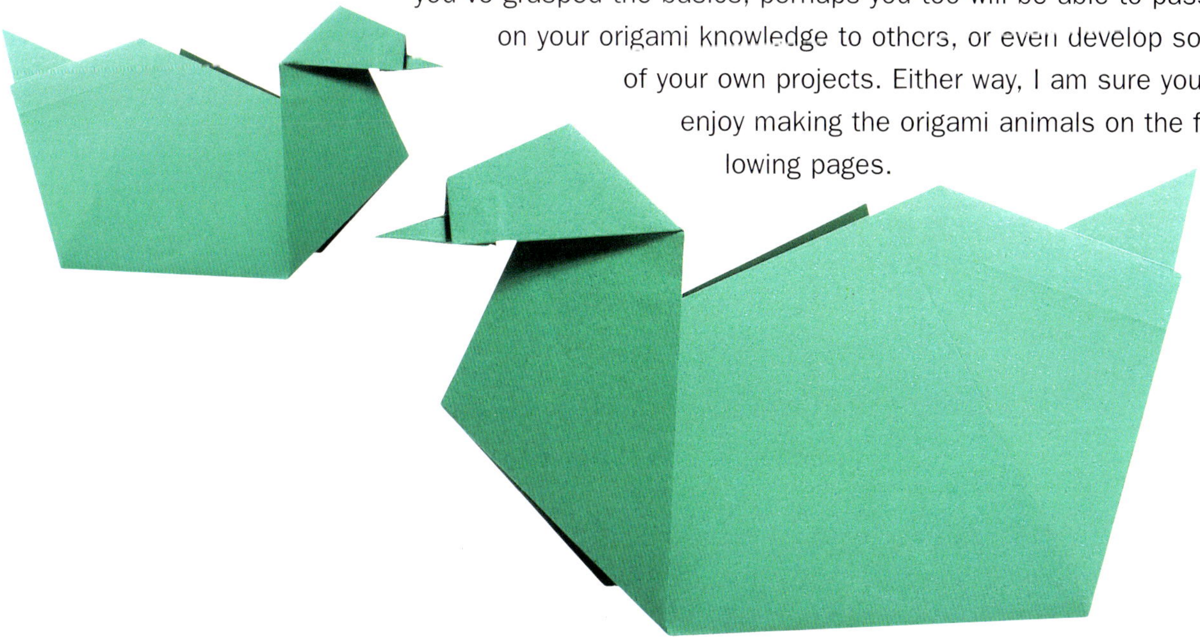

Types of Paper

Manufacturers and retailers of origami paper would like us to believe that you need special paper for folding, but this is not usually the case at all. Almost any kind of paper is suitable for origami. The trick is to find the right paper for the design you are folding, which is why paperfolders' houses are often crammed to the rafters with interesting types of paper.

Some designs work best with thin paper, some with thick; some work best with strong paper, some with soft. Brief guidance on the best type of paper to use for folding the designs in this book is given in the individual project introductions.

Almost all the designs in this book should be made from standard dyed paper, the sort you might use for photocopying. Dyed paper is the same color on both sides (and all the way through). If the instructions refer, for instance, to green paper, it is green dyed paper that you should use.

Bull's Head has been included to show you what can be achieved using differentiated paper, basically white paper that has been overprinted with a single plain color on just one side. Much commercial origami paper is of this kind.

All the folding instructions in this book begin from squares. Commercial origami paper normally comes in this shape, but if you are using dyed paper you will probably need to cut it down to size before you begin folding. If your first attempt at a design comes out a bit floppy try starting from a smaller square. If it is too stiff to finish use a larger one. A way to make four smaller squares out of one large one is given in the instructions for the Easy Hen and Chicks.

How to Cut Squares from Rectangles

The one-crease method—using scissors.

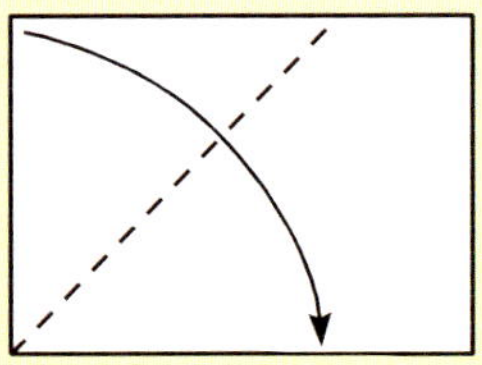

1. Fold the left-hand edge onto the bottom edge. Hold the edges together and crease firmly all along the fold line.

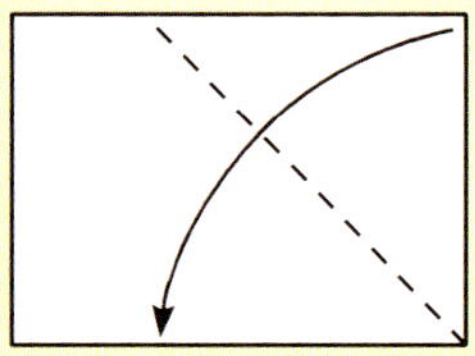

1a. If you are left-handed you will probably find it easiest to make the fold in this direction, but the cut should still be made from bottom to top.

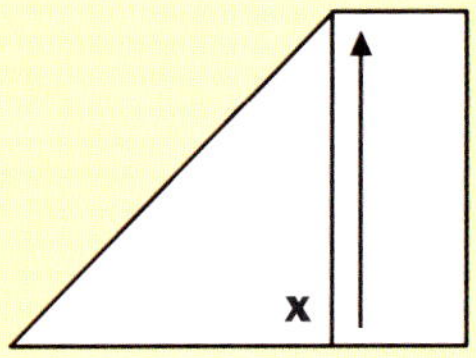

2. Hold the folded sheet firmly, especially at point "x," and cut along the edge of the square, working from the bottom to the top.

The no-crease method—using a craft knife, metal rule, and cutting mat

1. Neatly line up the top and right-hand edges of two identical sheets of paper. Hold both sheets firmly in place.

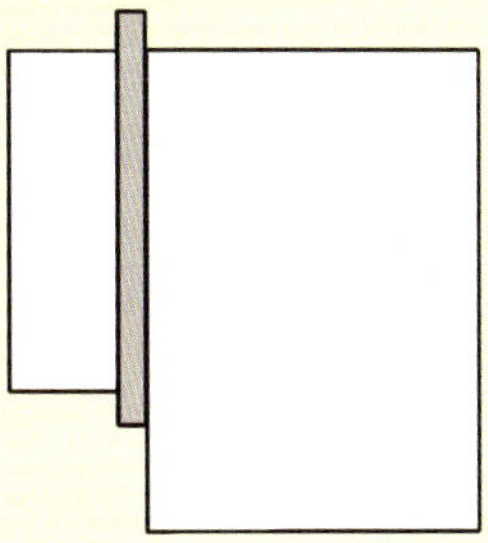

2. Lay the metal rule exactly along the left-hand edge of the top sheet. Hold the rule firmly in place.

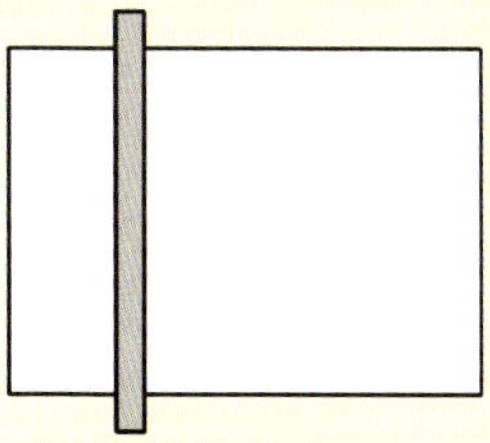

3. Remove the top sheet. Cut along the right-hand edge of the metal rule, taking great care that neither the rule nor the paper moves.

4. The result should be a perfect square. If your knife is sharp enough you can cut several squares at a time in this way.

How to Understand Origami Diagrams

Origami diagrams are drawn as a sequence of "before" and "after" pictures. Each picture is numbered to show the sequence in which they should be read. The "before" pictures are marked with folding symbols that show you which part of the paper moves during the fold, where it ends up, and where the crease will form. The "after" pictures show you what the paper will look like once the fold has been made.

The secret of following origami diagrams successfully is to always look one step ahead. If you know what the result of the fold should look like, before you start to make it, you are much more likely to get it right first time.

Almost all the pictures are accompanied by a written explanation of what is shown. As you become more familiar with origami diagrams you will begin to rely less on the written instructions, so that the pictures will eventually guide you on their own, but at first it's a good idea to read through the words before you start to fold. Incorrect folds can always be unfolded, but your finished design will be crisper and cleaner if you only make folds where they need to be made.

The following diagrams can be used as a visual dictionary, explaining the meaning of all the symbols you will come across while following the folding instructions in this book.

The edges of the paper are shown as solid lines.

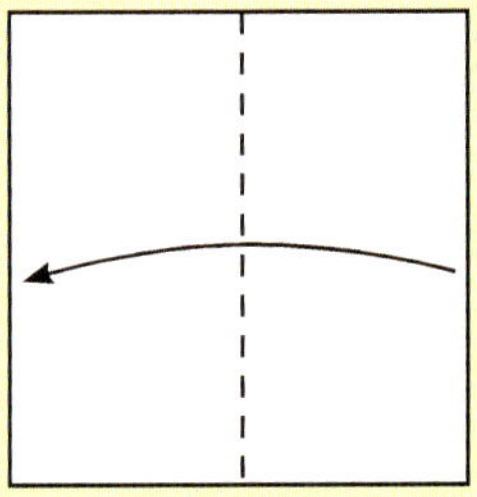

A folding instruction consists of a movement arrow and a fold-line.

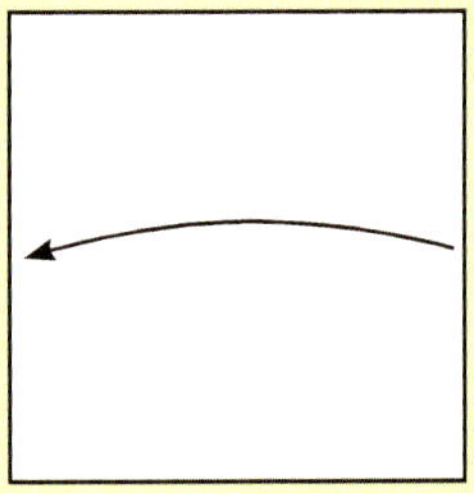

The movement arrow shows the direction in which the fold is made.

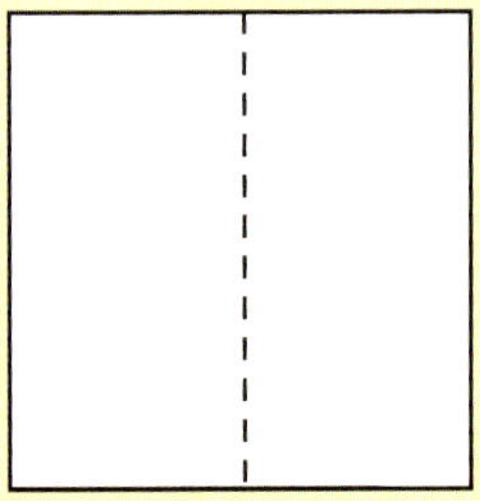

The fold-line shows where the new crease will form. A dashed fold-line means that the fold is made toward you.

Edges which lie exactly on top of each other as the result of a fold are normally shown slightly offset on the "after" diagram.

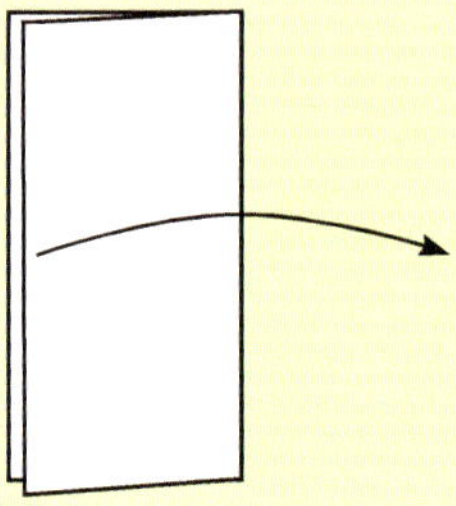

A movement arrow without a fold-line means unfold in the direction indicated.

Creases you have already made are shown as thin lines.

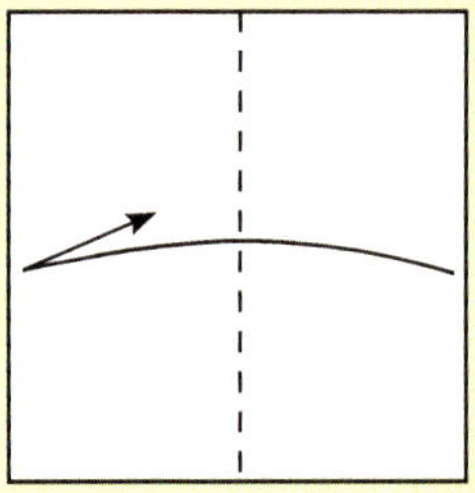

This version of the fold arrow means fold, crease firmly, then unfold.

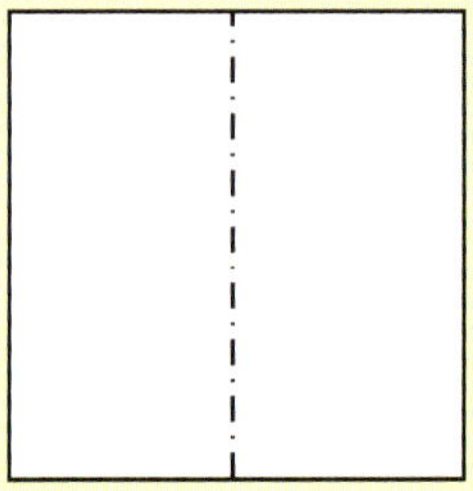

A dashed and dotted fold-line means that the fold should be made away from you.

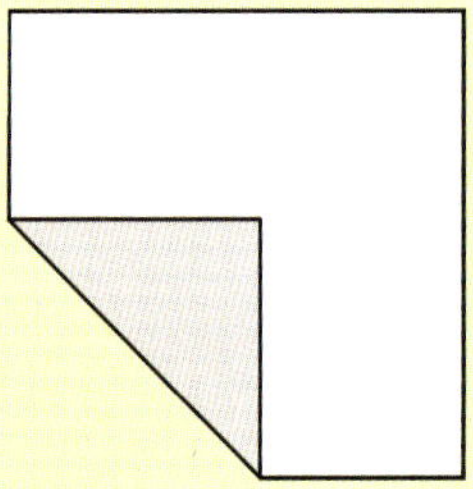

Shading is sometimes used to distinguish one side of the paper from the other.

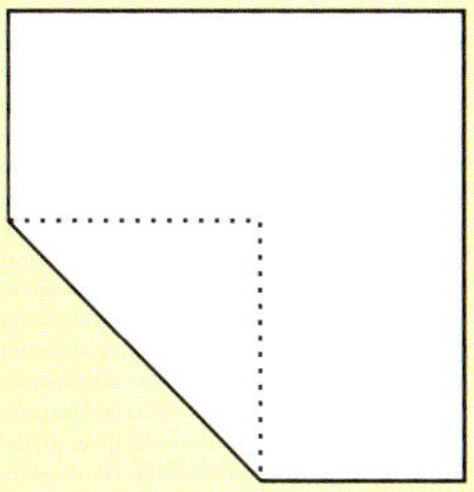

Dotted lines are used to show hidden or imaginary lines.

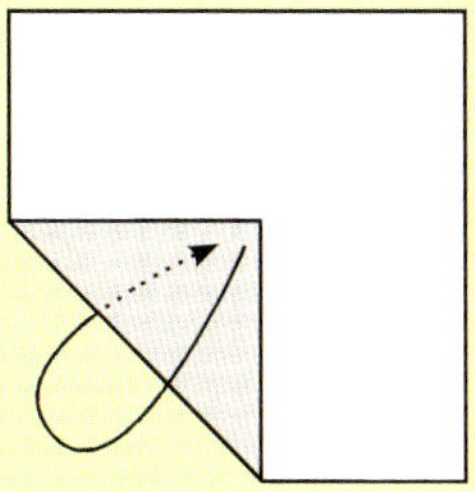

Dotted lines are also used to show the shafts of fold arrows where they pass behind one or more layers of paper. Here it tells you to swivel the flap to the back by reversing the direction of the crease.

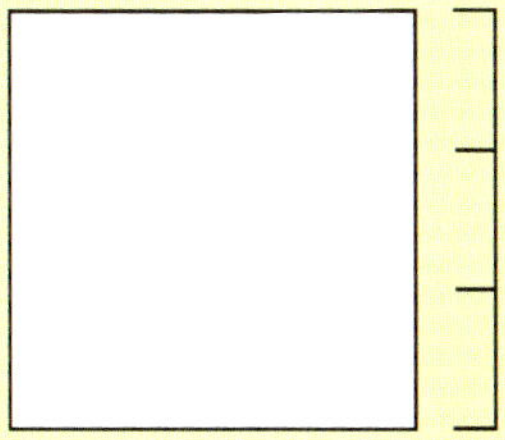

This symbol shows how the adjacent edge can be seen as divided into a number of equal sections to help you locate a fold.

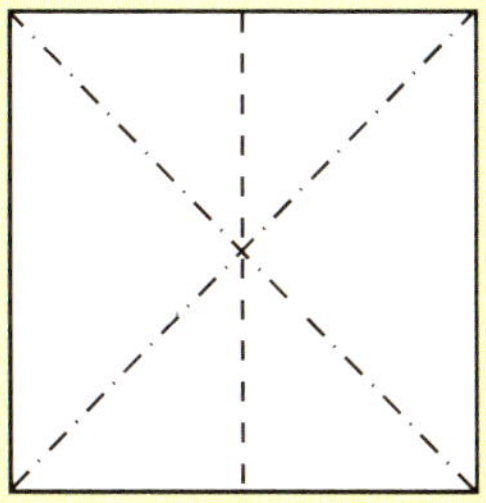

This combination of symbols shows you how existing creases can be used to collapse the paper into a different shape.

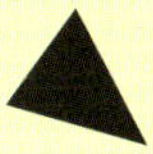

This symbol tells you to apply gentle pressure to the paper in the direction the arrowhead is pointing.

This symbol tells you to move the paper gently in the direction of the arrow.

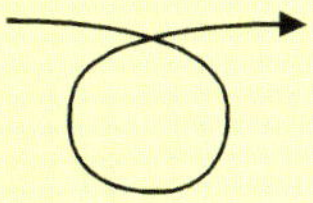

This symbol tells you to turn the paper over sideways.

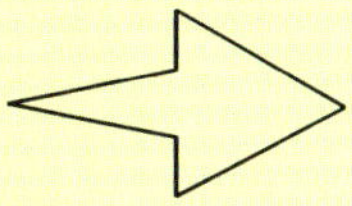

This symbol indicates that the next diagram has been drawn to a larger scale.

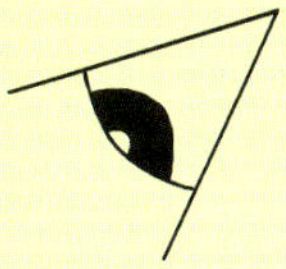

This symbol shows you that the next picture has been drawn from a different viewpoint.

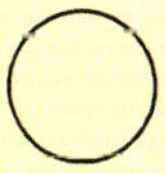

A circle is used to draw attention to a particular area referred to in the written instructions.

Origami Clubs

For those who want to take things further there are specialist origami clubs that arrange meetings, publish magazines, and discuss new designs. The two main English speaking clubs are the British Origami Society and Origami USA, both of which are non-profit making organisations run entirely by volunteers. Both clubs have a worldwide membership base.

Easy Hen and Chicks

If you have never tried your hand at origami before, the Easy Hen is a wonderful place to begin. Once you understand how it is done you will be able to fold a hen (or chick) in just a few seconds. Fold a square of paper in half diagonally, push in one point to form the head, tuck the loose edges under so that the hen will sit, and it's done!

The diagrams, of course, explain how to do this in much greater detail, taking you through the process, one simple step at a time. They also show you how to vary the final folds so that you can create Broody, Watchful, and Feeding Hens—or Chicks!

You will need a square of yellow or light brown paper for each hen or chick. The design will work well from almost any thickness of paper.

Adaptation of a traditional design.

The Broody Hen

Begin with your paper arranged in the way shown in picture 1.

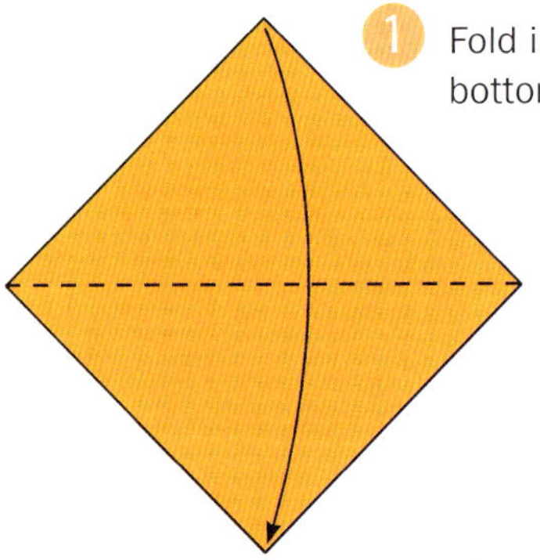

1 Fold in half diagonally from top to bottom.

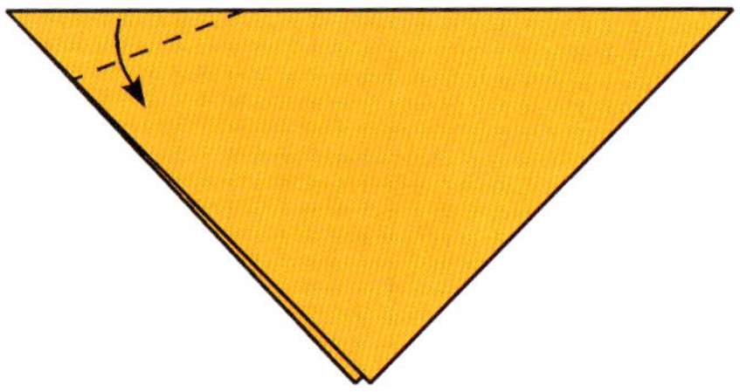

2 Fold the top of the left hand point over in the way shown here. Picture 3 shows what the result should look like. Crease firmly.

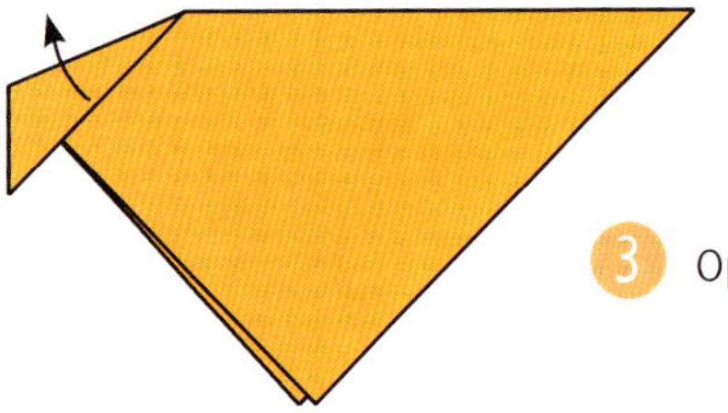

3 Open out the fold made in step 2.

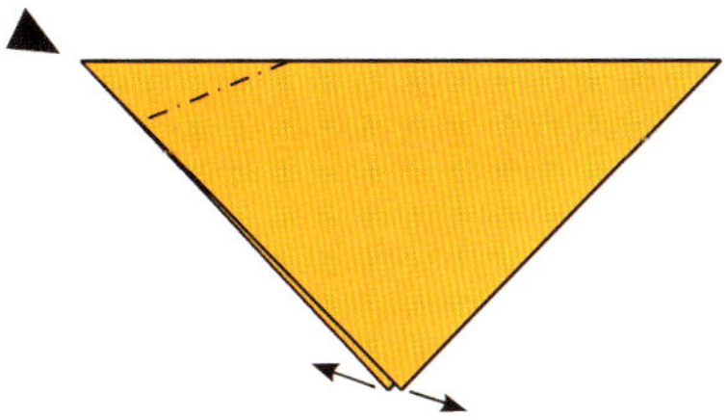

4 Open out the two sides of the model slightly then push gently on the top of the left hand point until it turns inside out between the other layers. The creases you need to achieve this were made in step 2. In technical origami language, this move is called an inside reverse fold. Picture 5 shows what the result should look like.

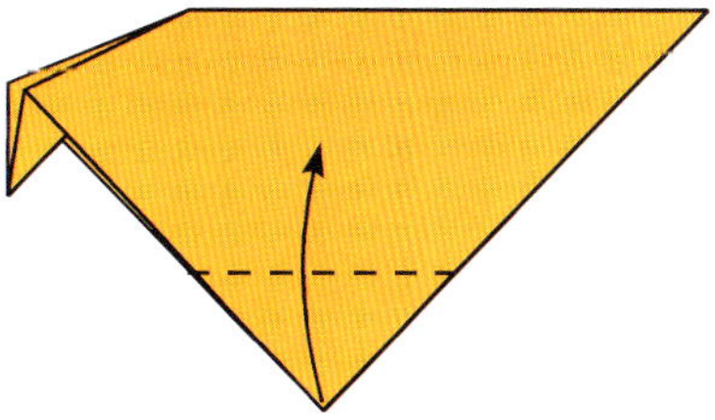

5 Hold the two bottom points together and fold them both upwards like this. Picture 6 shows what the result should look like. Crease firmly.

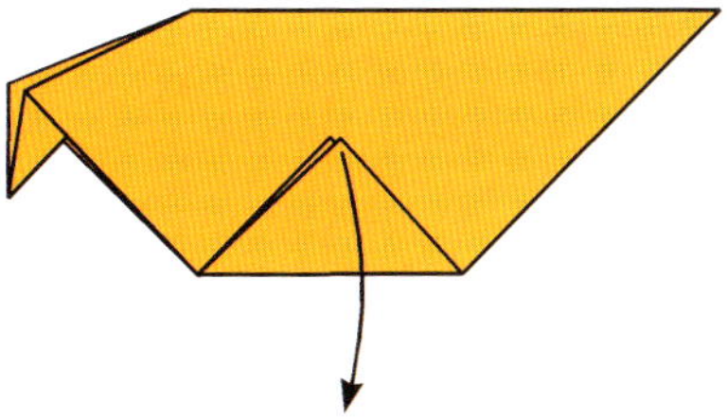

6 Open out the folds made in step 5.

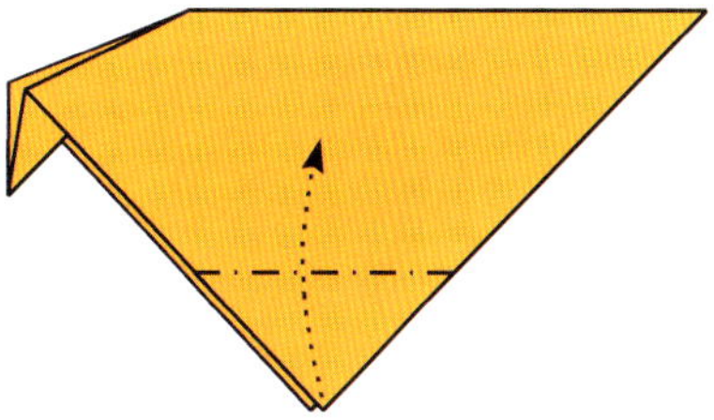

7 Fold the front layer inside the body by reversing the crease made in step 5.

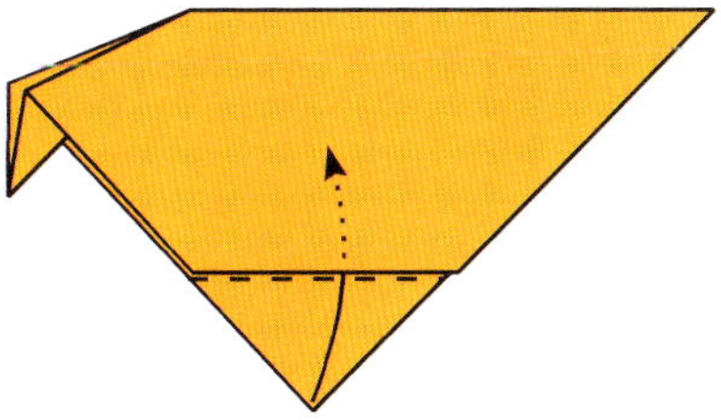

8 Fold the back layer inside the body using the crease made in step 5.

9 The Broody Hen is finished. You can create Feeding and Watchful Hen variations by varying the angle of the fold made in step 5.

Watchful Hen

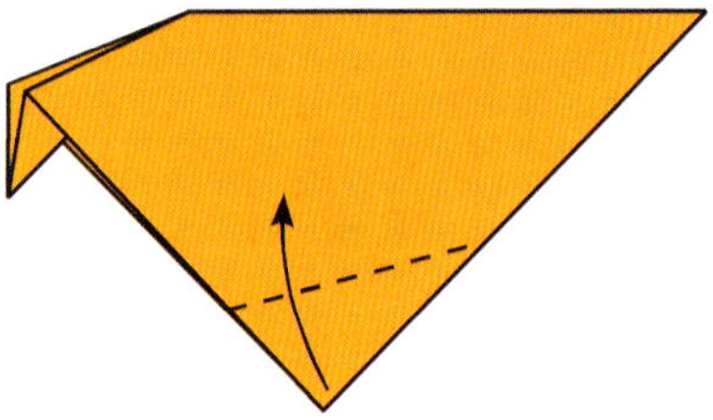

5a Make this fold so that the crease is slightly higher up the body on the right than on the left.

The finished Watchful Hen.

Feeding Hen

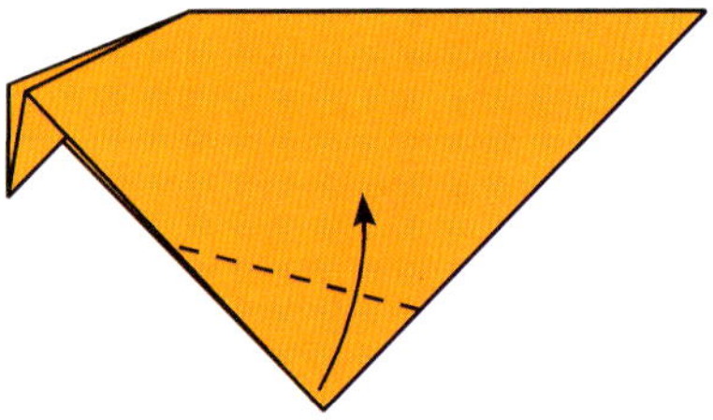

5b Make this fold so that the crease is slightly higher up the body on the left than on the right.

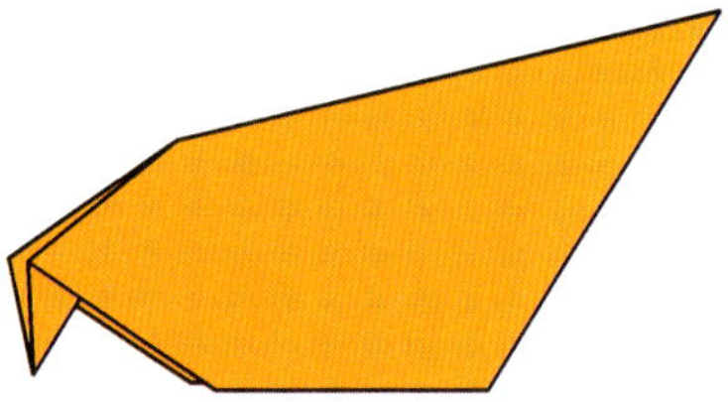

The finished Feeding Hen.

Chicks

You can create chicks simply by starting with smaller squares of paper. Here's how to make quarter size squares.

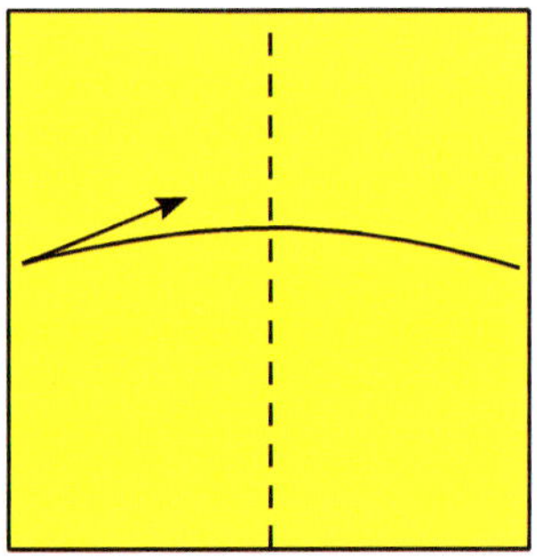

1 Fold in half from right to left, crease firmly, then unfold.

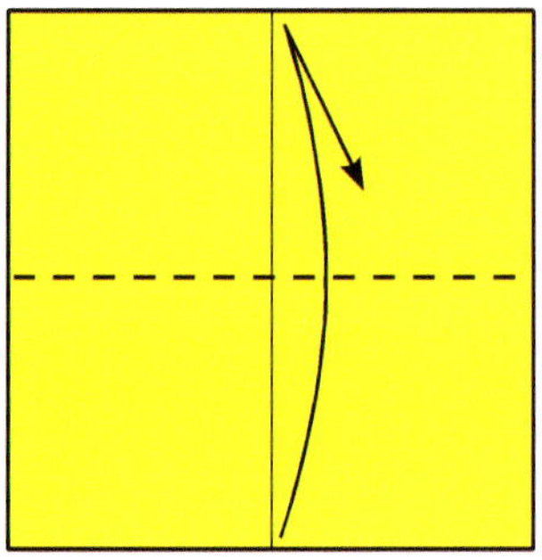

2 Fold in half from bottom to top, crease firmly, then unfold.

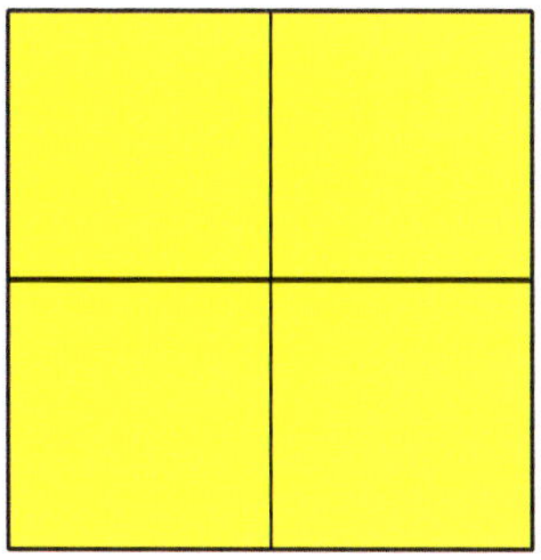

3 Divide the large square into quarters by cutting along the creases.

4 Fold your chicks from these four small squares.

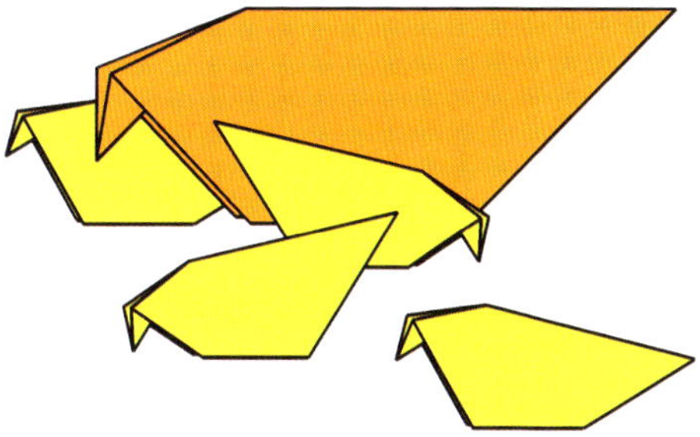

The finished Hen and Chicks.

Quick Crow

The Quick Crow is just that. Quick. All you need to do is make a Feeding Hen out of black paper, then sit it upright on its tail. Hey Presto!—the hen turns into a crow. In origami it is surprising what a big difference a very tiny change can make.

The Quick Crow is made in exactly the same way as the Feeding Hen except that you need to begin with a square of black or dark gray paper. The design will work well from almost any thickness of paper.

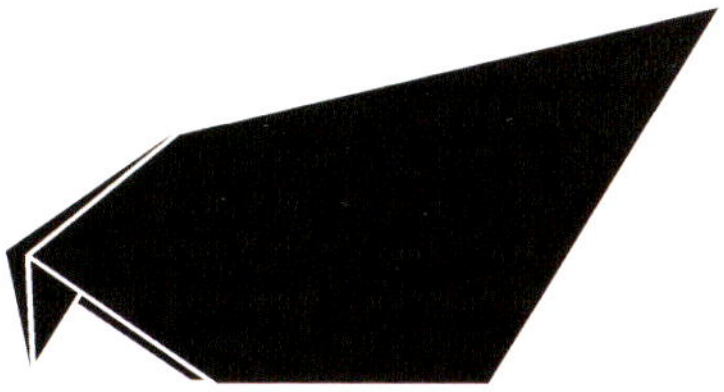

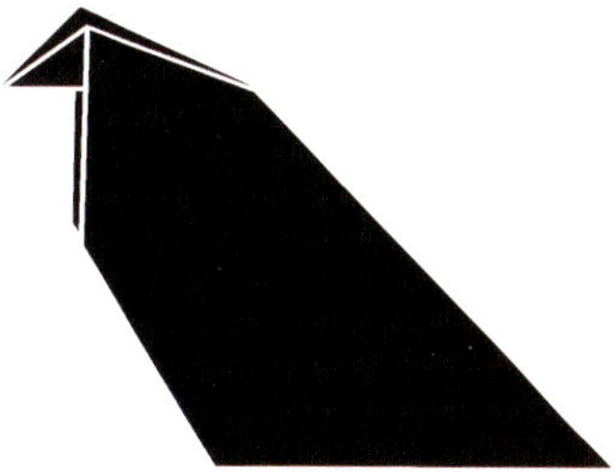

1 This is the Feeding Hen. To create the Quick Crow simply push the tip of the tail downwards until the model stands upright.

2 The Quick Crow is finished.

Secret Chickens

The secret of the Secret Chickens is that they have pockets hidden within the folds in which messages or other tiny objects can be concealed. The head of the Secret Chicken is made in the same way as the head of the Easy Hen, but the body and tails are made using much more sophisticated folding techniques. The way the shape of the body is produced in steps 14 and 15 is one of the best moves in the repertoire of traditional origami. Enjoy it!

You will need a square of yellow or light brown paper for each Secret Chicken. For best effect use fairly thin paper.

Basic Secret Chicken and Swallowtail Secret Chicken are traditional Japanese designs.
Fantail Secret Chicken is a modern variation by David Mitchell.

Basic Secret Chicken

Begin with your paper arranged in the way shown in picture 1.

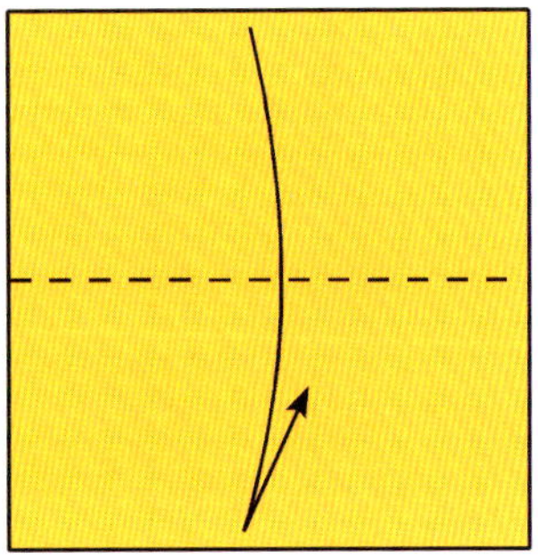

1 Fold in half from top to bottom, crease firmly, then unfold.

2 Turn over sideways.

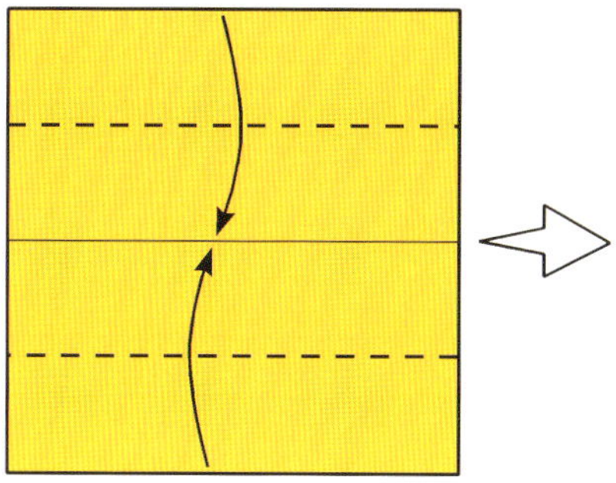

3 Fold both the top and bottom edges inward to lie along the crease made in step 1. The next picture has been drawn to a larger scale.

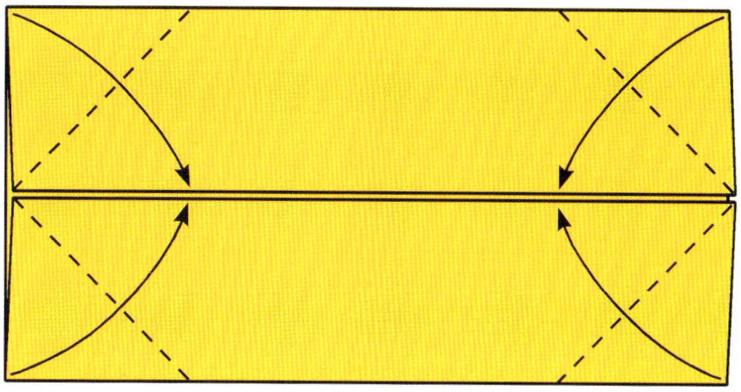

4 Fold all four corners inward as shown.

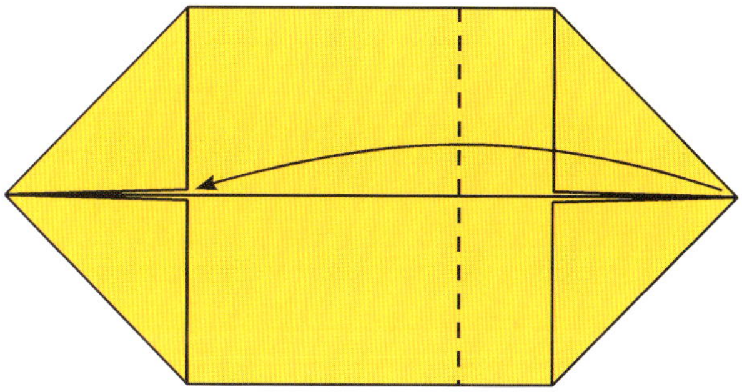

5 Fold the right-hand point inward to the left as shown.

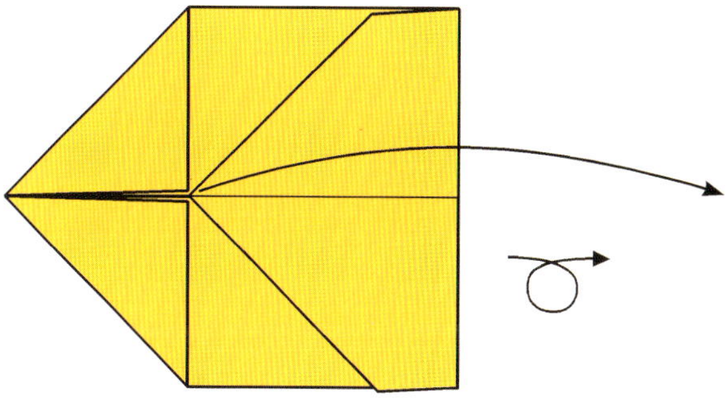

6 Open out the fold made in step 5. Turn over sideways.

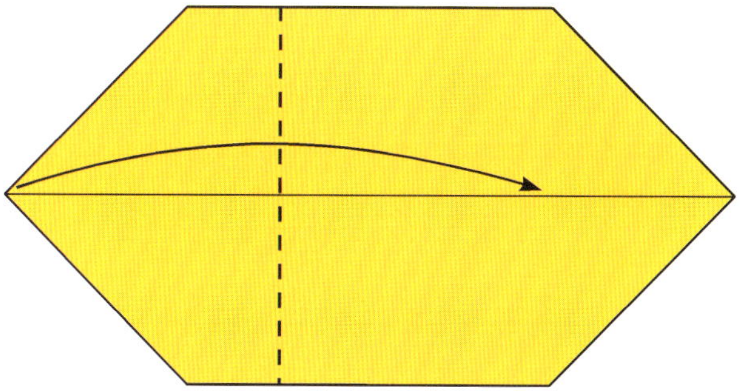

7 Fold the left hand point inward to the right by reversing the direction of the crease made in step 5.

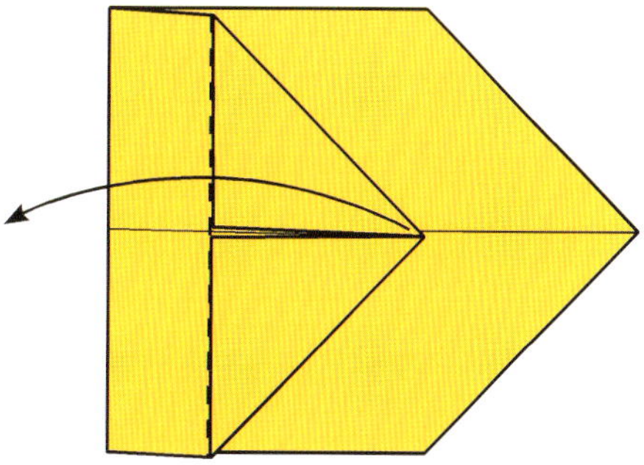

8 Fold the front layers back out to the left using the vertical edges of the small triangular flaps as a guide to where the crease should form.

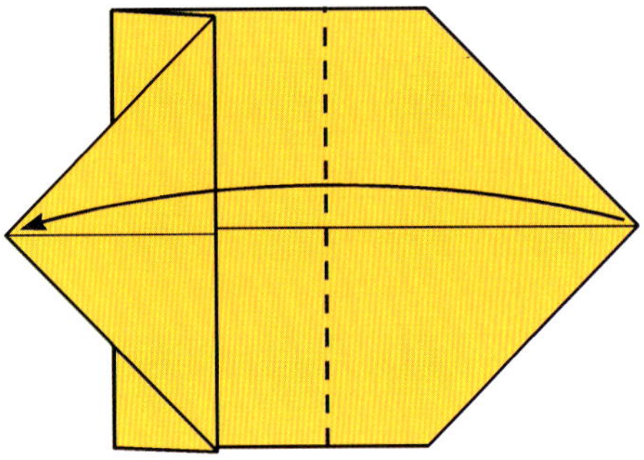

9 Fold the right-hand point onto the left-hand point. Crease firmly.

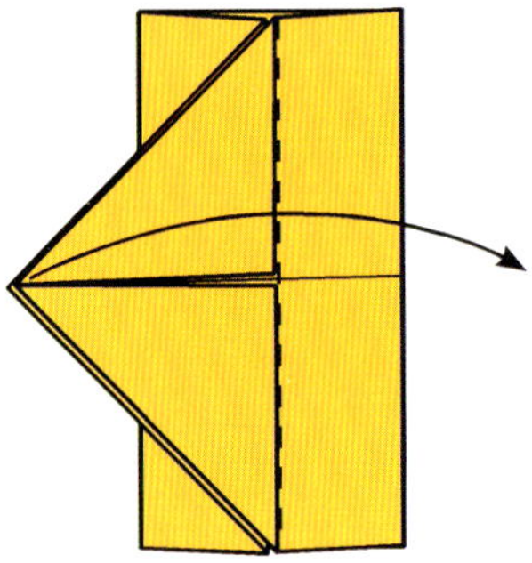

10 Fold the right-hand point back out to the right, using the vertical edges of the small triangular flaps as a guide to where the crease should form.

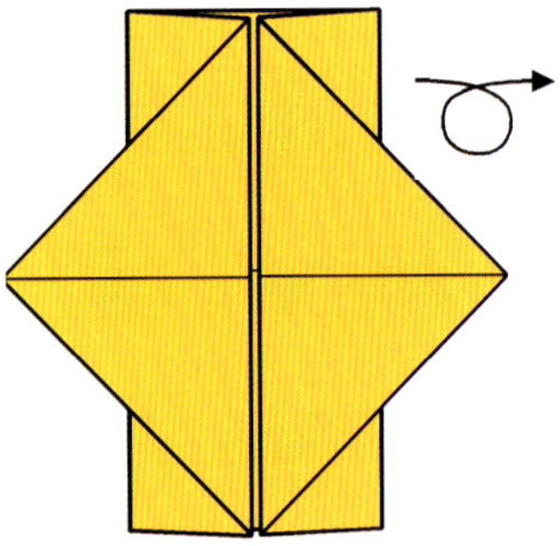

11 Turn over sideways.

12 The Secret Chicken has concealed pockets in which secret messages or other tiny objects can be hidden.

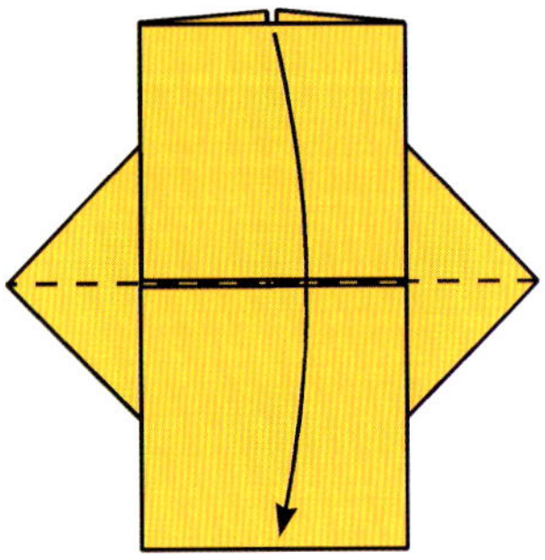

13 Fold in half from top to bottom to hide the pockets.

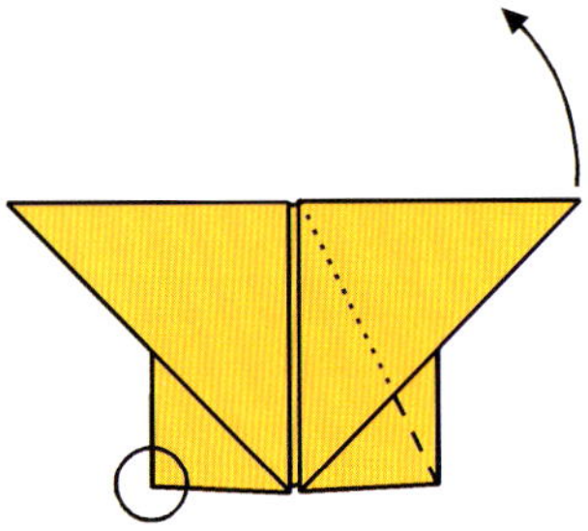

14 Hold the lower left-hand corner with your left hand and use your right hand to pull the top right-hand point upward as far as it will go. Picture 15 shows how it should look.

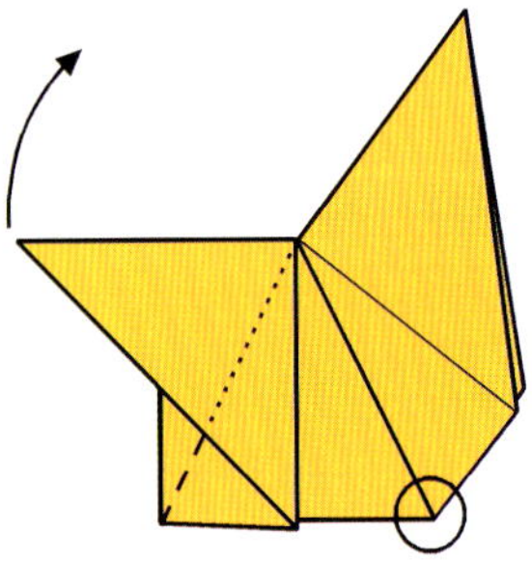

15 Repeat step 14 on the left-hand side of the paper.

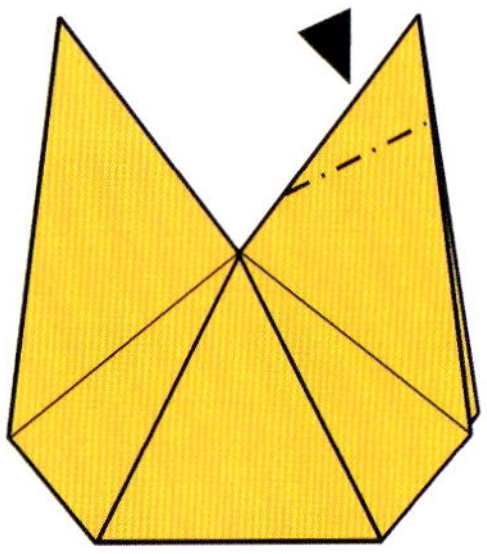

16 Turn either of the top points inside out to form the head and beak. (See steps 2 to 4 of the Easy Hen.)

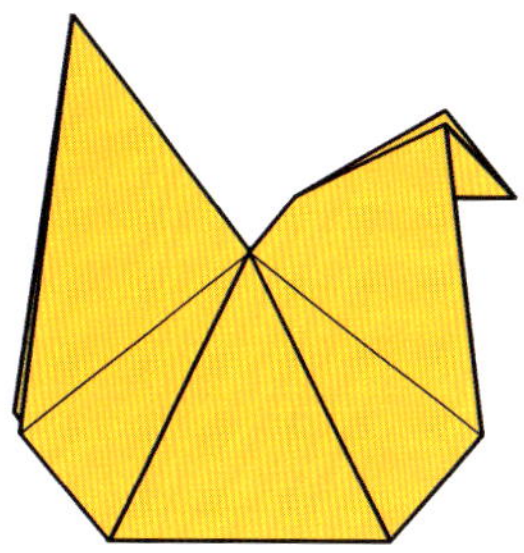

17 The finished Basic Secret Chicken.

Swallowtail Secret Chicken

Begin by folding a Basic Secret Chicken. Then continue with steps 18–21 shown below to create the Swallowtail Secret Chicken.

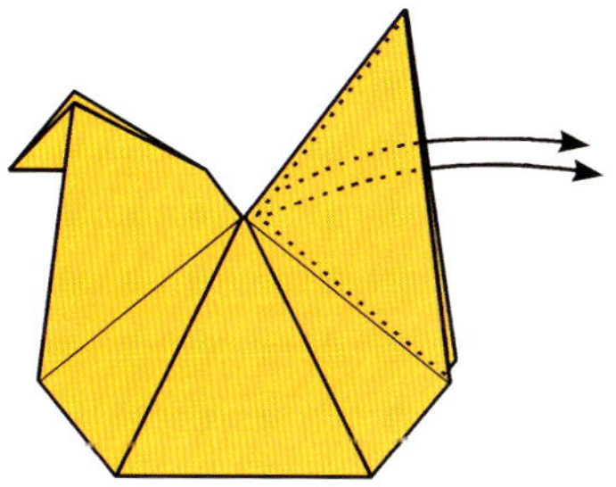

18 Pull out both the flaps hidden inside the tail.

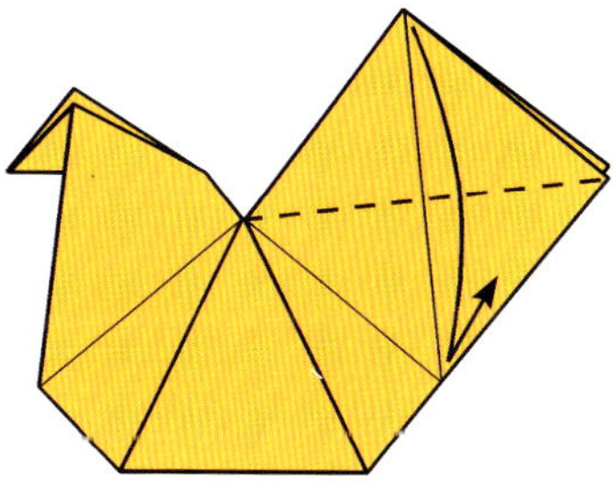

19 Fold the tail in half from top to bottom, crease firmly then unfold.

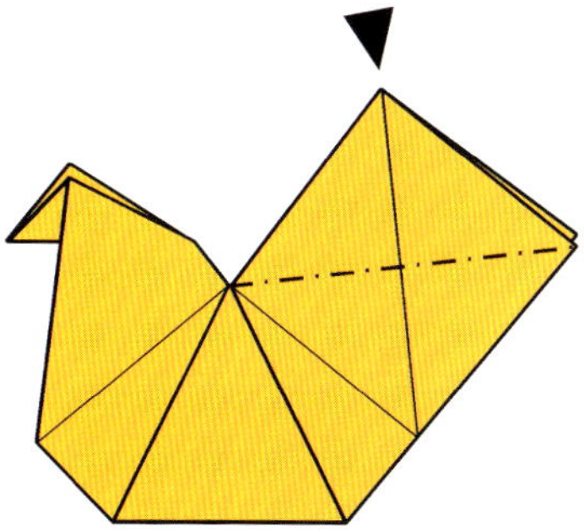

20 Turn the top half of the tail inside out between the layers using the crease made in step 19.

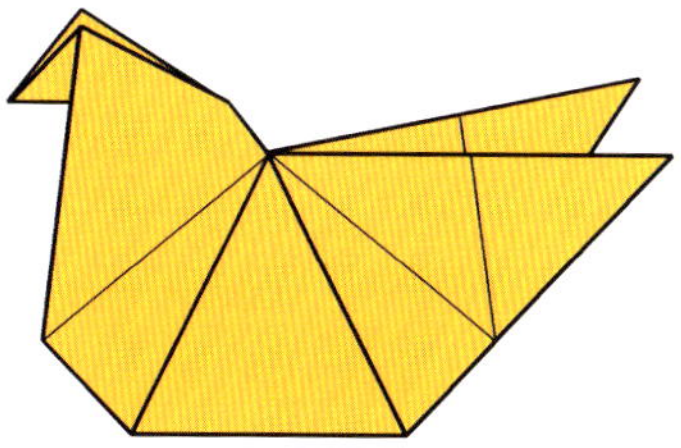

21 Spread the tail to taste. The Swallowtail Secret Chicken is finished.

Fantail Secret Chicken

Begin by following steps 1 through 5 of the Basic Secret Chicken then follow steps 22 through 35 below.

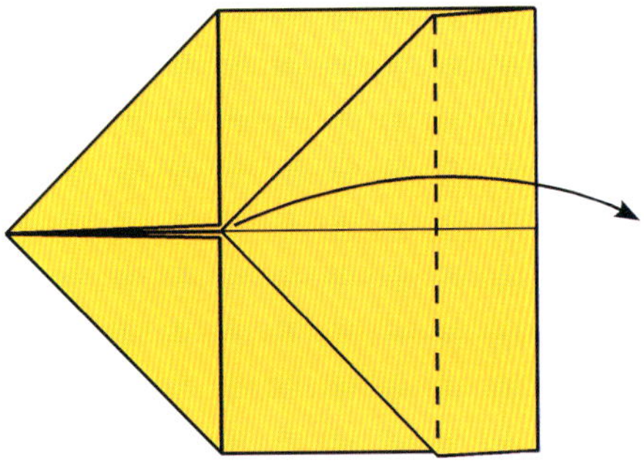

22 Fold the front layers back out to the right using the vertical edges of the small triangular flaps as a guide to where the crease should form. Picture 23 shows what the result should look like.

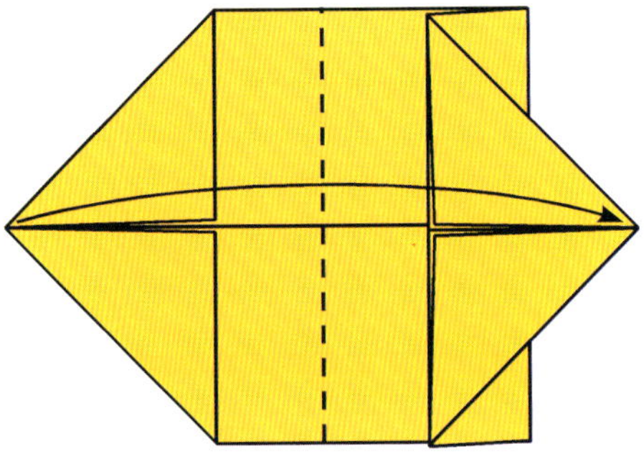

23 Fold the left hand point onto the right-hand point.

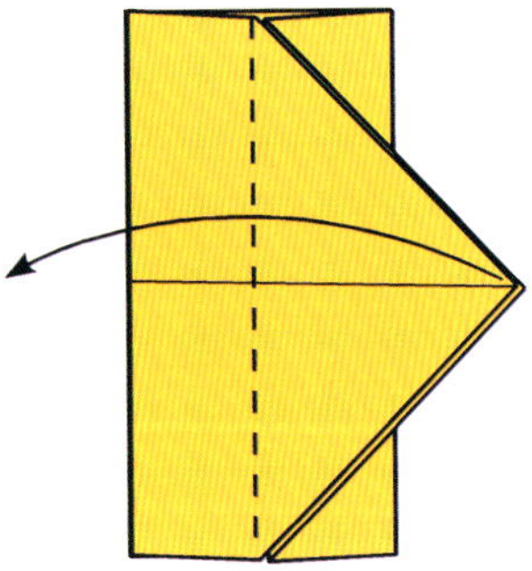

24 Fold the front layers back out to the left, using the vertical edges of the small triangular flaps as a guide to where the crease should form. This is a repeat of step 22.

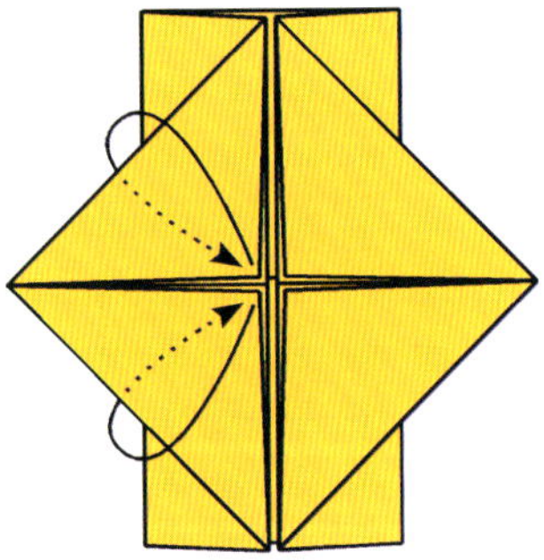

25 Fold the left-hand pair of triangular flaps away into the pocket behind them.

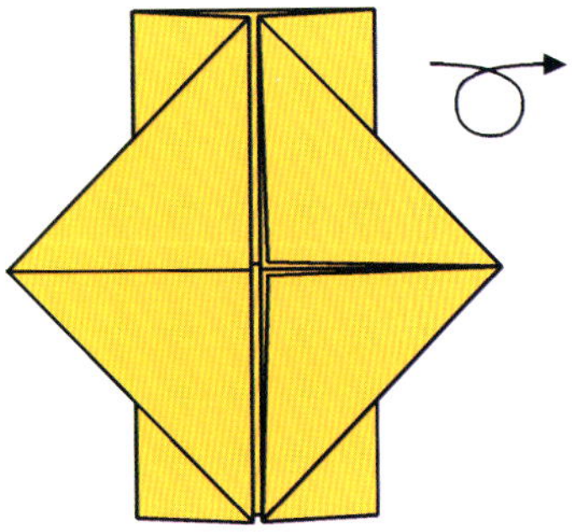

26 Turn over sideways.

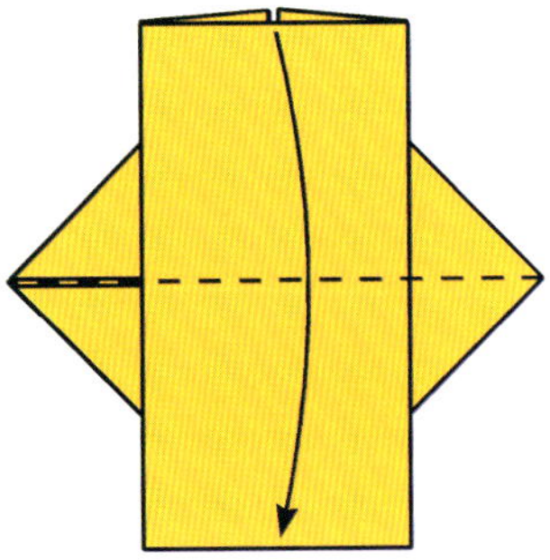

27 Fold in half from top to bottom.

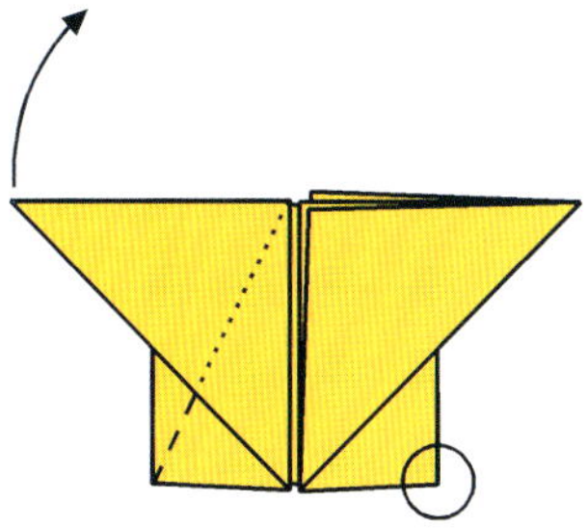

28 Hold the lower right-hand corner with your right hand and use your left hand to pull the top left hand point upwards as far as it will go. Picture 29 shows the result.

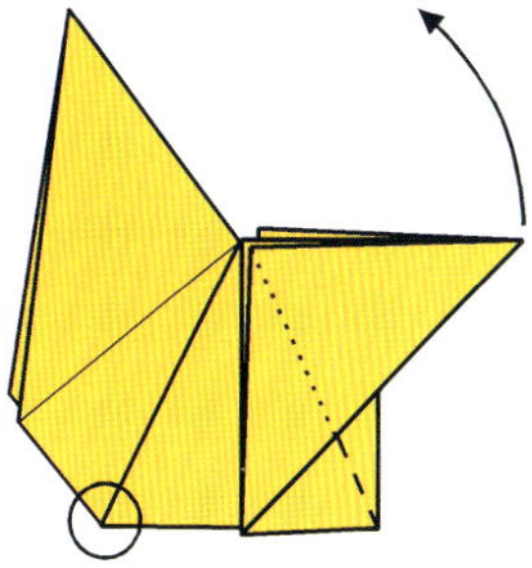

29 Repeat step 28 on the right hand side of the paper.

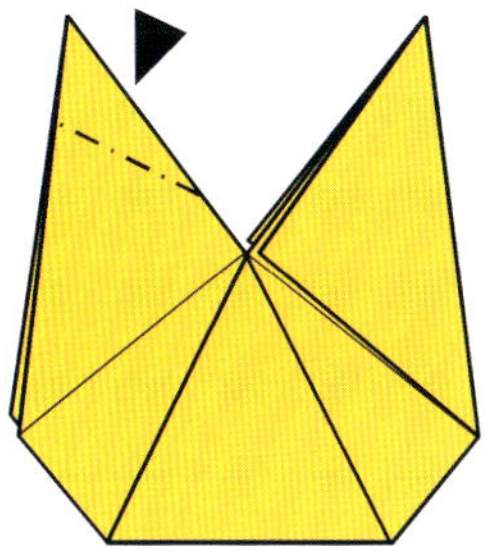

30 Turn the left hand top point inside out to form the head and beak.

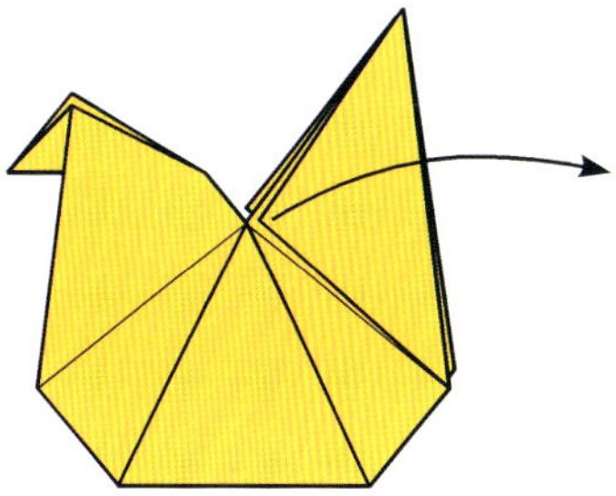

31 There are triangular flaps in front of and behind the tail. Swing the front flap across to the right.

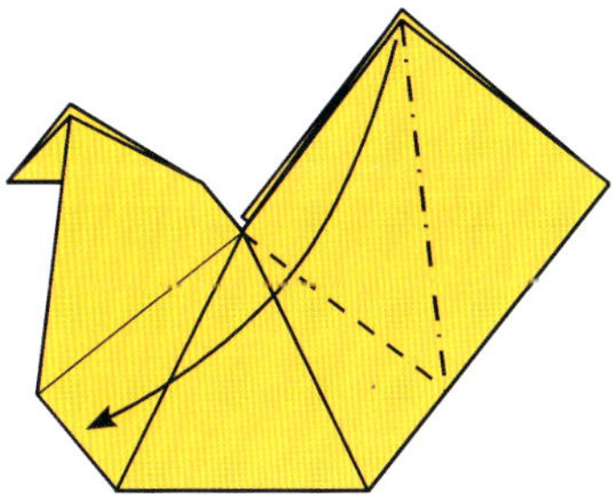

32 Fold the tip of the front layer of the tail across to the left as shown. All the creases you need are already there.

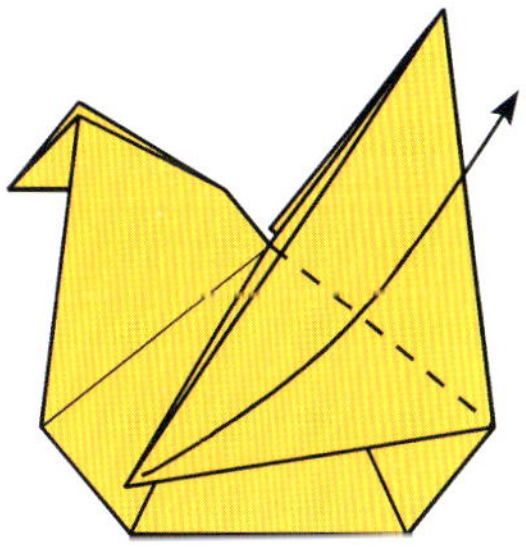

33 Fold the tip of the front layer of the tail back across to the right.

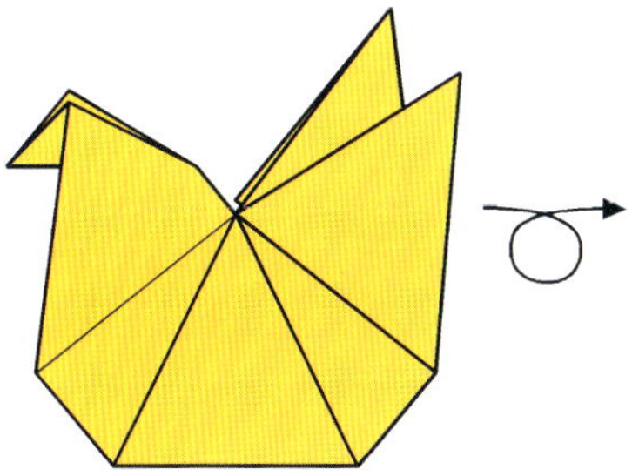

34 Turn over sideways and repeat steps 31 through 33 on the other side of the design.

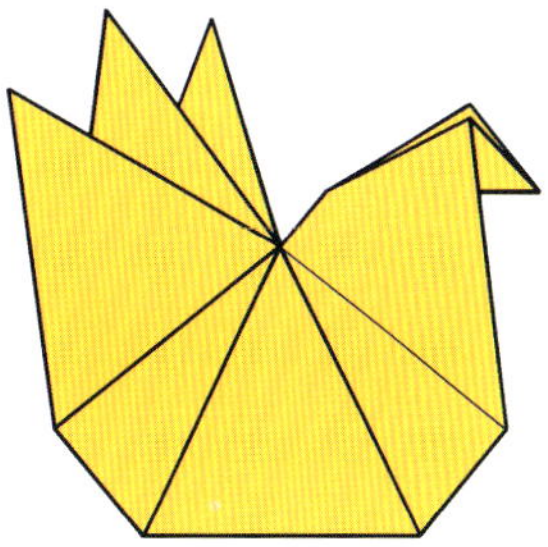

35 Spread the tail to taste. The Fantail Secret Chicken is finished. This Secret Chicken still has hidden pockets but now they are really well concealed.

Basic Duck

The Basic Duck is made from a standard intermediate fold known as the Kite Base (pictured in step 4). It can be varied and improved in many ways. The diagrams show you how to make the most basic of Basic Ducks and then how to improve the head and the tail to produce a much more life-like result.

Origami is not only about following diagrams to accurately reproduce a design. It is also about experimenting for yourself to find out what difference a small change here and there can make. If you want to do this then the Basic Duck is a great design to experiment with.

One of the experiments you might like to try is folding the Basic Duck from paper that is white one side and colored the other. Many different partly white and partly colored Basic Ducks can be made.

You will need a square of green, brown or white paper for each Basic Duck. The design will work well from almost any thickness of paper.

Adaptation of a traditional design.

Begin with your paper arranged in the way shown in picture 1.

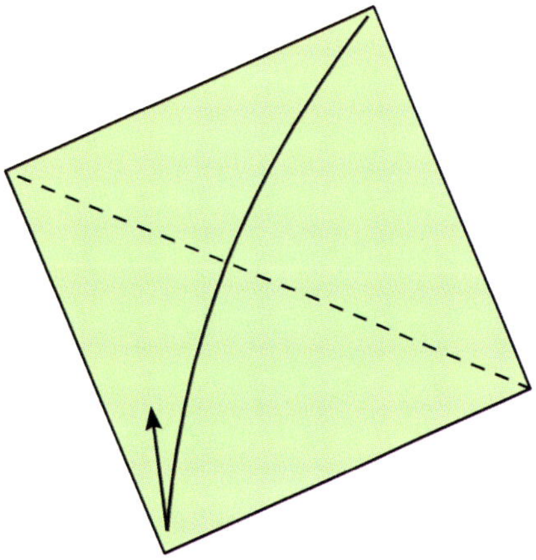

1 Fold in half from top to bottom, crease firmly, then unfold.

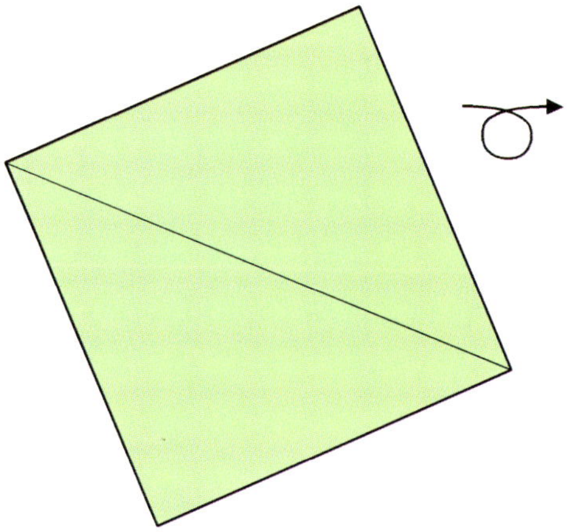

2 Turn over sideways.

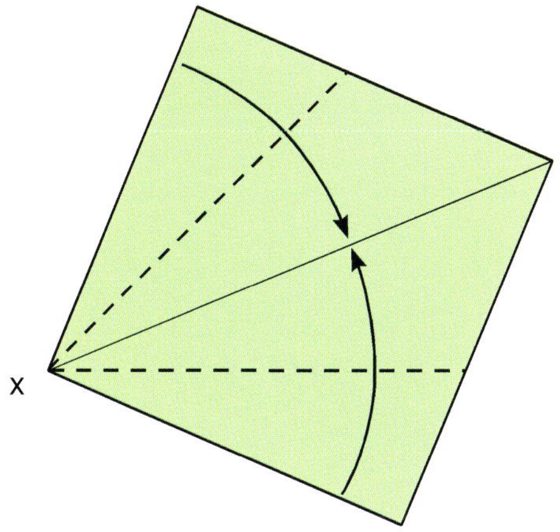

3 Fold both the bottom and right-hand edges inward to lie along the crease made in step 1, leaving a tiny gap between the edges. Try to make sure point x remains sharp.

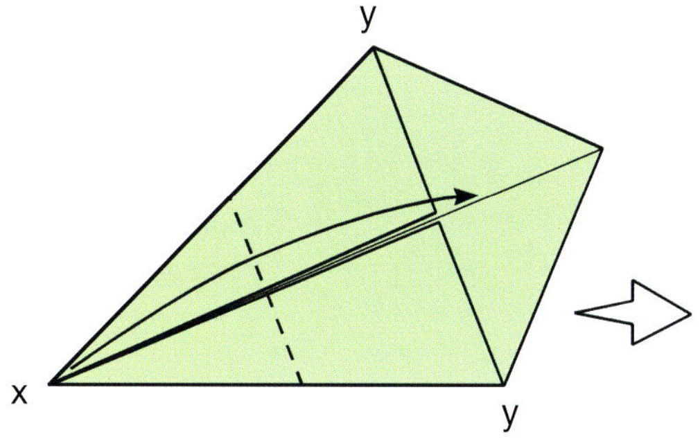

4 Make this fold softly. Point x ends up just a little to the right of line yy. Picture 5 shows what the result should look like. (Making a fold softly means not pressing the crease completely flat.) The next picture has been drawn to a larger scale.

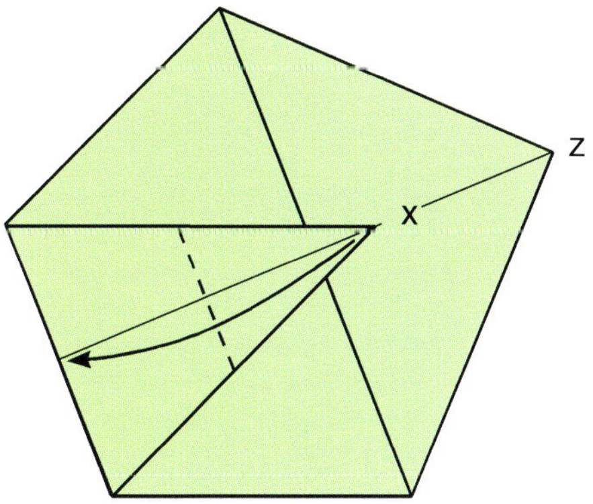

5 Make the next fold softly as well.

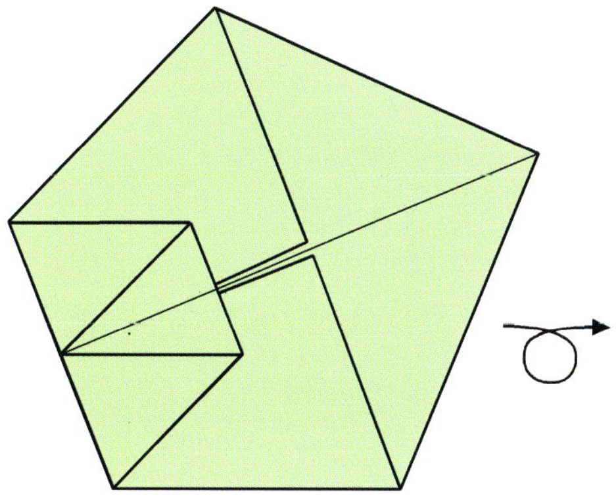

6 Turn over sideways.

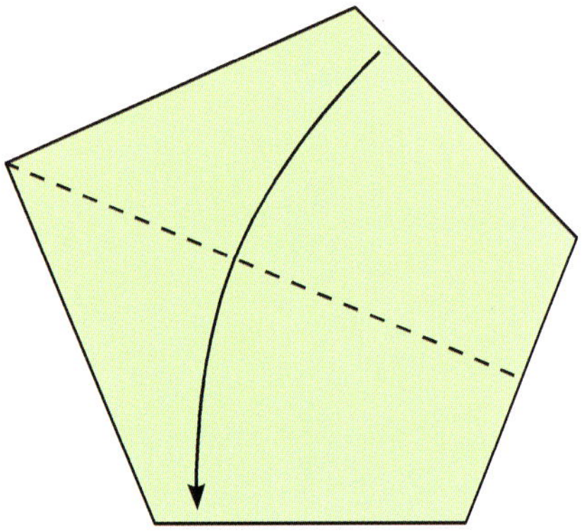

7 Fold in half from top to bottom as shown.

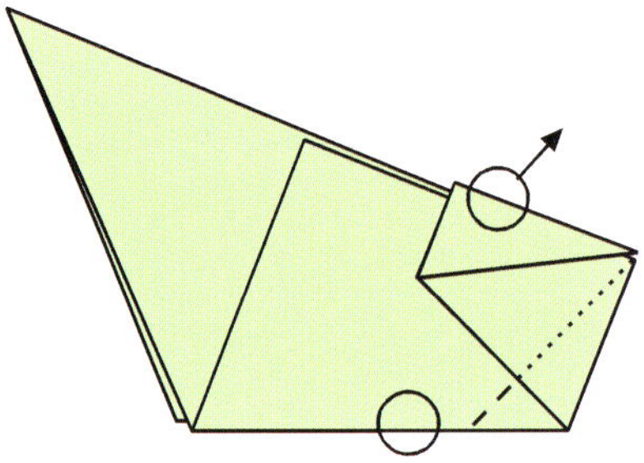

8 Hold the bottom of the paper in one hand. With your other hand grip the top of the head and pull gently upward to separate the neck from the body. Flatten to form a new crease, as shown in picture 9.

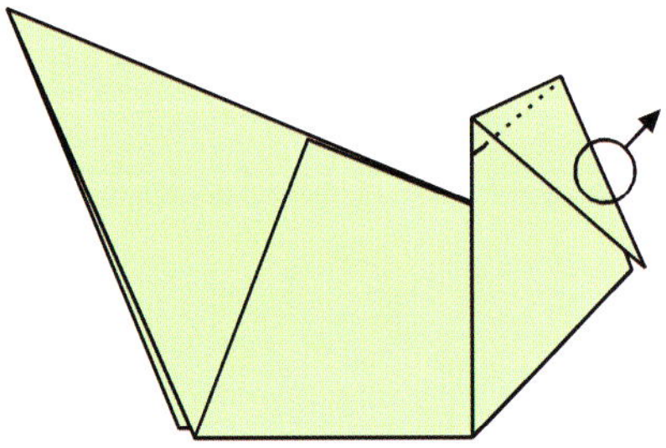

9 Lift the beak upward and flatten to form a new crease, as shown in picture 10.

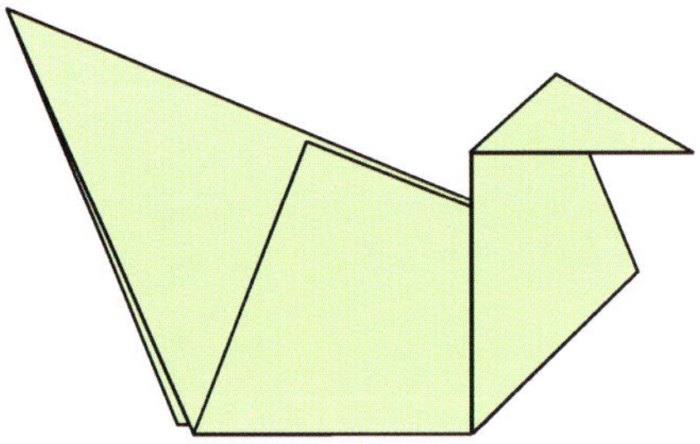

10 The Basic Duck is finished. You can change the relative proportions of body, neck, and head by varying the position of folds 5 and 6. Repeating fold 5 and making point x move closer to z increases the amount of paper available to form the neck and head.

Improving the Head

Begin by making a duck with a head that looks too big compared to the size of its body. See step 10 for how to achieve this.

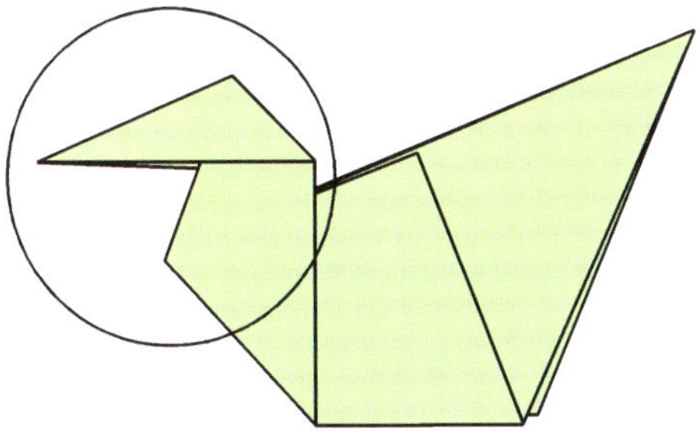

11 To improve the Duck's head follow the instructions in the enlargements.

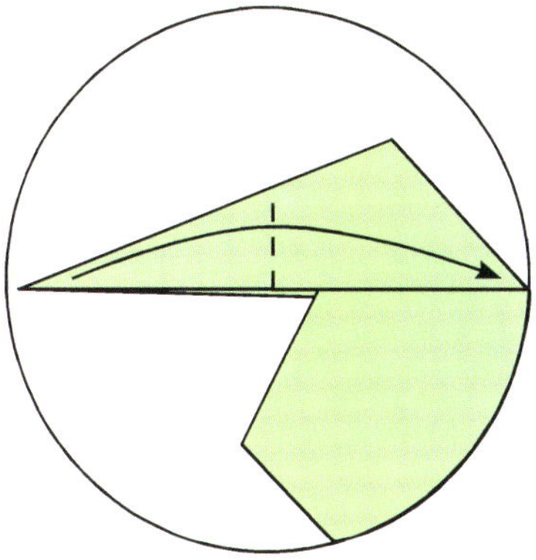

12 Fold the tip of the beak to the back of the head as shown.

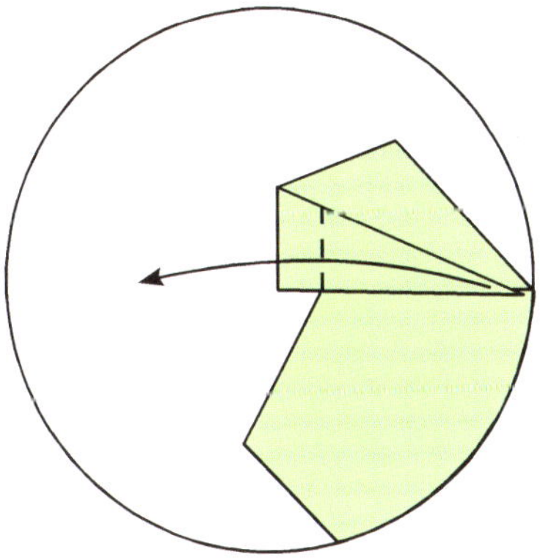

13 Fold the tip of the beak back out to the left.

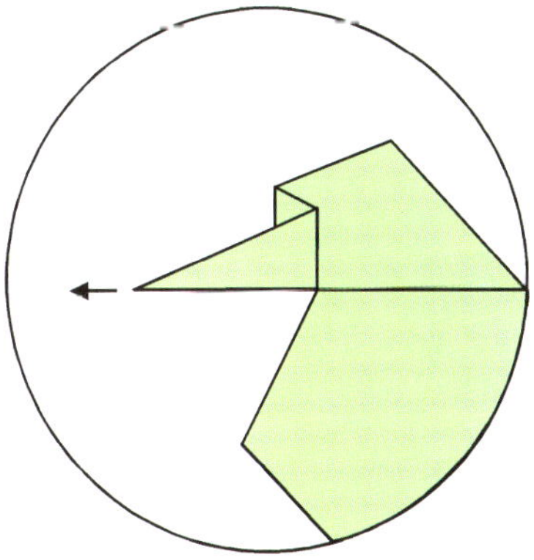

14 Open out the folds made in steps 12 and 13.

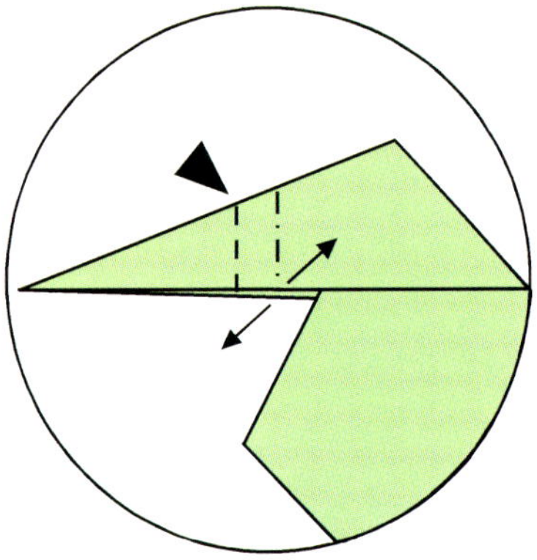

15 Open the layers at the bottom of the head and tuck the folds into a zigzag between the layers of the head, using the creases made in steps 12 and 13. Picture 16 shows what the result should look like.

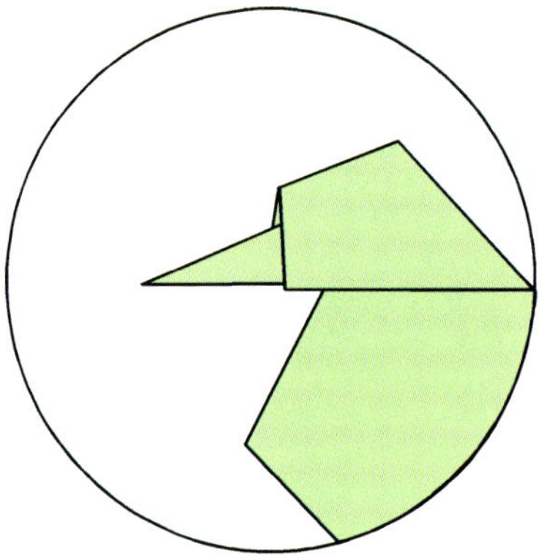

16 The improved head is finished.

Improving the Tail

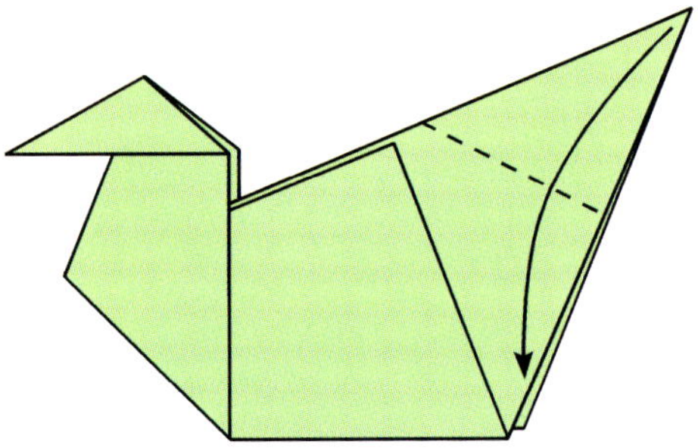

17 Fold the tip of the tail downward.

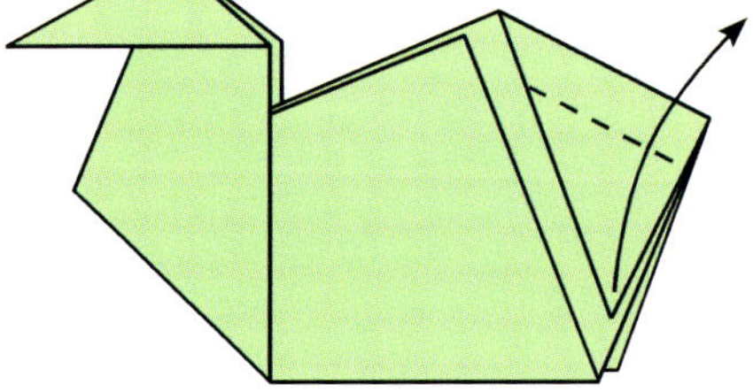

18 Fold the tip of the tail upward again as shown.

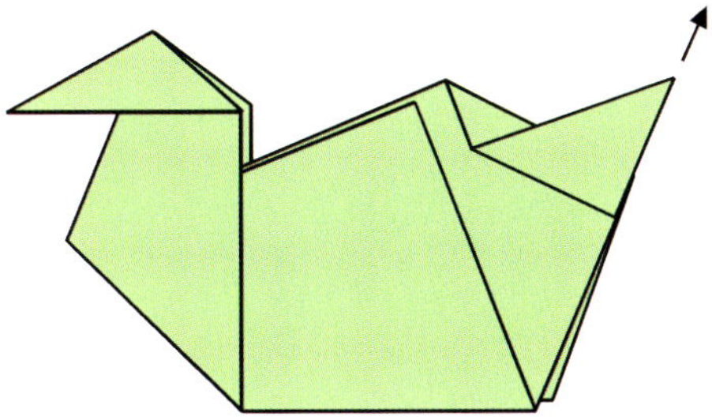

19 Open out the folds made in steps 17 and 18.

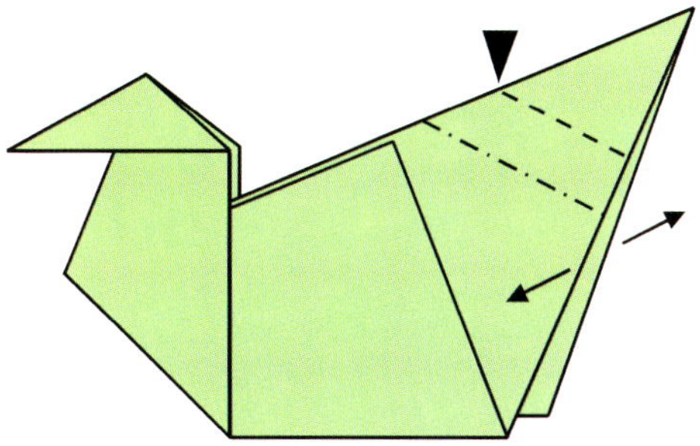

20 Separate the layers of the tail and tuck the paper into a zigzag in between the layers of the body, using the creases made in steps 17 and 18. Picture 21 shows you what the result should look like.

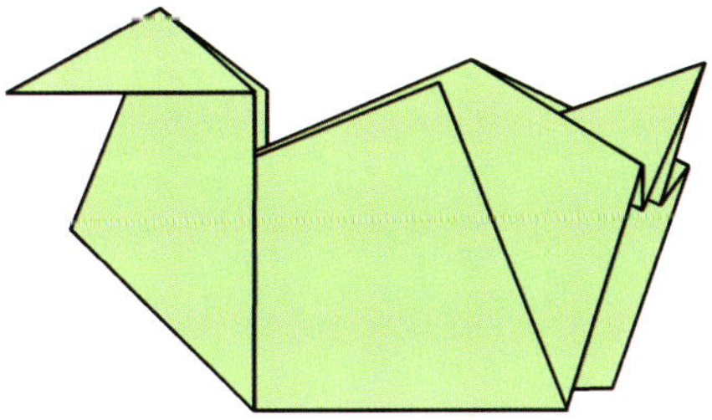

21 The improved tail is finished.

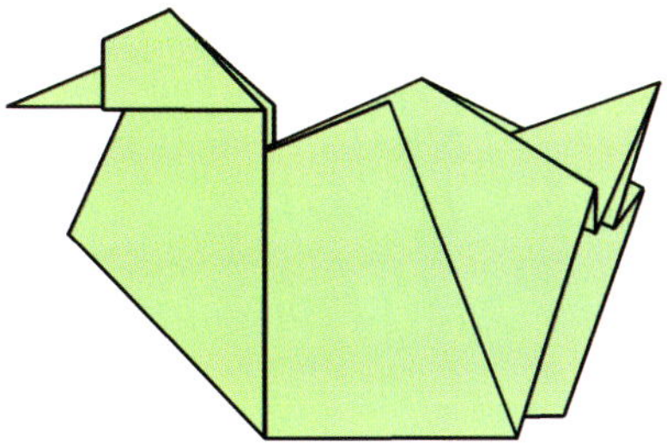

22 A not so basic Basic Duck with improved head and tail.

Turkey

The Turkey is a development of the Basic Duck. The character of the design is completely changed by reshaping the tail. You can try to give the Turkey an improved head, but you will find that there is little paper to spare.

It is worth comparing the way in which the folds that form the head and neck are created with the way the same folds were created for the Basic Duck. Either method will work. The diagrams for the Basic Duck explain a method suitable for absolute beginners that will only work on very basic designs. The diagrams for the Turkey explain an alternative method that can be used on more complex designs as well. You will need a square of brown paper for each Turkey. The design will work well from almost any thickness of paper.

Adaptation of a traditional design.

Begin by following steps 1 through 3 of the Basic Duck, then arrange the paper in the way shown here in the first picture.

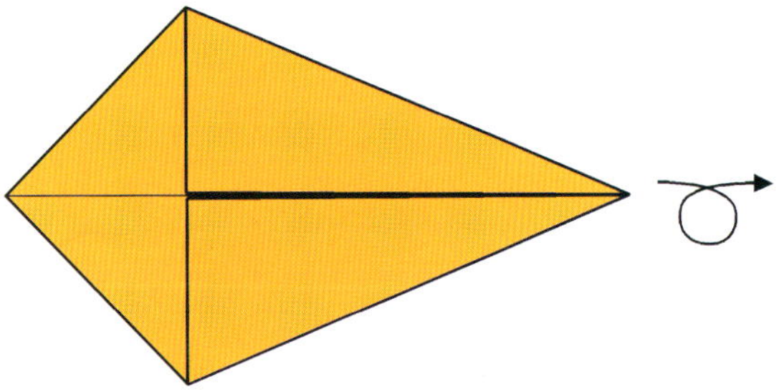

1 Turn over sideways.

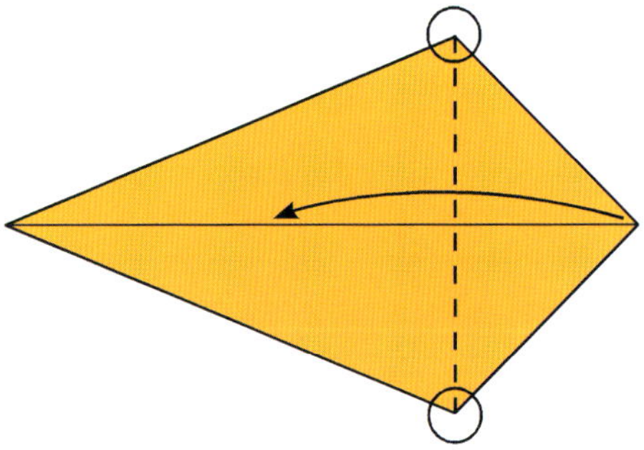

2 Fold the right-hand point inward using the top and bottom corners to locate the position of the crease.

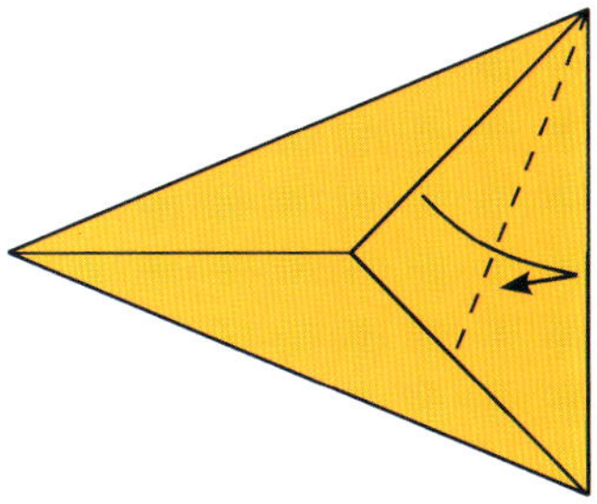

3 Fold the upper right-hand edge of the triangular flap across to lie along the left-hand edge, crease firmly, then unfold.

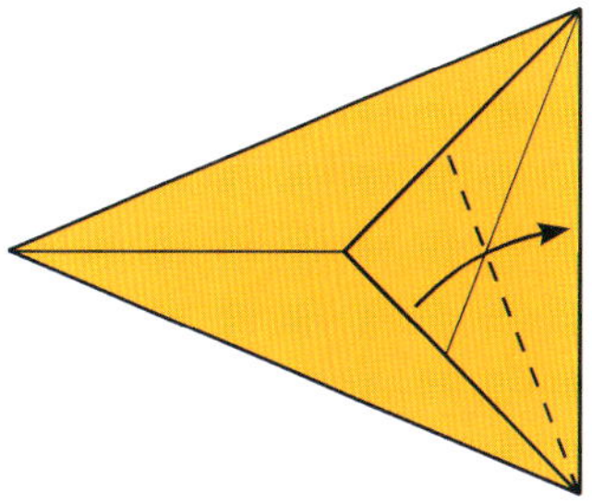

4 Fold the lower right-hand edge of the triangular flap across to lie along the left-hand edge in a similar way. Don't unfold this time.

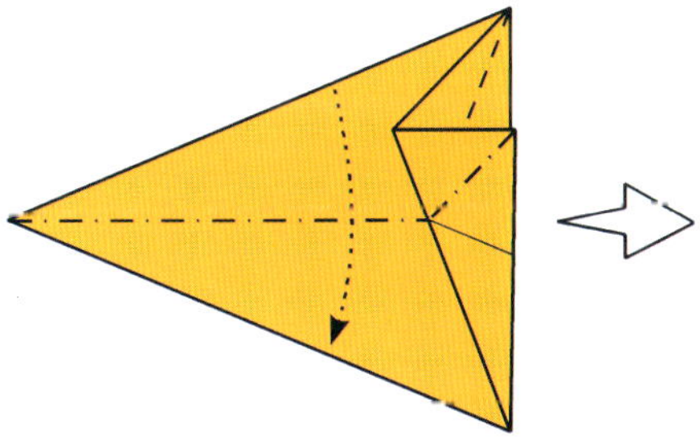

5 Pick the paper up and fold in half from top to bottom behind the model. Picture 6 shows you what the result should look like. The next picture has been drawn to a larger scale.

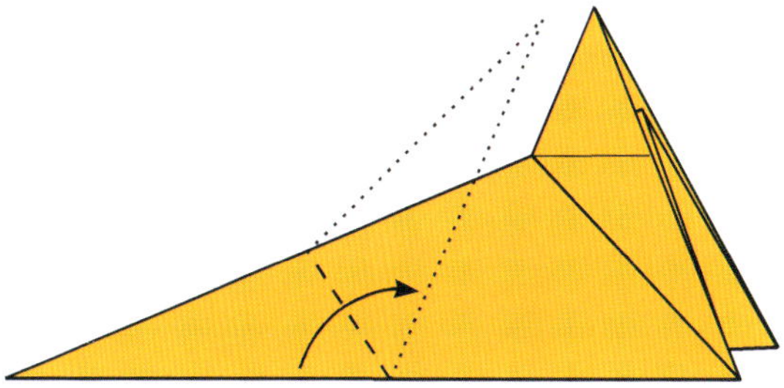

6 Begin to form the neck by folding the left-hand point across to the right. The dotted line shows where the paper should end up.

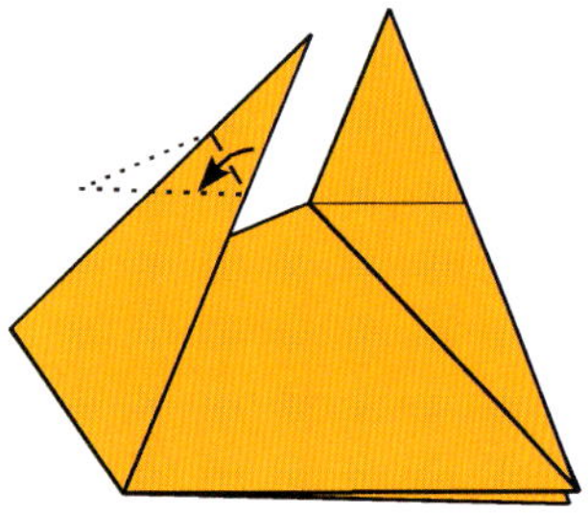

7 Begin to form the head by folding the tip of the left-hand point across to the left. The dotted line shows where the paper should end up.

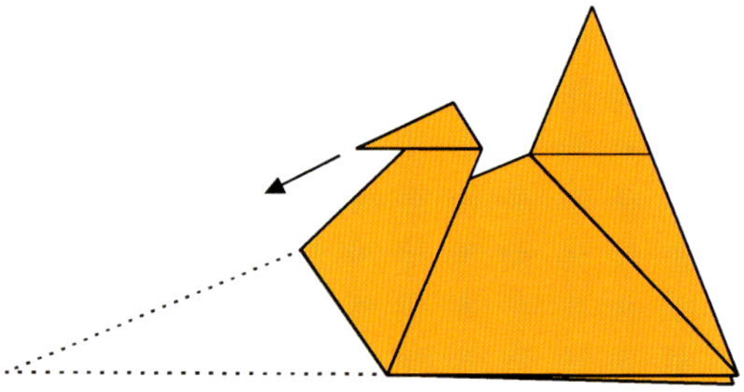

8 Open out the folds made in steps 6 and 7.

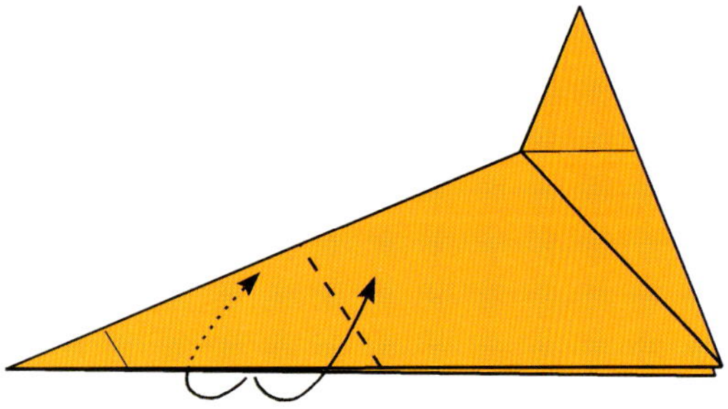

9 Turn the neck inside out using the creases made in step 6. In technical origami language this move is known as an outside reverse fold.

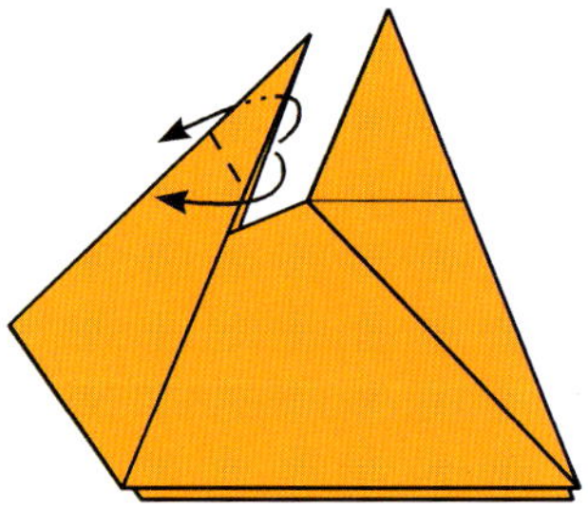

10 Make a second outside reverse fold to turn the head and beak inside out using the creases made in step 7.

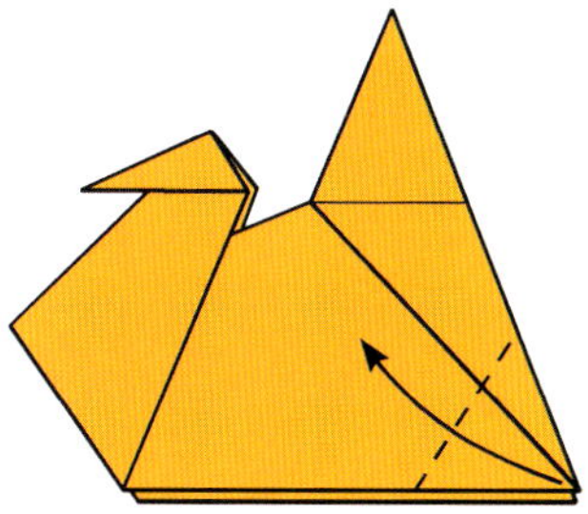

11 Make this fold through all the layers to begin to shape the body.

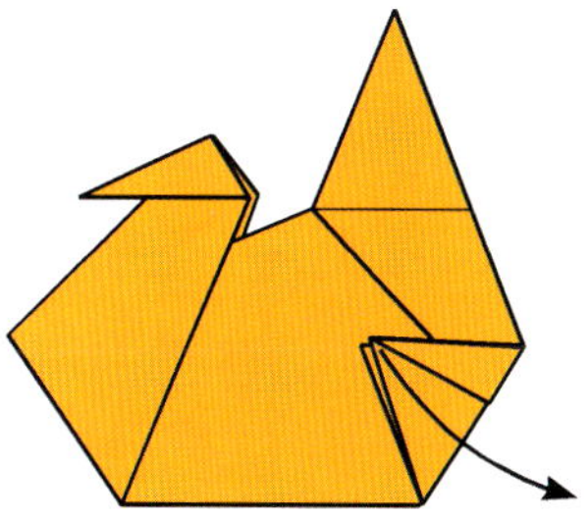

12 Open out the folds made in step 11.

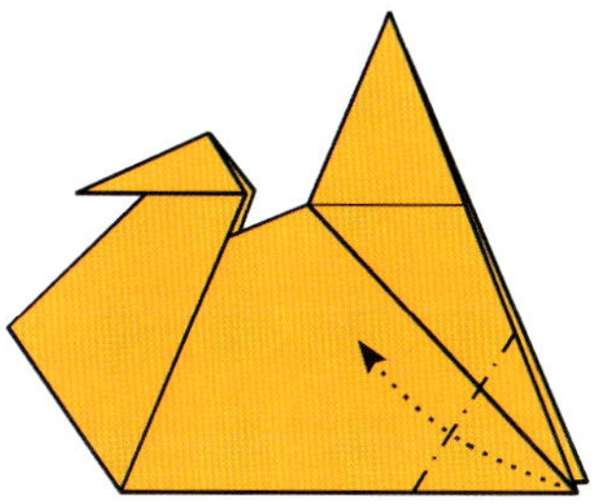

13 Fold the front layer away inside the body by reversing the crease made in step 11.

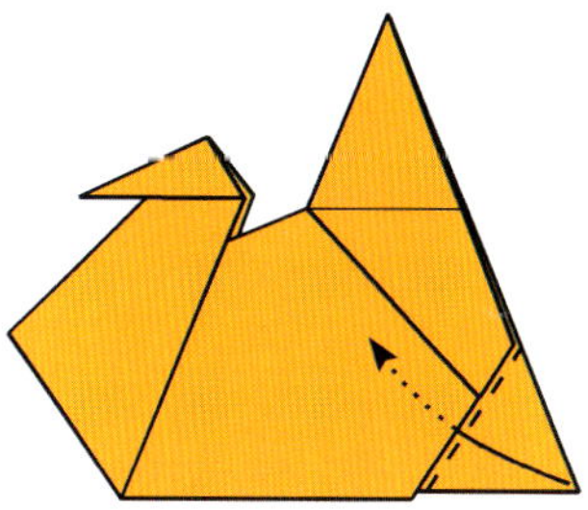

14 Fold the back layer away inside the body using the crease made in step 11.

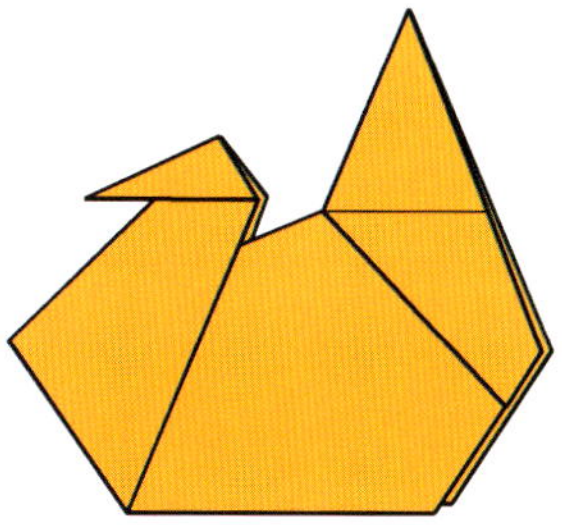

15 The Turkey is finished.

Swan

Like the Turkey, the Swan is also a development of the Basic Duck, though a much more sophisticated one. Swans have much longer necks, heads, and beaks than ducks or turkeys and so the length of paper allocated to making them has to be increased (while the length allocated to the tail and body remains about the same). The extra length is found by thinning the kite-shaped base in step 4 of the Basic Duck. The other significant difference between the designs is that an extra fold is added to suggest the graceful arc of a swan's neck.

Once you understand how the design works you might like to experiment with forming the neck and head folds using the method explained in the diagrams for the Basic Duck. It's all about getting the proportions just right.

You will need a generous square of white paper for each Swan. For best effect use fairly thin paper.

Adaptation of a traditional design.

Begin by following steps 1 through 3 of the Basic Duck then arrange the paper in the way shown in the first picture.

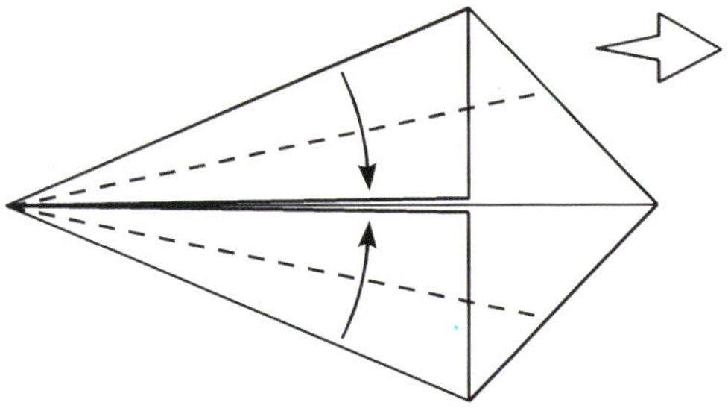

1 Fold both the sloping right-hand edges inward to lie along the crease (made in step 1 of the Basic Duck), leaving a tiny gap between the edges. The next picture has been drawn on a larger scale.

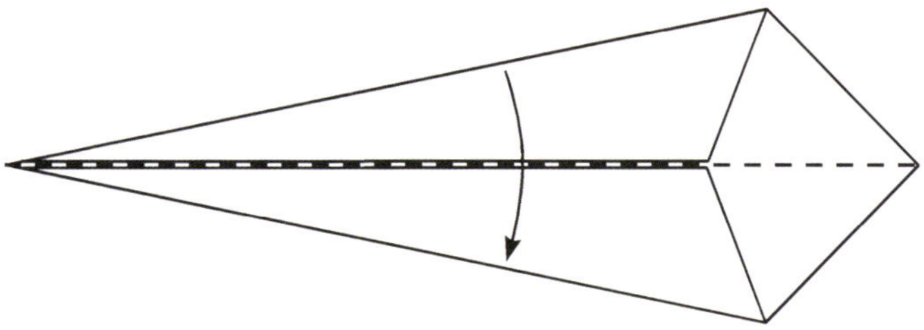

2 Fold in half from top to bottom and flatten firmly. If you have left small gaps between the edges (made in step 3 of the Basic Duck) you should be able to do this without splitting the center of the paper.

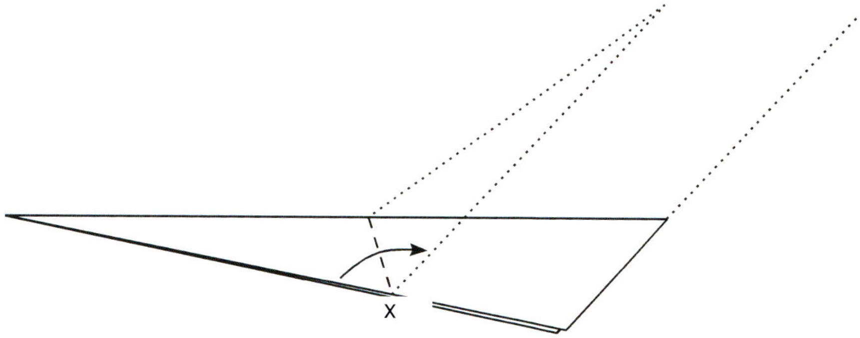

3 Fold the front point across to the right to begin to form the neck and head. There are no location points for this fold so you have to make it by eye. The left-hand set of dotted lines show you where the point should end up. The right-hand dotted line shows you how to line up edge x with the line of the tail. Make the fold softly at first and only crease firmly once you are sure you have the fold in the right place. Laying your model on the diagrams to compare lengths and angles may help.

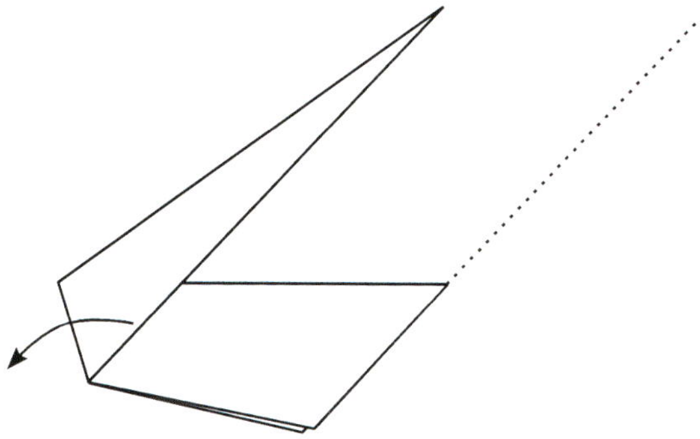

4 Open out the fold made in step 3.

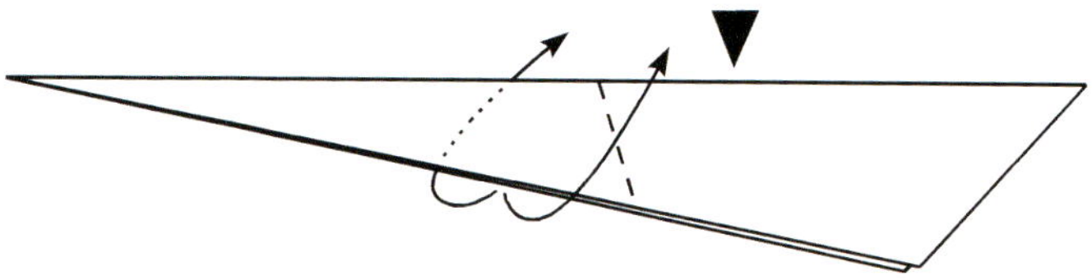

5 Pick the model up, flatten slightly to separate the bottom edges, then turn the right-hand point inside out, outside the other layers, using the creases you made in step 3.

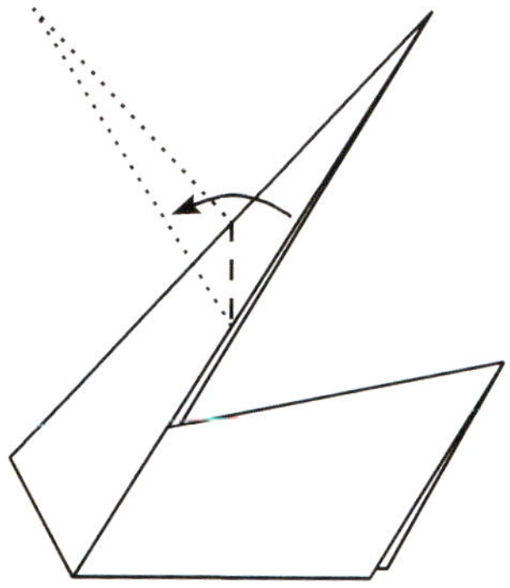

6 Continue to form the neck and head by making this fold in a similar way to fold 3. Note that the line of the crease is more or less upright.

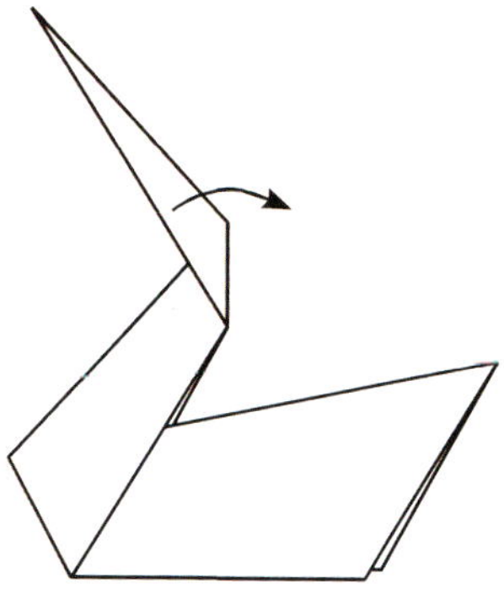

7 Open out the fold made in step 6.

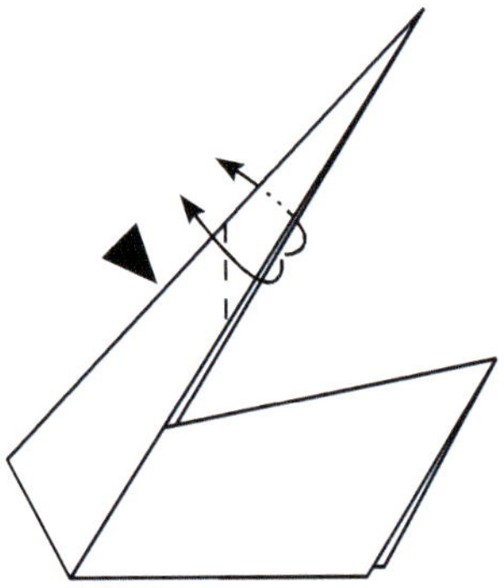

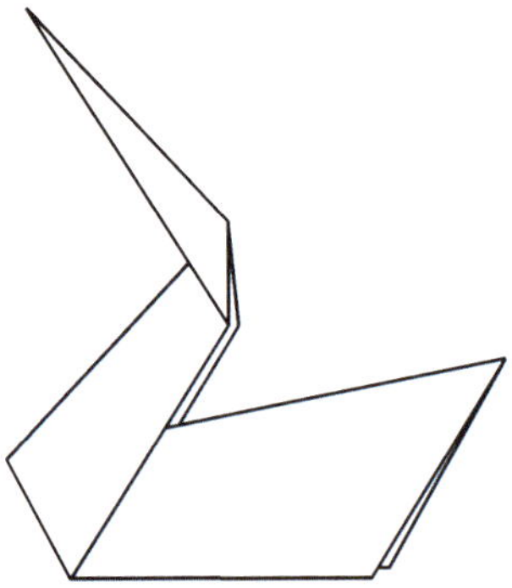

8 Pick the model up and turn the top point inside out outside the other layers of the neck using the creases you made in step 6.

9 Crease firmly then open out the folds made in steps 2, 3, and 6.

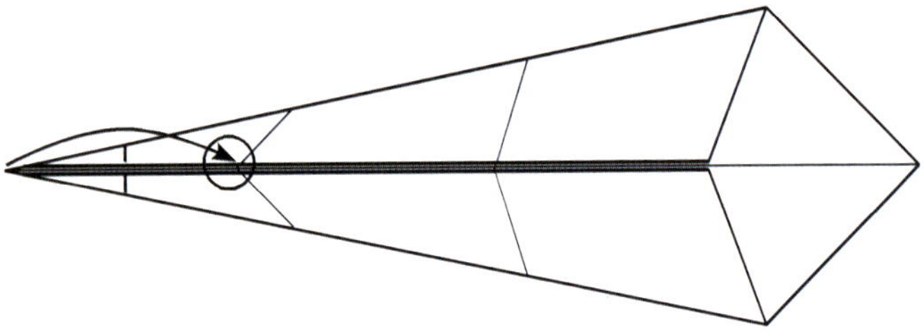

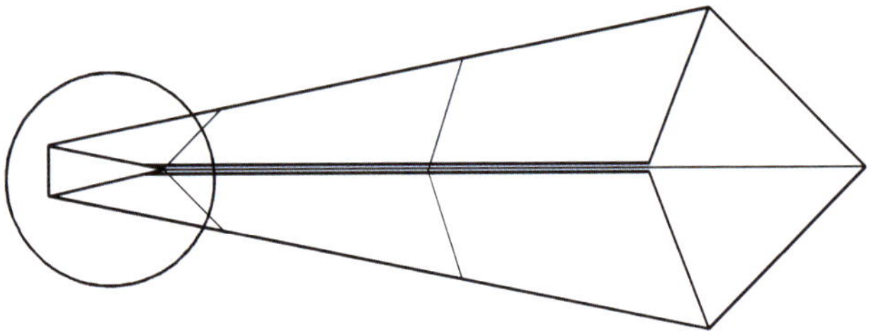

10 Begin to form the beak by folding the tip of the left-hand point inward. You can use the creases made in step 6 to locate this fold.

11 Make another tiny fold (see enlargements 11a and 11b) to form the beak, then remake folds 2, 3 and 6.

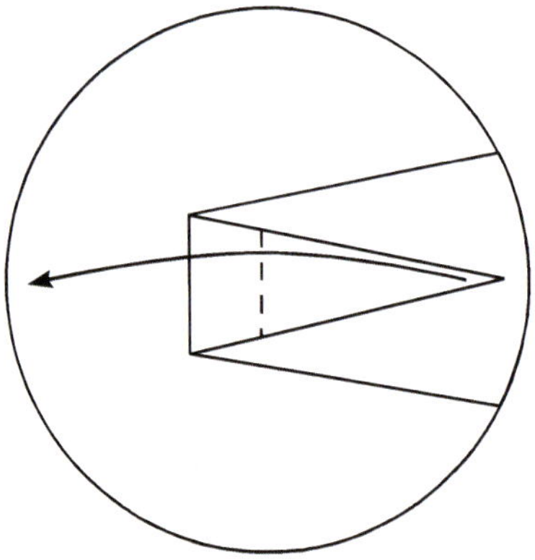

11a

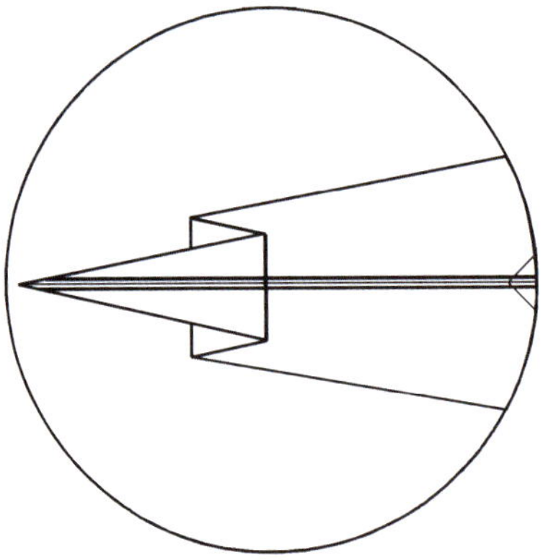

11b

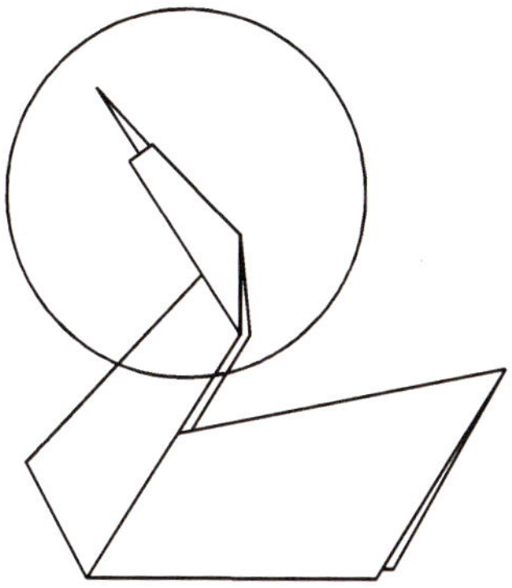

12 Your Swan should now look like this. Finish off the head and neck by making two more tiny folds in the way shown in the enlargements.

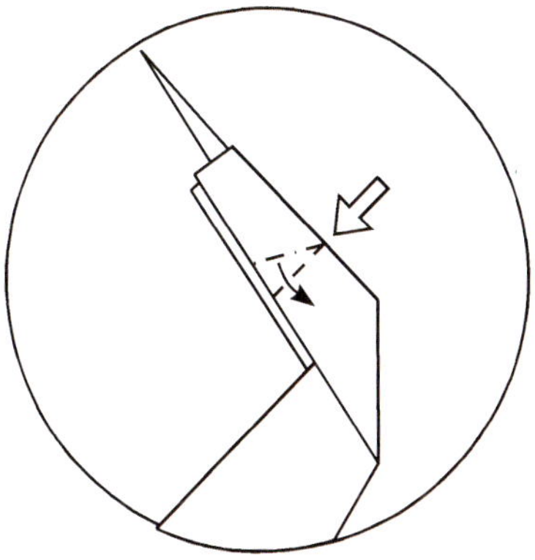

12a Pick the model up. Hold the top of the head in your right hand and grip the beak and front of the head with your left. Move your left hand downward to change the angle of the head. Allow the top edge of the head to break at the point marked with an arrow and the layers of the head to fold outside the layers of the neck. Picture 12b shows you what the result should look like. In technical origami language this type of fold is called a crimp.

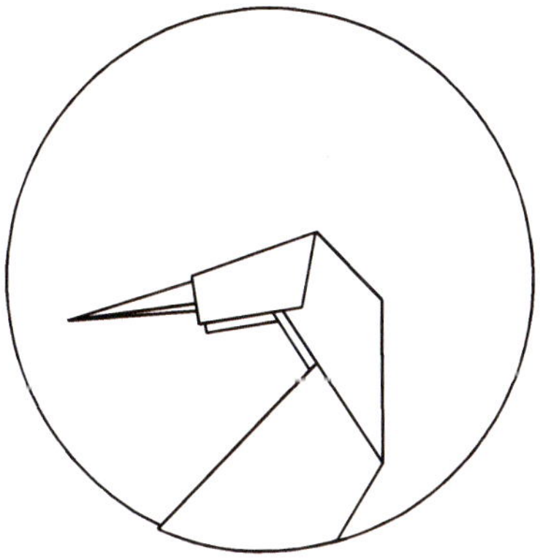

12b

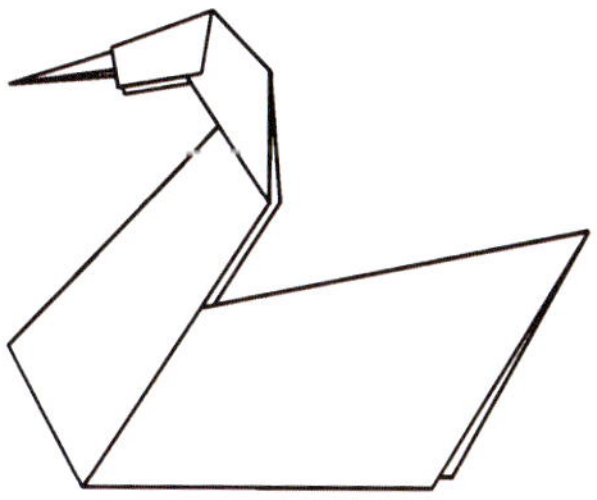

13 If you wish you can stop at this point or you can improve the tail in the way shown in Basic Duck.

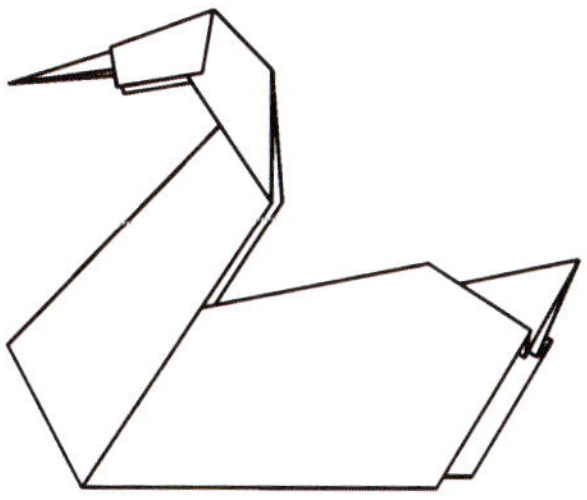

14 Here is the finished Swan, with improved tail.

Rooster

The Rooster is a lively design made from a standard intermediate fold known as the Diamond Base (shown in picture 2), which is created by thinning the fat end of the Kite Base to a point. Many great paperfolds begin in this way.

The design of the Rooster shows how a vocabulary of simple folds can be used to create an overall effect greater than the sum of its parts.

You will need a square of red paper for each Rooster. The design will work well with almost any thickness of paper.

Adaptation of a traditional design.

Begin by following steps 1 through 3 of the Basic Duck then arrange the paper in the way shown here in picture 1.

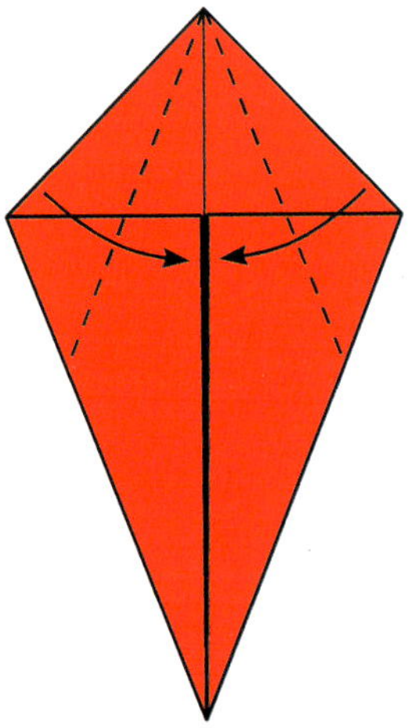

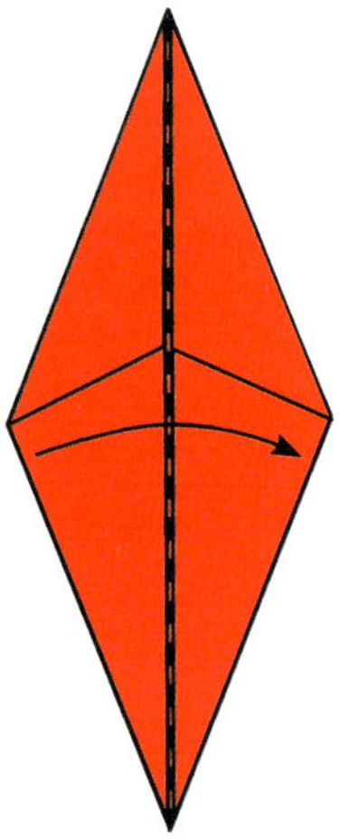

1 Fold both upper sloping edges inward in a similar way, once again leaving a tiny gap between the edges.

2 Fold in half from right to left. This fold will be easier to make if you have left gaps between the edges in steps 3 and 4 of Basic Duck.

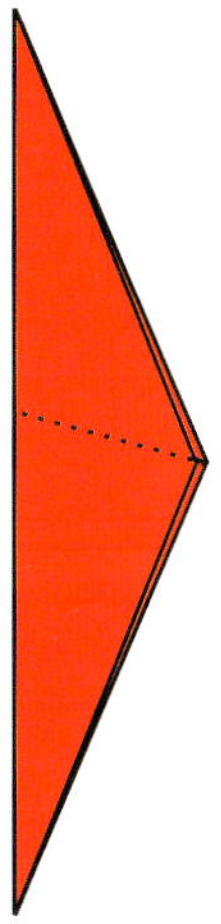

3 The dotted line marks the edges of the flaps created in step 1 which are now hidden inside the design. You should be able to feel these through the outer layers of the paper.

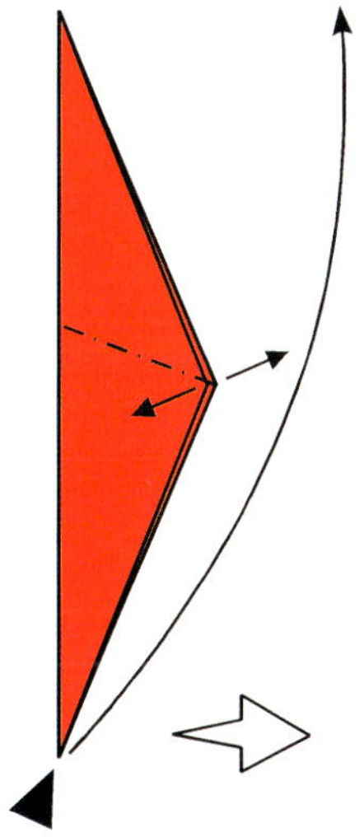

4 Open up the layers on the right-hand side then turn the entire bottom point inside out upward between them until you meet the resistance of the internal flaps formed in step 1. The new creases should be formed along the line of the internal edges of these flaps. This is difficult to describe but quite easy to do. Make sure your creases are in the right place before you crease firmly. Picture 5 shows what the result should look like.

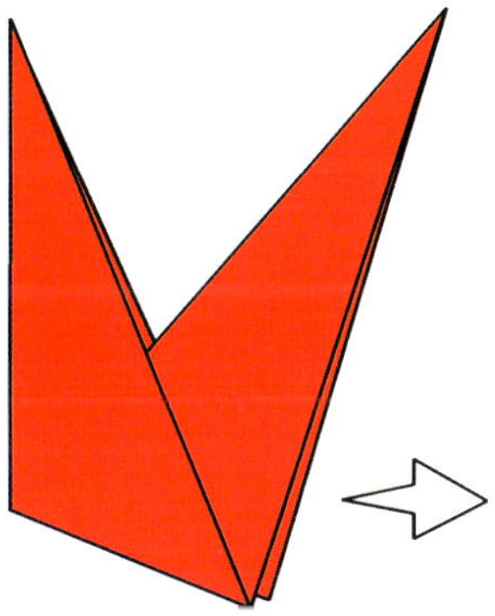

5 This is the result. Rotate slightly anticlockwise and arrange like picture 6.

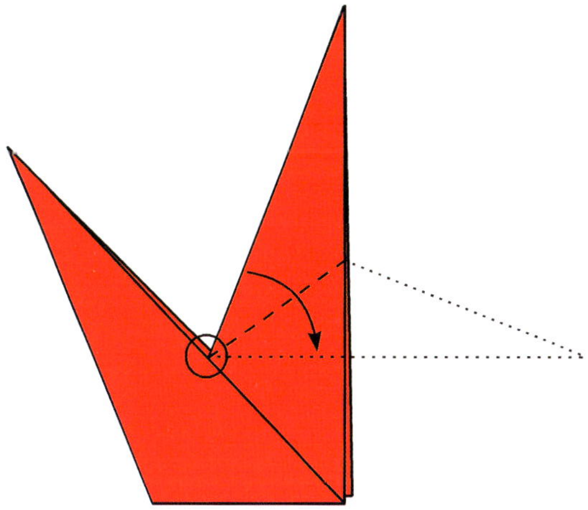

6 Begin to form the tail by folding the right-hand point down to the right in the way shown here. The dotted line shows where the paper should end up.

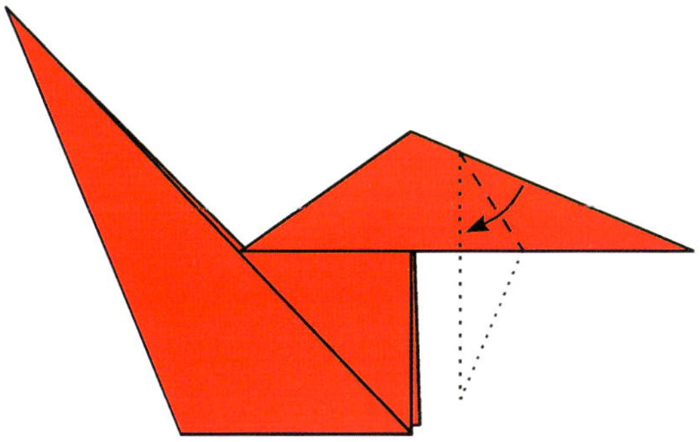

7 Make a second smaller but similar fold to complete the outline of the tail.

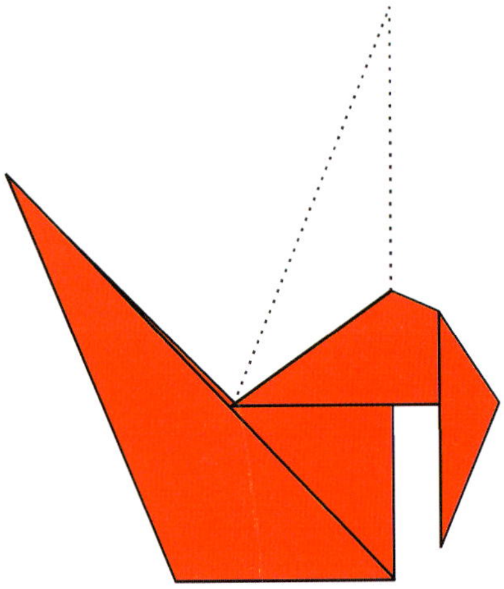

8 Open out the folds made in steps 6 and 7.

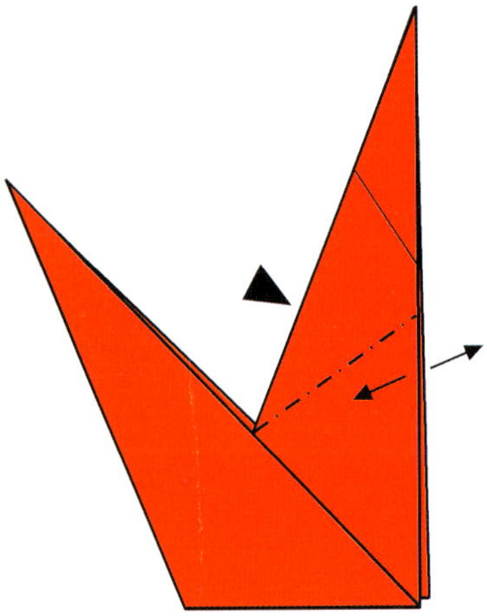

9 Open up the layers on the right-hand side then turn the top point inside out between them using the creases made in step 7.

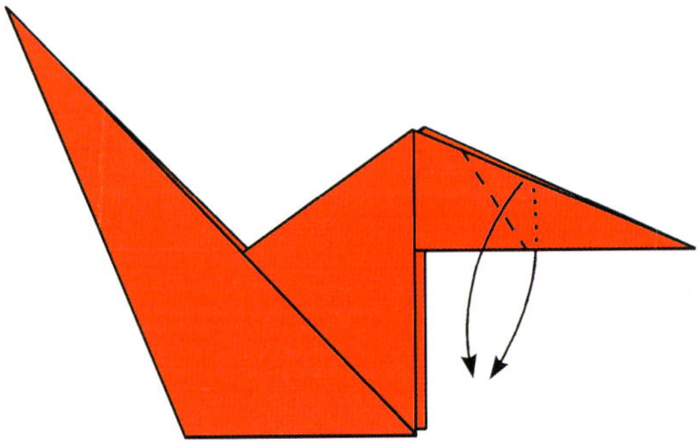

10 Turn the tip of the tail inside out using the creases made in step 8.

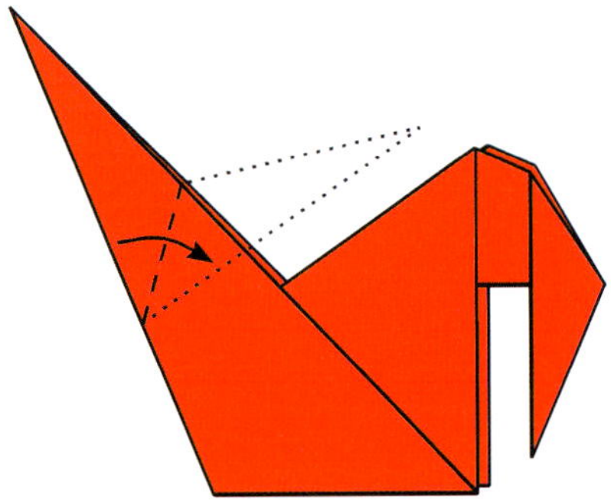

11 Begin to form the head by folding the left-hand point across to the right in the way shown here. The dotted line shows where the paper should end up.

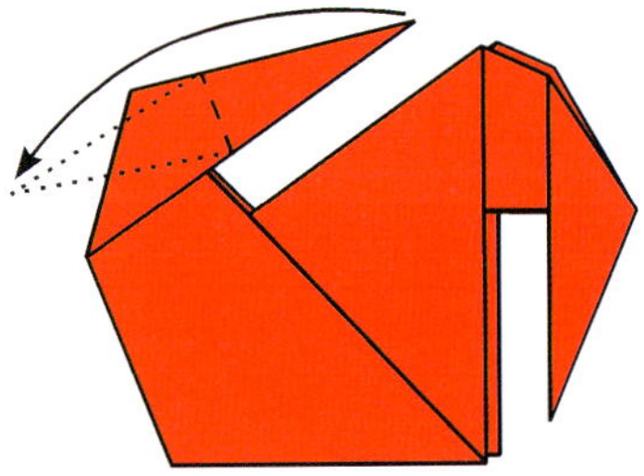

12 Begin to form the crest and beak by folding the same point back across to the left.

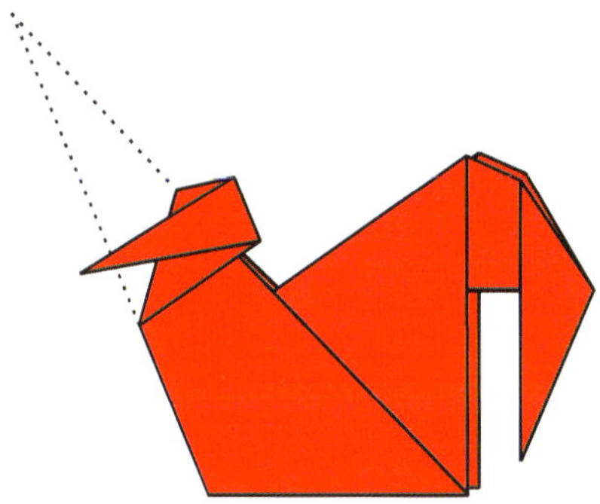

13 Open out the folds made in steps 11 and 12.

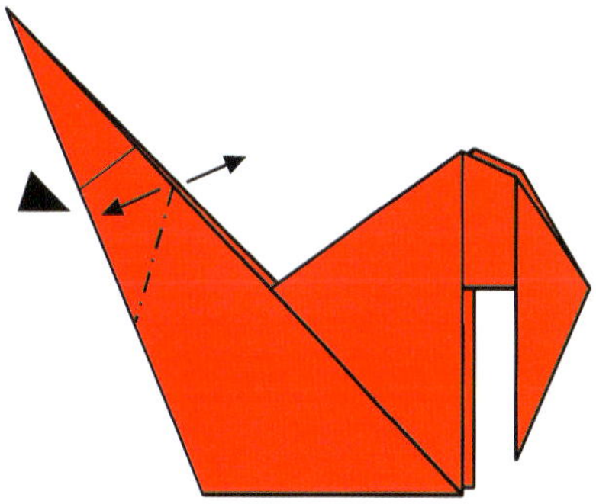

14 Open up the layers of the neck then turn the point inside out between them using the creases made in step 11.

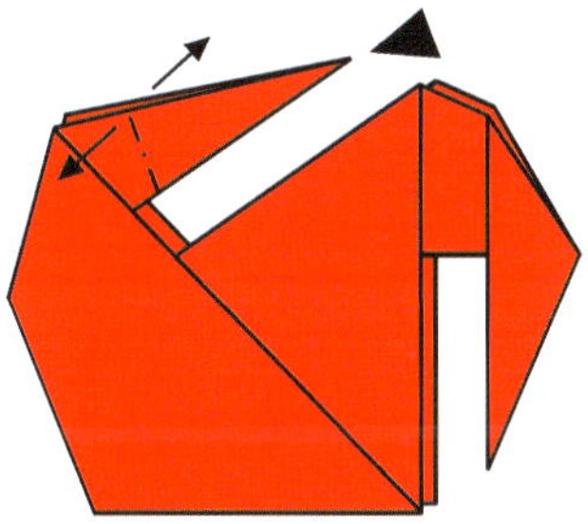

15 Open up the layers at the top of the head then turn the point of the beak inside out between them using the creases made in step 12.

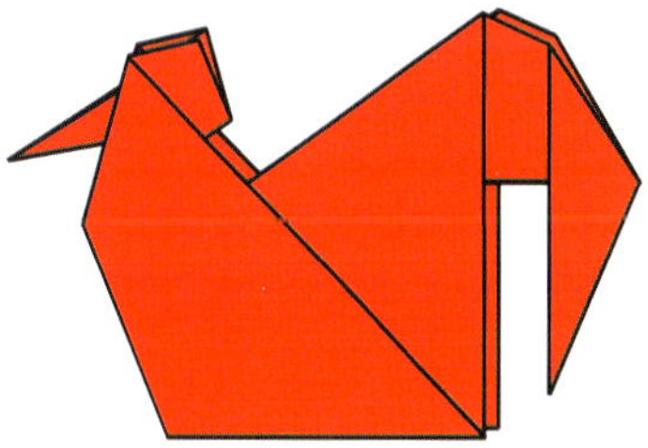

16 The Rooster is finished.

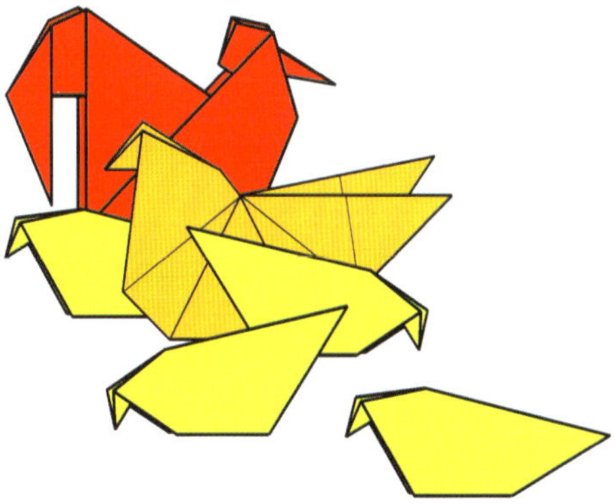

Super Rooster

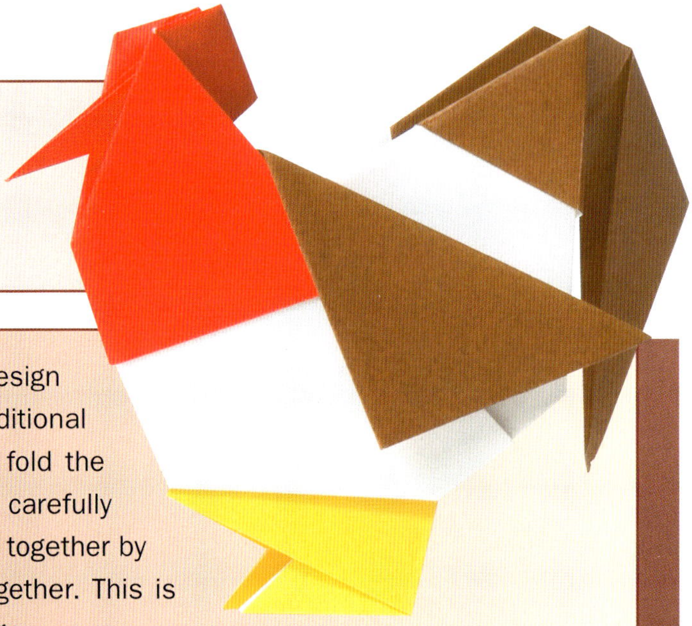

The Super Rooster is a colorful five-piece design created by clothing and accessorizing the traditional Rooster explained earlier in the book. If you fold the pieces accurately and follow the instructions carefully you will find that all five pieces will hold firmly together by themselves. You won't need to glue them together. This is the hallmark of good multi-piece origami design.

Once you have folded this design and understand how it is done you will find it easy to add extra pieces to some of the other designs in this book in a similar way.

You will need … five squares of paper altogether. All the squares should be the same size. For the color scheme shown here you will need one white, one red, one yellow and one brown square. There is however no reason why you should not design a custom color scheme of your own. You will need to use thin strong paper for this design.

Begin by folding a traditional Rooster from the white square in the way shown on pages xx to xx then follow the instructions below.

Accessorized by David Mitchell.

Preparing the Paper

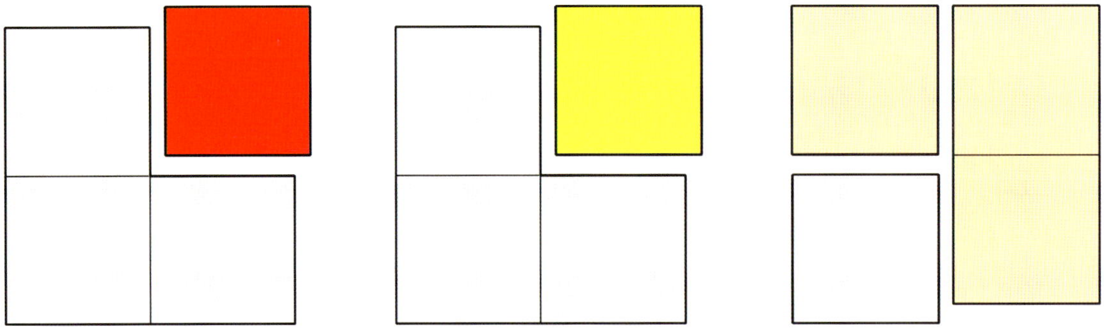

You will first need to create three small squares and a 2x1 rectangle from the remaining three large squares in the way shown here. Those parts of the large squares which are shown colored gray are not needed for this design.

Clothing the Head and Tail

Begin by folding both the small brown and small red squares to step 3 of the Basic Duck.

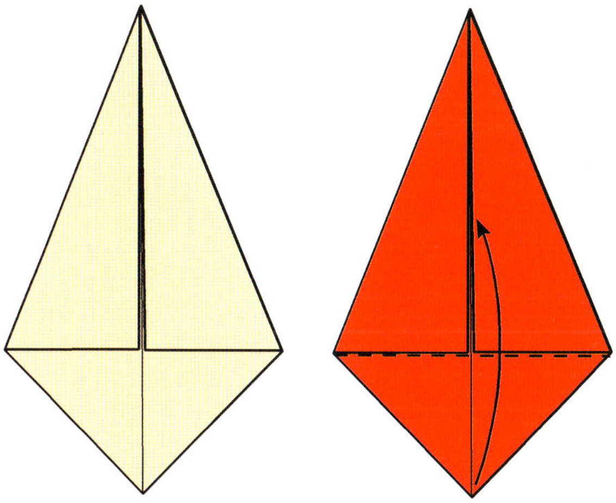

4 The brown piece will be used as it is. Fold the bottom point of the red piece upwards as shown.

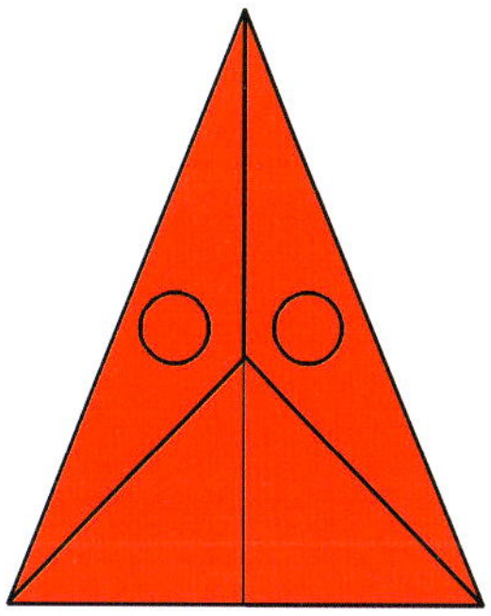

5 Rearrange the layers to bring the flaps marked with circles to the front.

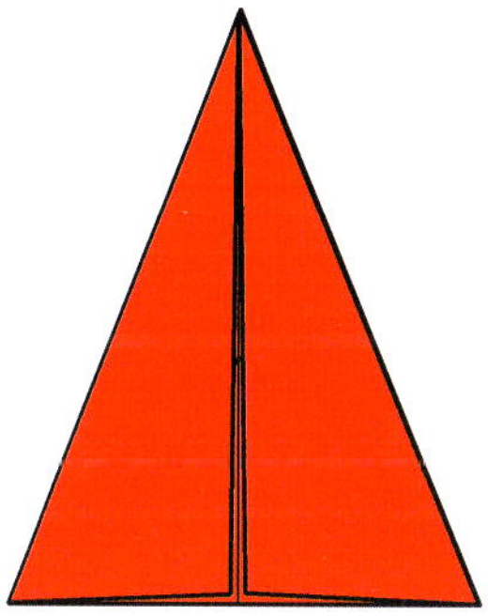

6 This is the result.

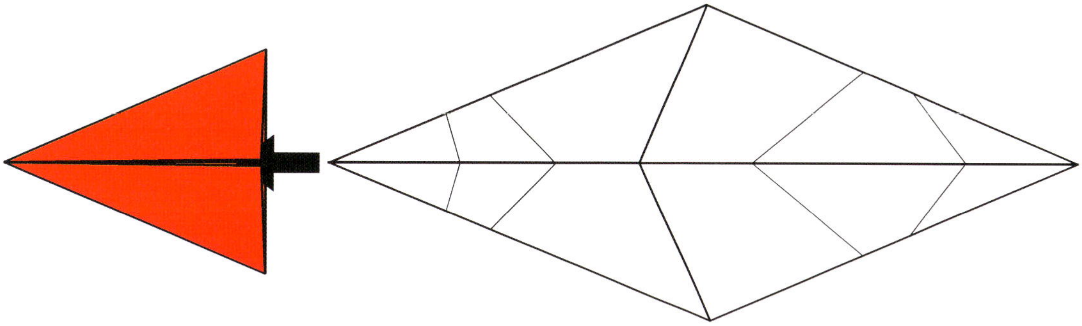

7 Unfold your Rooster to step 5 and insert the head and neck of the Rooster inside the cladding in the way shown here.

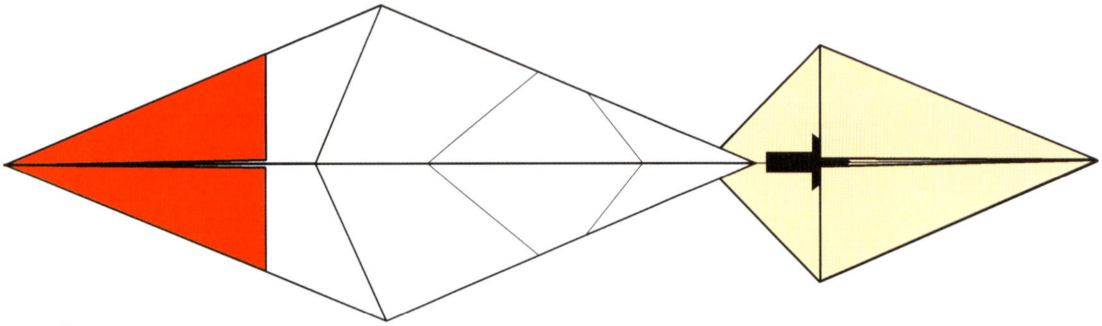

8 Insert the tail of the Rooster inside the tail cladding in a similar way.

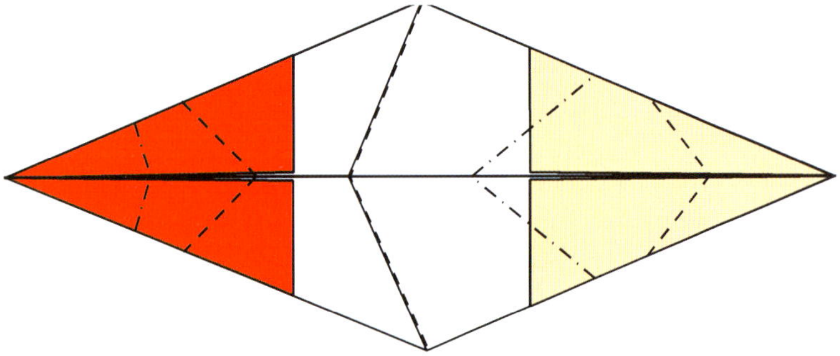

9 Refold the Rooster, making sure the claddings do not slip out of alignment as you do so.

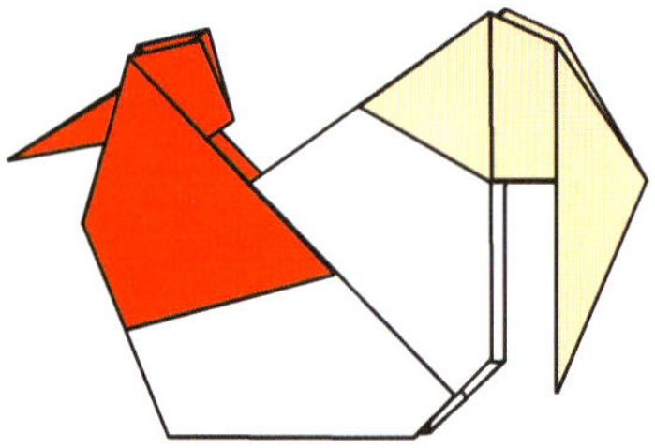

10 This is the result.

Creating the Wings

Begin with the brown rectangle arranged in the way shown in picture 28.

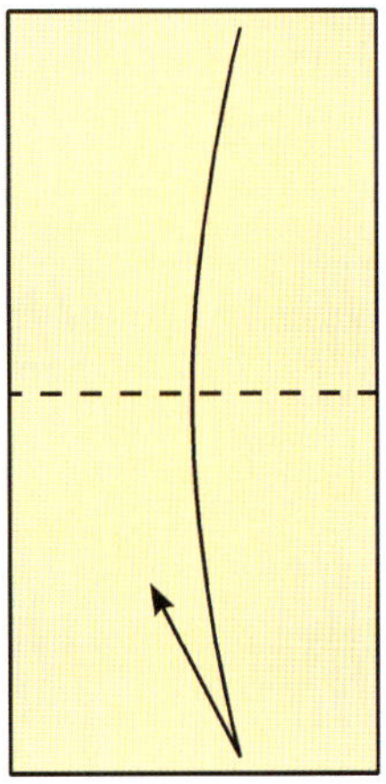

11 Fold in half from top to bottom, crease firmly, then unfold.

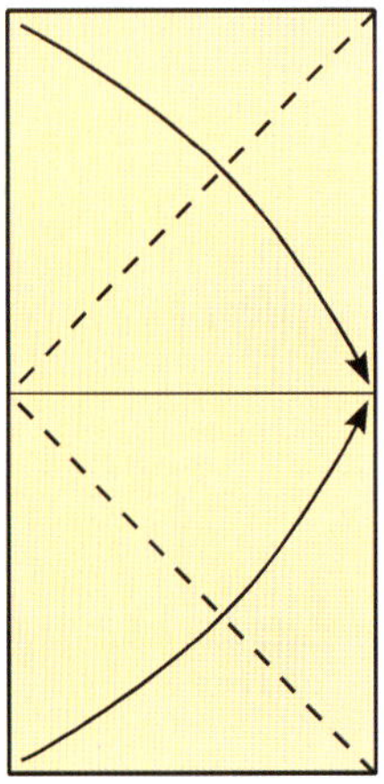

12 Fold both halves of the paper in half diagonally as shown.

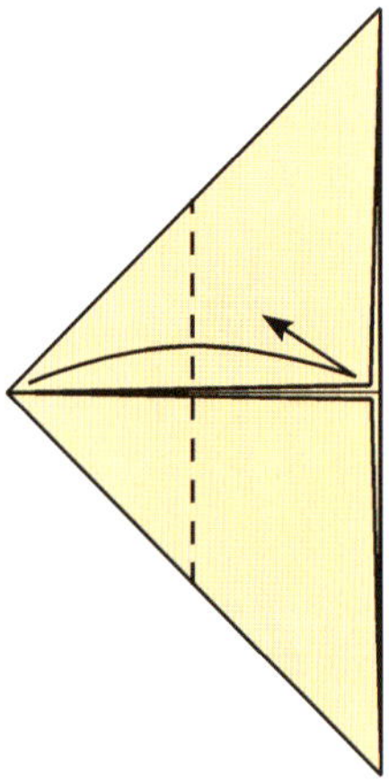

13 Fold the left-hand point across to the middle of the right-hand edge, crease firmly, then unfold. The next picture is drawn to a larger scale.

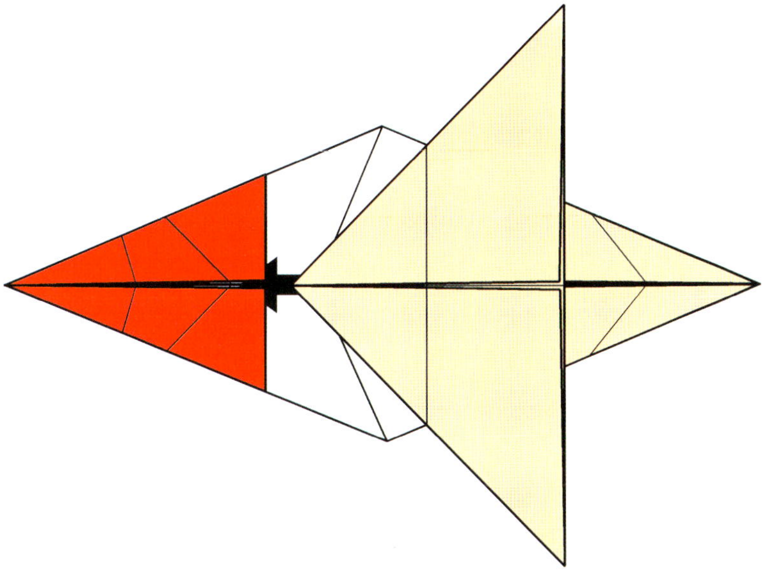

14 Insert the point of the wing piece underneath the flaps of the head piece in the way shown here.

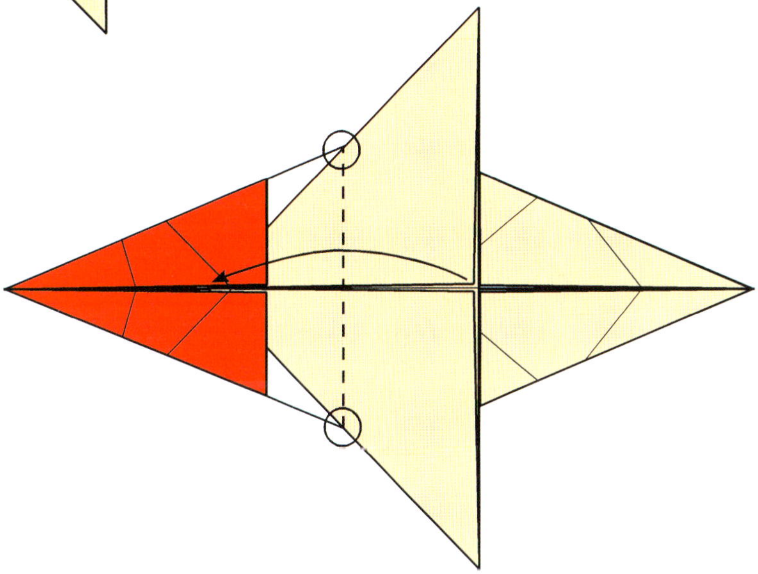

15 Align the wing piece to the rest of the model in the way shown here then fold the wing piece in half from right to left, using the crease made in step 30.

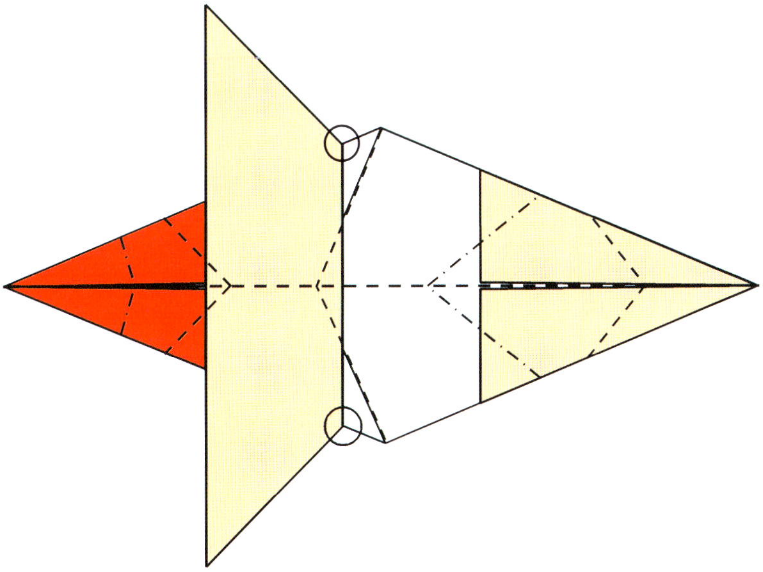

16 Refold the Rooster making sure the wing piece does not slip out of alignment.

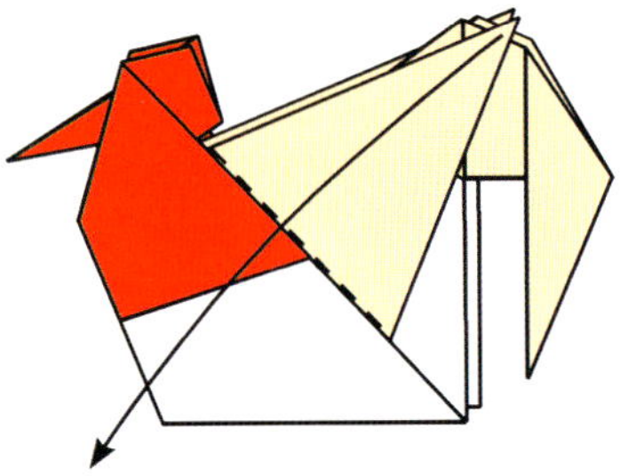

17 Fold the front wing down over the folded edge in front of it in the way shown. Repeat this fold on the wing at the back of the model.

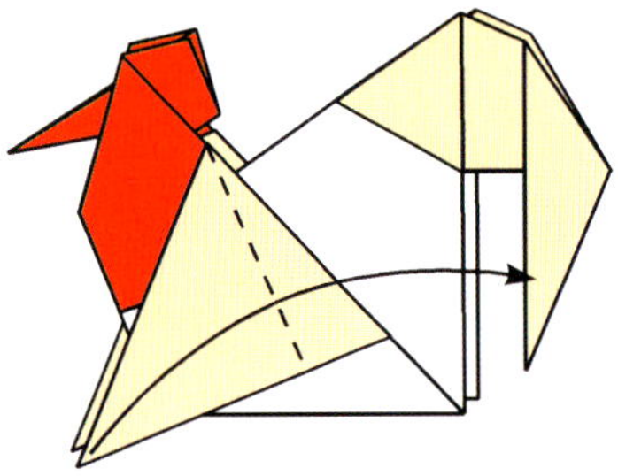

18 Fold the front wing across to the right in the way shown. Repeat this fold on the wing at the back of the model.

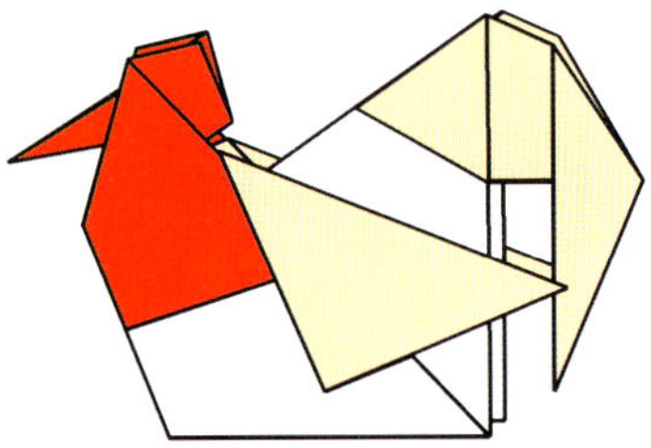

19 This the result.

Creating the Feet

Begin with the small yellow square arranged in the way shown in picture 37.

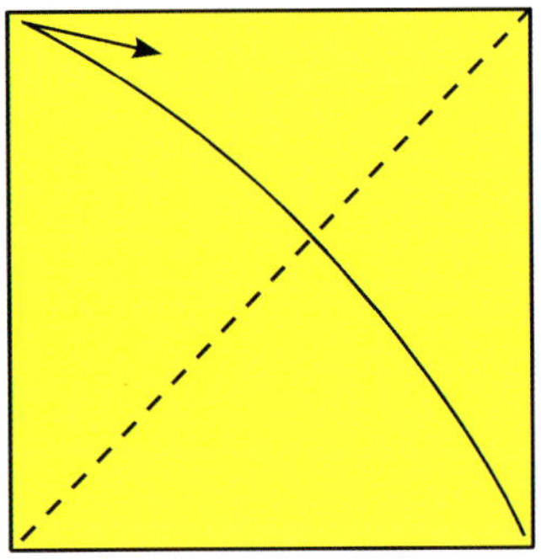

20 Fold in half diagonally as shown, crease firmly then unfold.

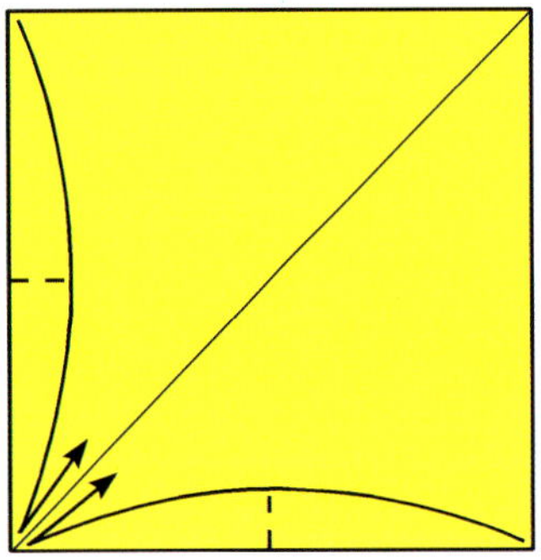

21 Make two tiny creases to mark the center of these two edges.

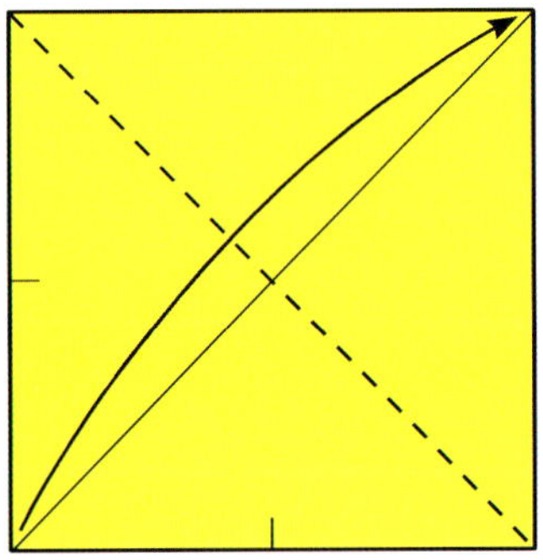

22 Fold in half diagonally in the other direction.

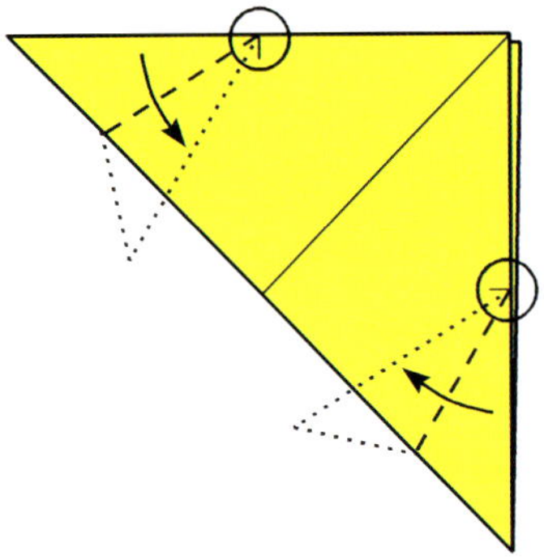

23 Form the feet by making these two small folds using the creases made in step 38 as location points. Try to make your result look as much like picture 41 as possible.

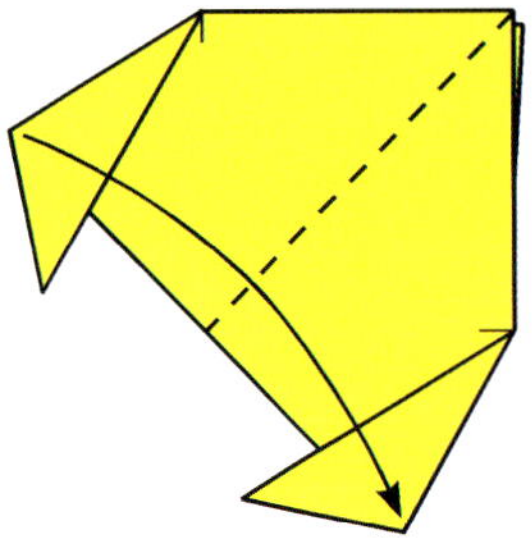

24 Fold in half using the crease made in step 37.

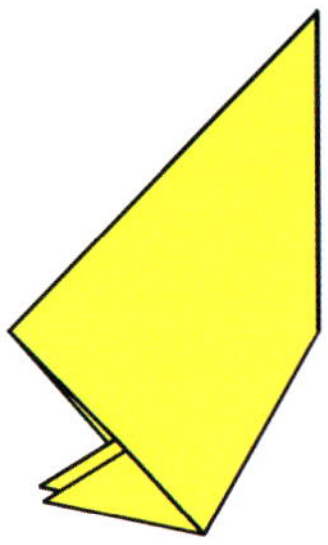

25 The feet are finished. Attach the feet to the rest of the Super Rooster in the way shown in picture 43.

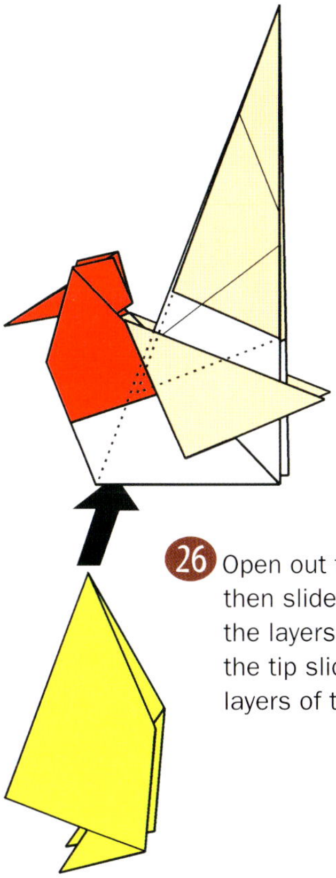

26 Open out the tail of the Rooster then slide the feet up inside the layers of the body so that the tip slides underneath the layers of the tail piece.

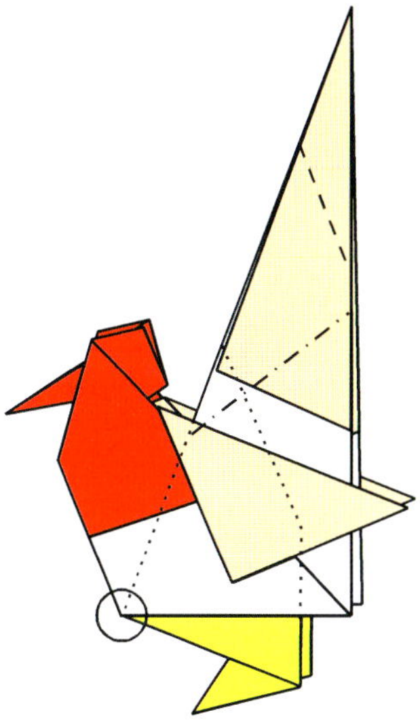

27 Continue sliding the feet inside the body until they are aligned like this. Refold the tail to trap the feet in place.

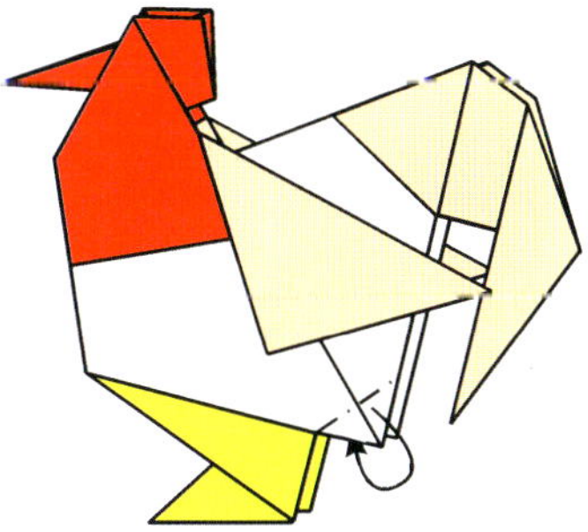

28 Shape the body by tucking the point of the front and back layers away inside the model.

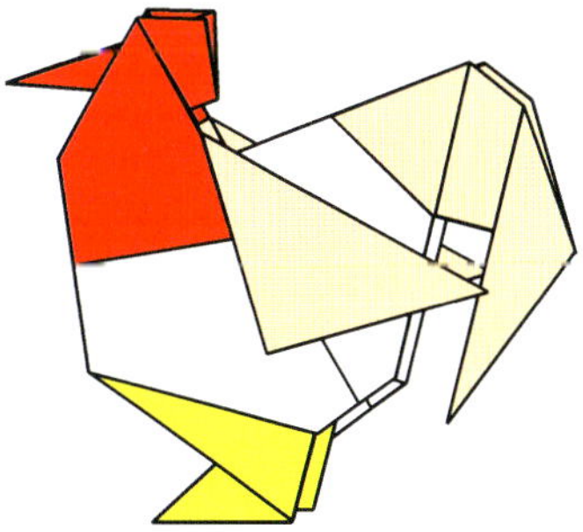

29 The Super Rooster is complete.

If your Super Rooster will not stand upright you can adjust the creases made in step 40 slightly to bring the center of gravity forward slightly until it does.

Woodpecker

The Woodpecker begins in the same way as the Rooster (from the Diamond Base) but there the similarities end. While the Rooster just sits there looking feisty, the Woodpecker is an action design. By squeezing the two bottom corners of the finished design together the Woodpecker can be made to peck into a hole in the opposite half of the paper. Relax the squeeze and the beak pulls back, ready to strike again. With practice, and stiff enough paper, you will be able to achieve a very satisfactory and life-like rat-a-tat-tat noise.

You will need a square of bright green or red paper. For best effect use stiff paper.

Designed by David Mitchell.

Begin by following steps 1 through 3 of the Basic Duck and 1 through 4 of the Rooster then continue with step 1 here.

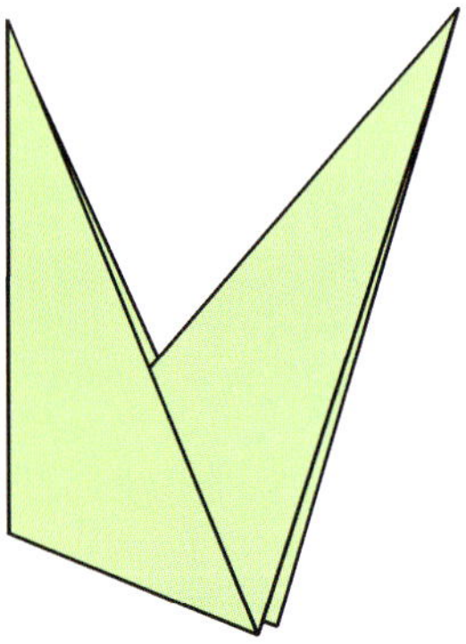

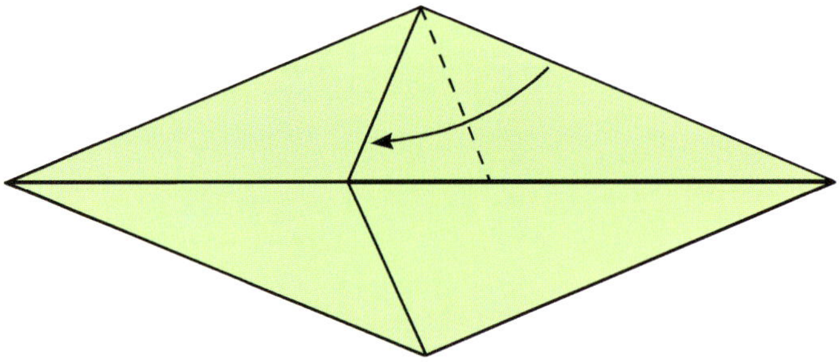

1 Crease firmly then open out the fold made in step 4 of the Rooster. Align the paper to picture 2 before continuing.

2 Fold the upper right-hand edge across to lie along the edge of the front layer of the paper as shown. Try to make sure your new crease stops halfway down the paper.

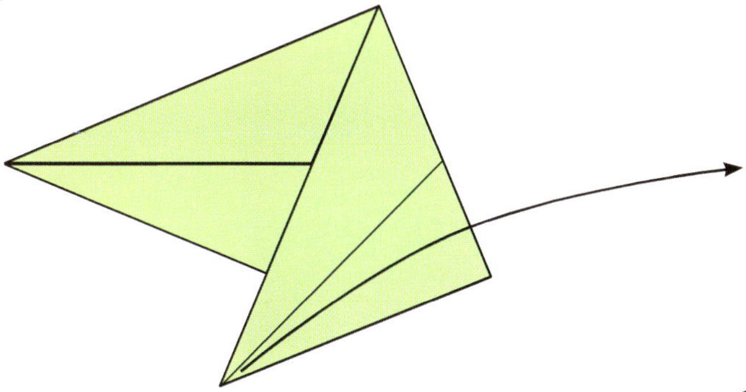

3 Open out the fold made in step 2.

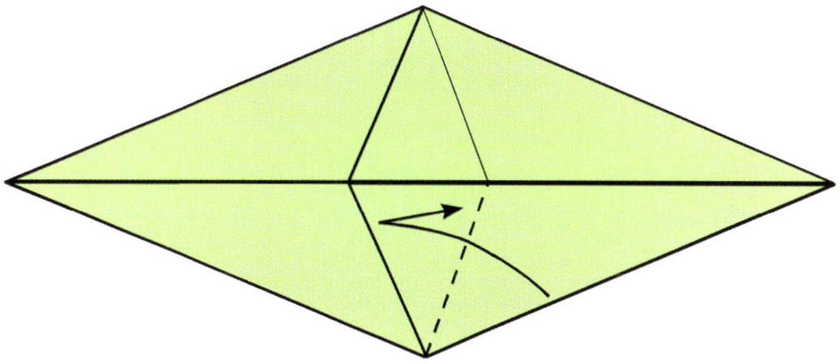

4 Repeat step 2 on the lower half of the paper, crease firmly, then unfold.

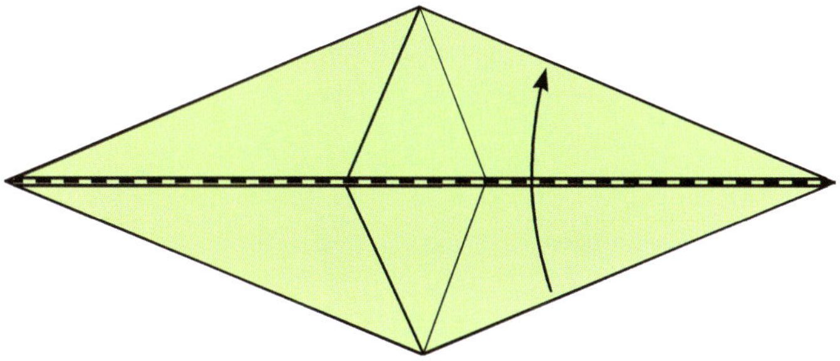

5 Fold in half from bottom to top.

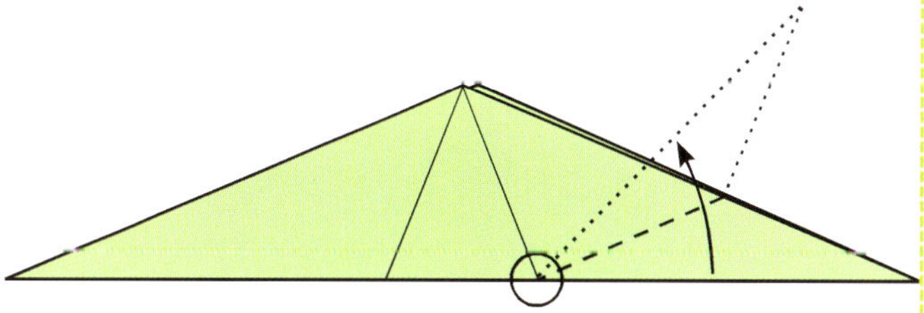

6 Make this fold as shown. The crease begins at the point where the crease made in step 4 intersects the bottom edge but the angle is a matter of judgement. Make the fold softly at first and check your result against picture 7 before creasing firmly.

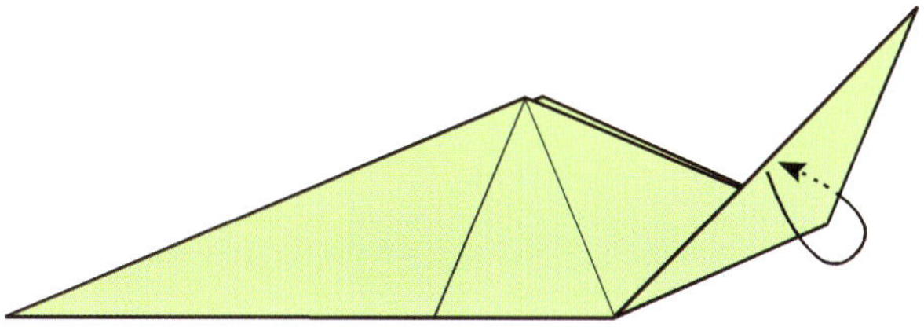

7 Pick the paper up and swing the flap around to the back by reversing the creases. Crease firmly again.

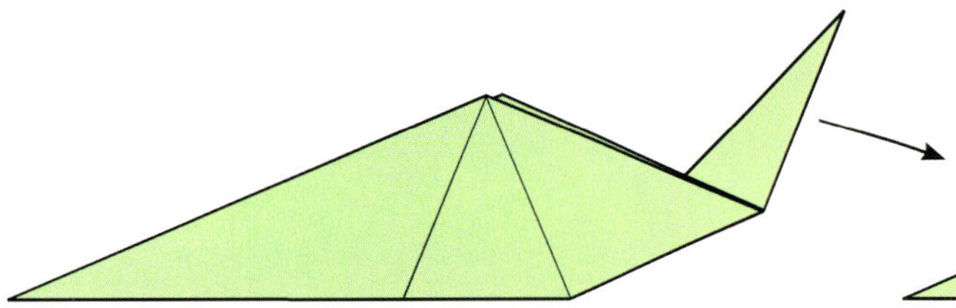

8 Open out the fold made in steps 6 and 7.

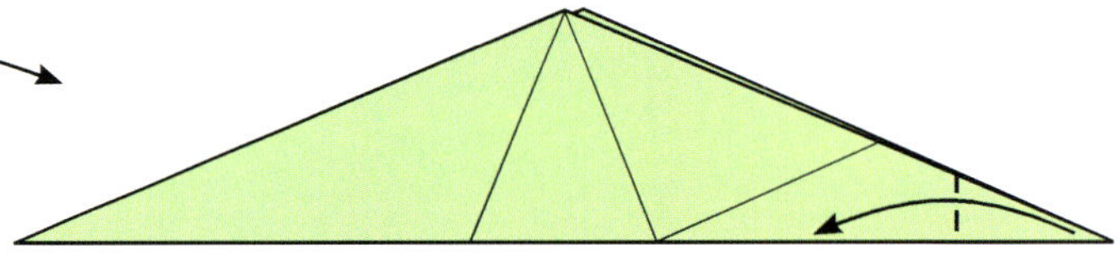

9 Fold the right-hand point inward as shown to begin to form the head and beak.

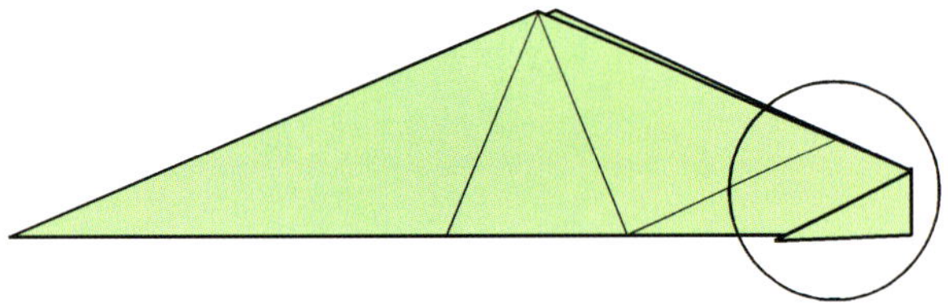

10 Make the fold shown in the enlargements.

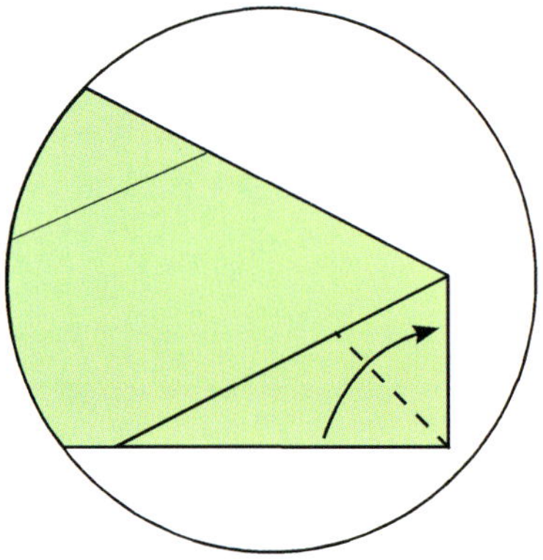

11a Fold the bottom edge of the triangular flap across to lie along the right-hand edge.

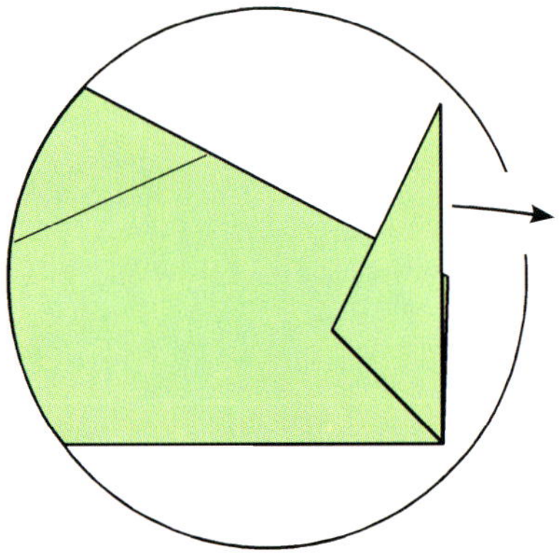

11b Open out the folds made in steps 9 and 11a.

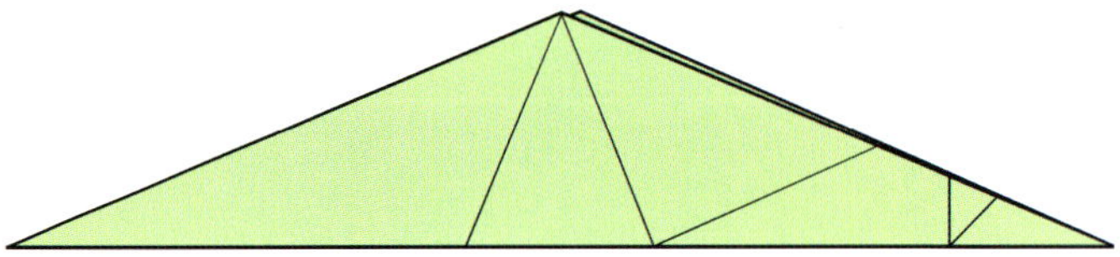

12 Form the head in the way shown in the enlargements.

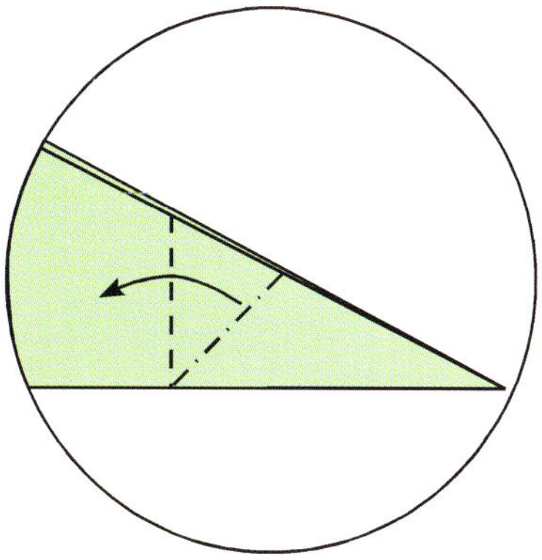

13a Crimp the head using the creases made in steps 9 and 11a.

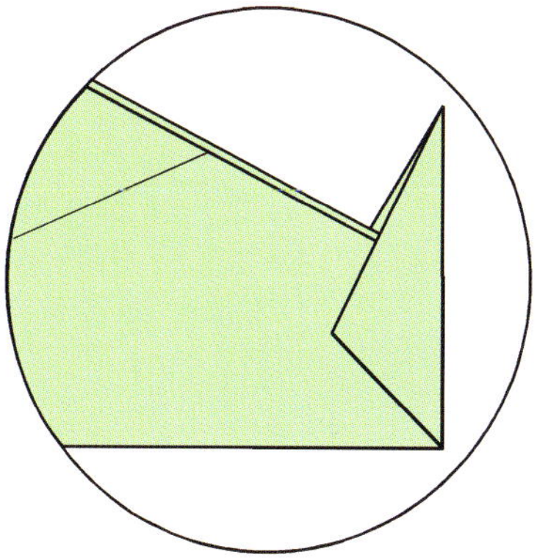

13b The Woodpecker's head is finished.

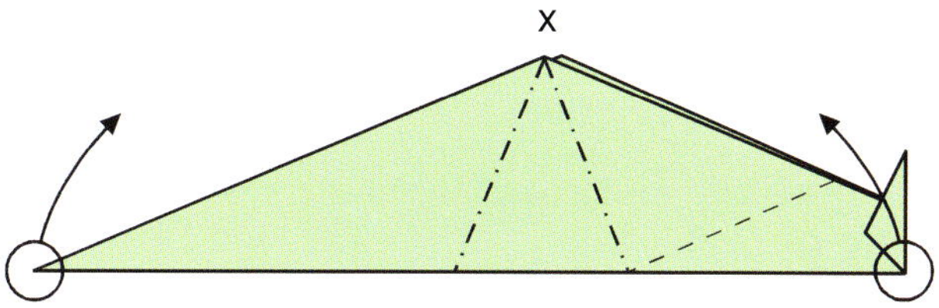

14 Pick up the design by the head and the tip of the left-hand point. Bring your hands together above the design allowing the layers at point x to separate. Picture 15 shows what the result should look like.

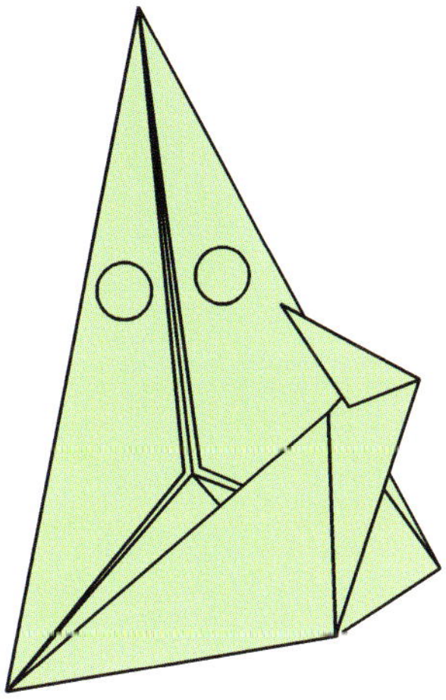

15 This is the result. Work around the design making sure all the creases are crisp and sharp. Bring the two flaps marked with circles forward slightly to create a hole for the Woodpecker to peck into.

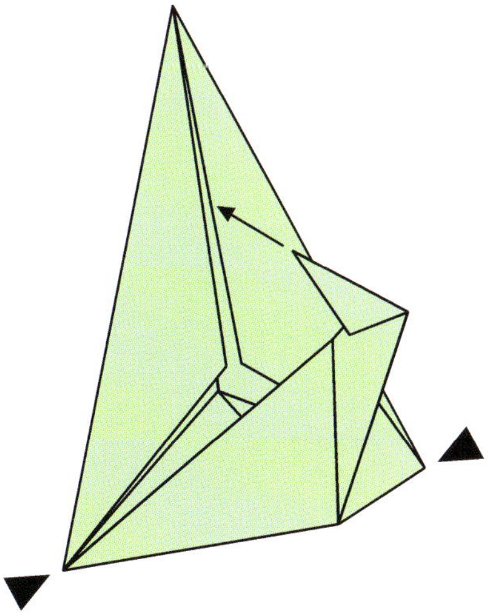

16 The Woodpecker is finished. If you squeeze the lower left and right-hand corners gently towards each other with the thumb and index finger of one of your hands the Woodpecker will peck. Relax your fingers and the beak will pull back. If you have creased carefully and used fairly thick paper the Woodpecker can be made to make a very satisfactory pecking noise.

Jumping Frog

The traditional Jumping Frog is one of the best-loved designs in the animal origami repertoire. The back legs of the frog are a simple but effective spring that will propel the Jumping Frog quite a surprising distance, especially if you make one from thin card. Make several Jumping Frogs and invent games to play with your family or friends. Frogliwinks (jumping frogs onto or into a target like an unfolded square of paper or a small box) is an established favorite, as is Frog Marathon (making Jumping Frogs race across the room is harder than you might think since they have a tendency to jump in unexpected directions) or Frog Gymnastics (persuading a frog to turn a single or double somersault and land the correct way up).

You will need a square of green or yellow paper for each Jumping Frog. For the best effect use stiff paper or even light card.

The Jumping Frog is a traditional Japanese design.

Begin with your paper arranged in the way shown in picture 1.

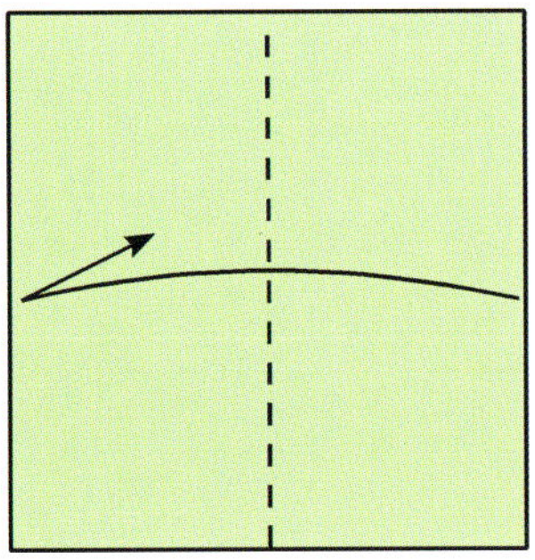

1 Fold in half from left to right, crease firmly, then unfold.

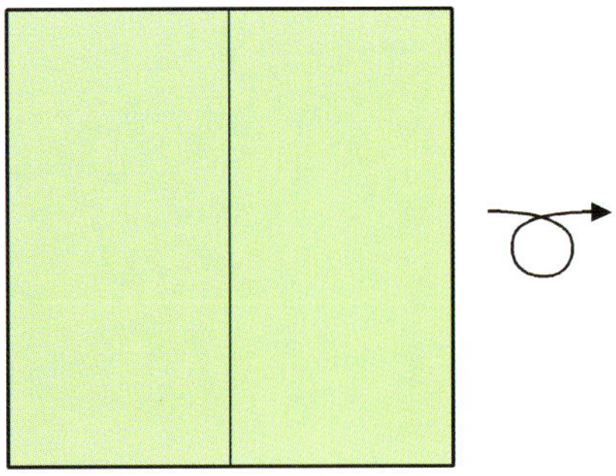

2 Turn over sideways.

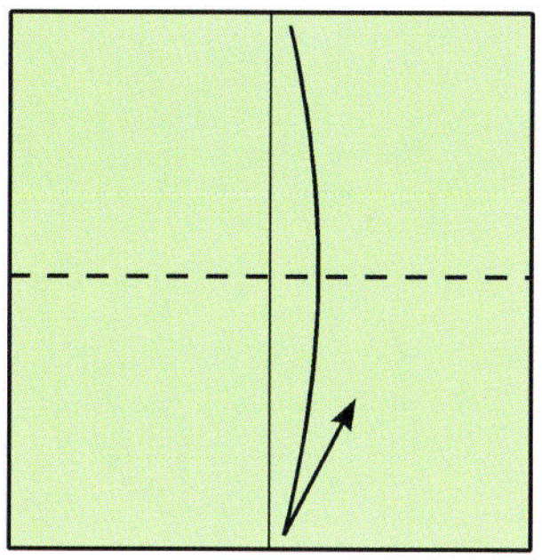

3 Fold in half from top to bottom, crease firmly, then unfold.

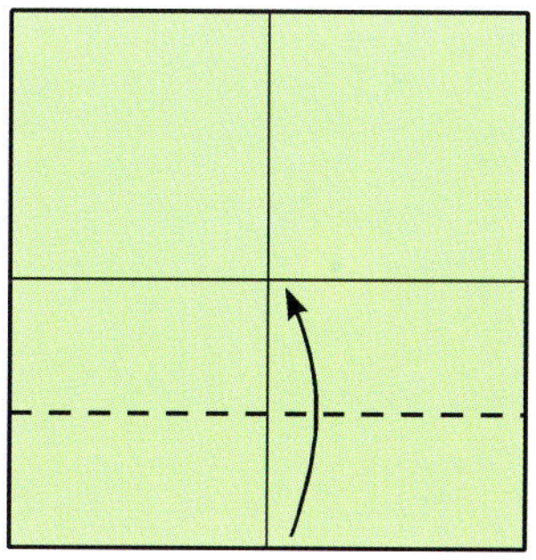

4 Fold the bottom edge upward to lie along the crease made in step 3.

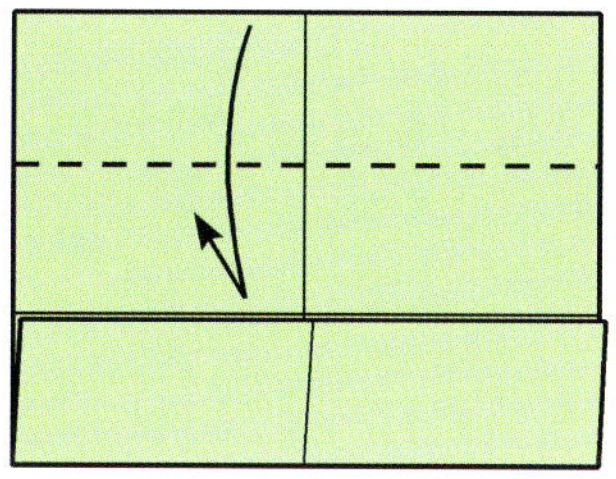

5 Fold the top edge downward to lie along the crease made in step 3, crease firmly, then unfold.

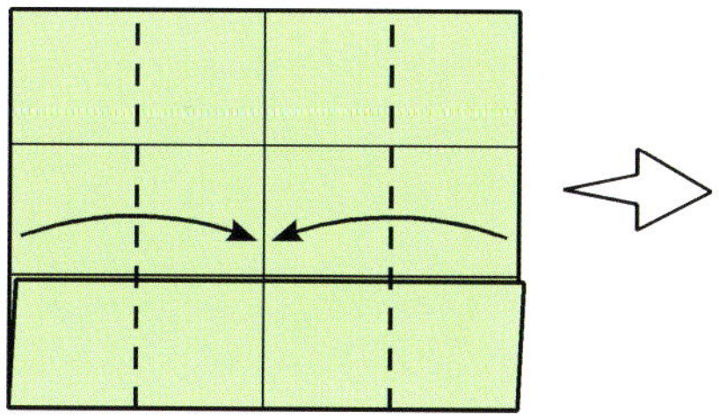

6 Fold both the left and right edges inward to lie along the crease made in step 1. Crease firmly. The next picture has been drawn to a larger scale.

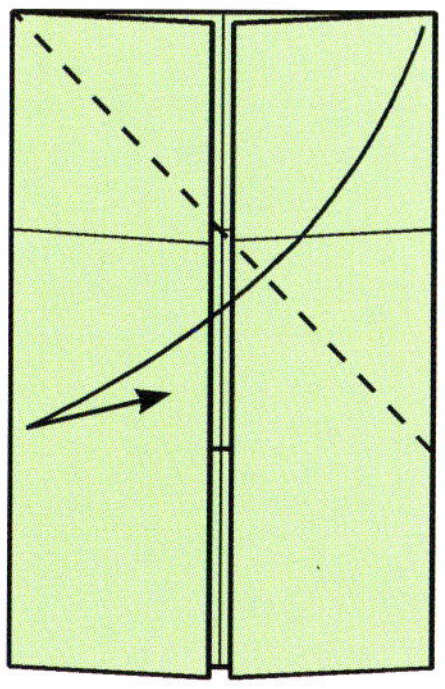

7 Fold the top edge diagonally downward to lie along the left-hand edge, crease firmly, then unfold.

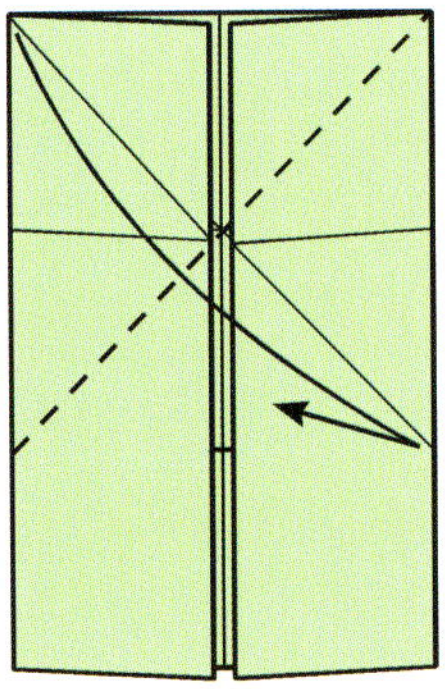

8 Fold the top edge diagonally downward to lie along the right-hand edge, crease firmly, then unfold.

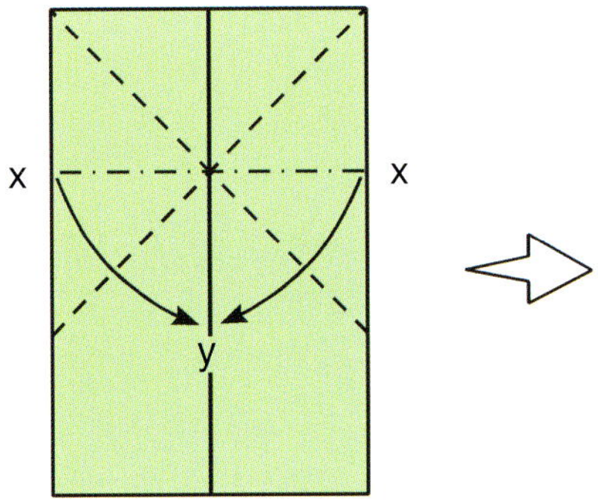

9 Use the existing creases to fold both points marked x to point y. If you have followed the instructions carefully the top two thirds of the model will collapse into the form shown in picture 10. The next picture has been drawn to a larger scale.

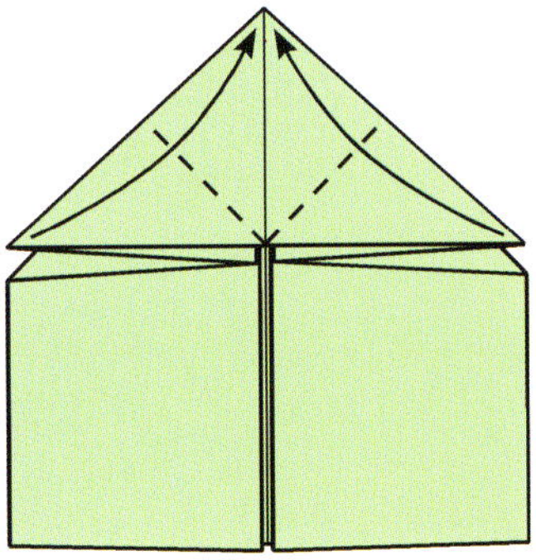

10 Fold the left and right-hand corners of the triangular flap inward and upward as shown.

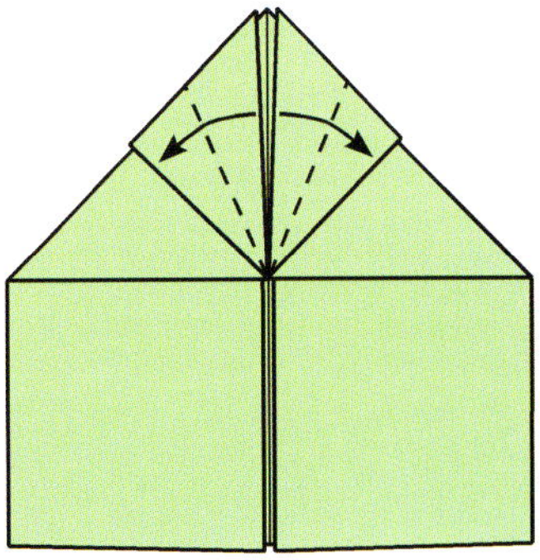

11 Fold the inside edges of both small triangular flaps outward again in the way shown here. Picture 12 shows what the result should look like.

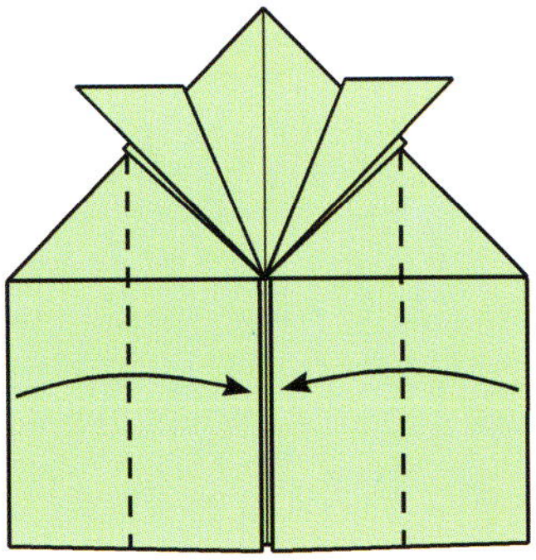

12 Fold the left and right-hand edges into the center. Make sure all the creases you have made to this point are firm and sharp.

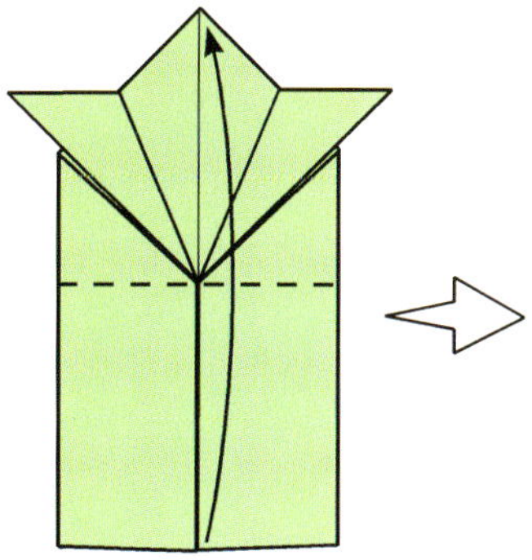

13 Fold in half from bottom to top. This fold should only be creased softly. The next picture has been drawn to a larger scale.

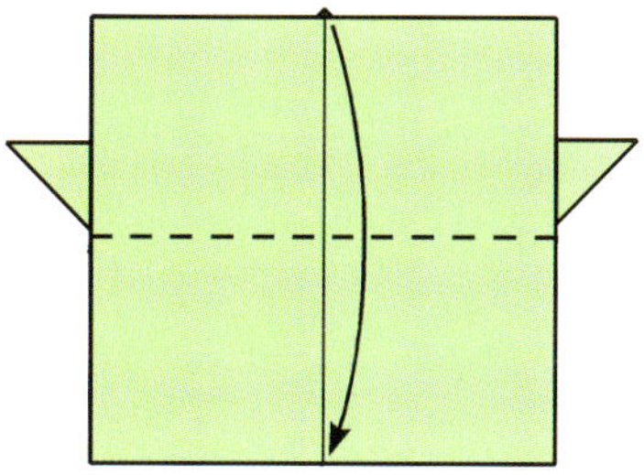

14 Fold the top layers in half from top to bottom. This fold should only be creased softly.

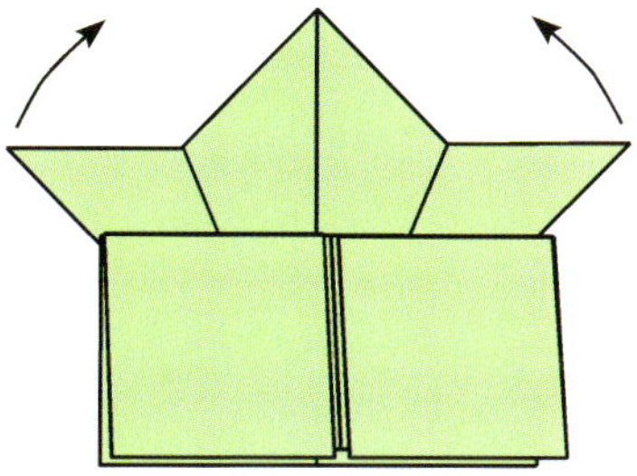

15 Allow the softly creased folds to spring open slightly and open up the front legs to support the body.

16 The Jumping Frog is finished. Stand upright in the way shown in picture 17.

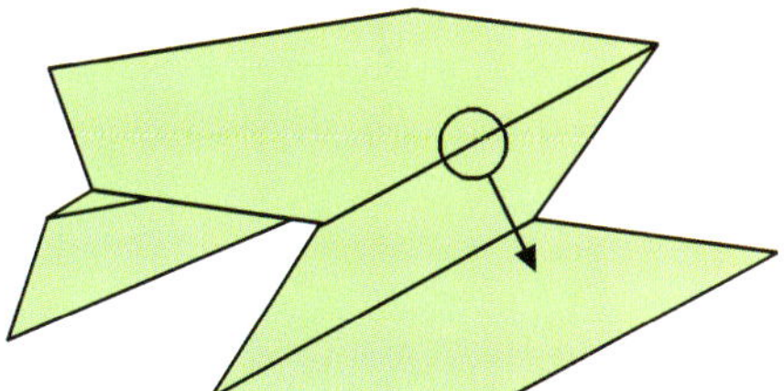

17 To make the frog jump first place the index finger of your right hand on the frog's back at the point marked with a circle then move it gently in the direction of the arrow. The spring will first compress, then release as your finger slips off. With practice you will be able to make the frog jump quite a surprising distance. You can make a frog that will jump even further if you use a small piece of cardboard such as a business card and begin folding from step 9.

Hound

Hound is the first of two related dog designs in this book. It is simple yet subtle. The folds are not precisely located, but have to be judged mostly by eye alone on the "right about there" principle. Small variations in the placing and angle of the folds can have large effects on the appearance of the finished design. If you want your Hound to look as much like the final picture shown here as possible make sure you carefully compare your results to the pictures at every stage. If this doesn't bother you then just experiment wildly. This is the best possible way to learn to understand the subtleties of animal origami design.

You will need a square of brown paper for each Hound. The design will work well with almost any thickness of paper.

Designed by David Mitchell.

Begin with your paper arranged in the way shown in picture 1.

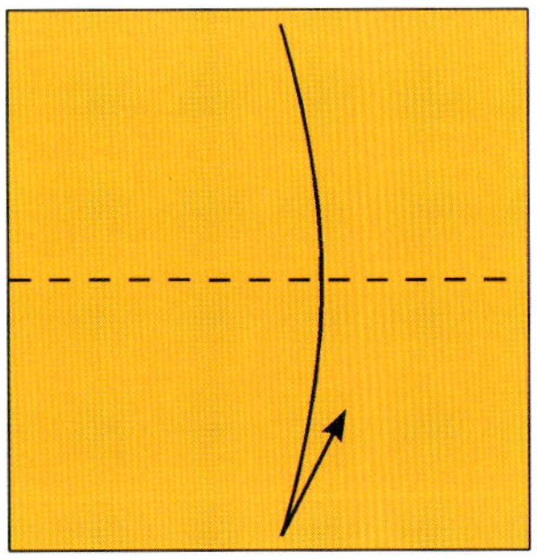

1 Fold in half from top to bottom, crease firmly, then unfold.

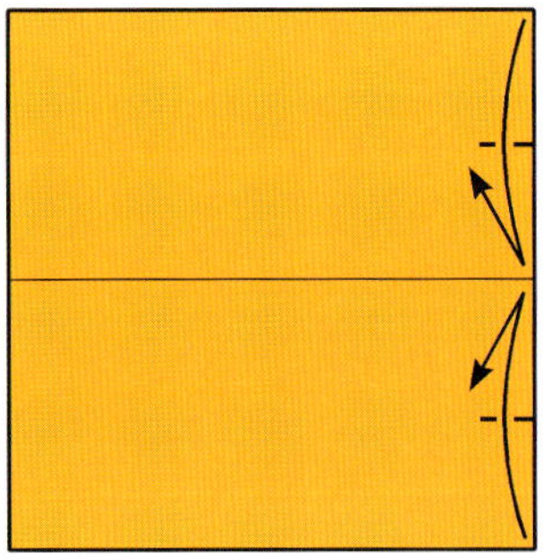

2 Fold both right-hand corners to the horizontal crease in turn, then unfold. Try to keep your creases as short and neat as possible.

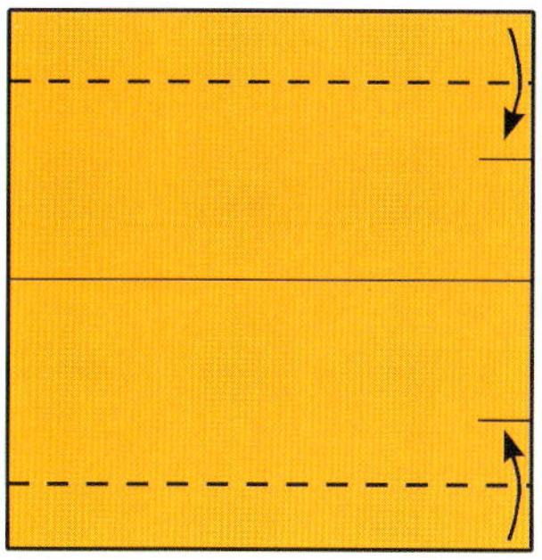

3 Fold the top and bottom edges inward using the tiny creases made in step 2 as your location points.

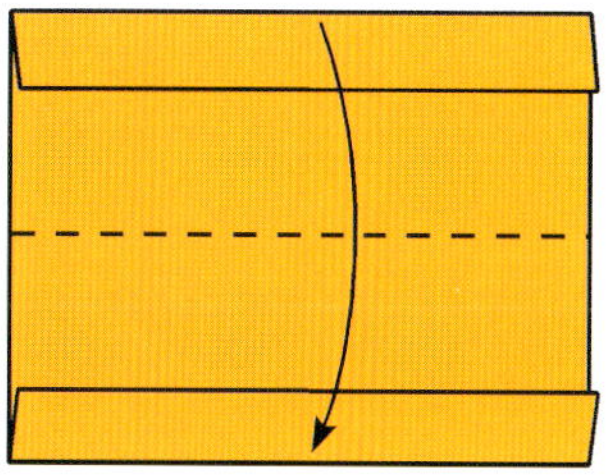

4 Fold in half from top to bottom, making sure that the folds made in step 3 remain on the outside.

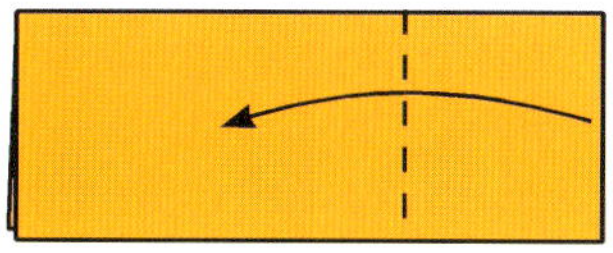

5 Fold approximately one third of the paper across to the right. Make this fold softly at first and only crease it firmly when you are sure you have got the crease positioned correctly. Picture 6 shows what the result should look like.

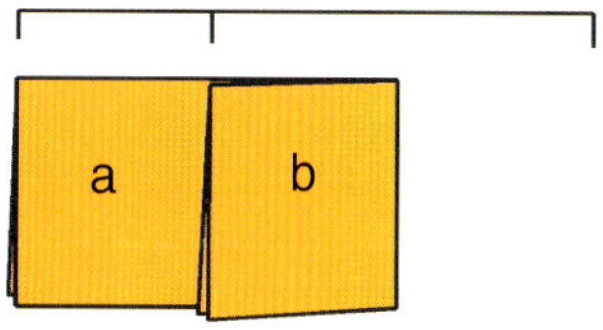

6 When the crease is in the correct position the two rectangles a and b should be the same size. Nearly the same size is good enough. Crease firmly.

7 Fold the top flap back out to the right in the way shown here. Note that the crease passes through the top right-hand corner and is made at a very shallow angle. Picture 8 shows what the result should look like.

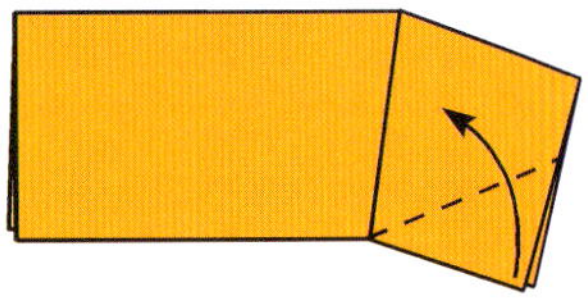

8 Fold both layers of the front flap upward as shown. Make sure the crease begins where the bottom edge of the design changes angle. One way of checking if you have got your angles right is to lay your model on top of the diagrams.

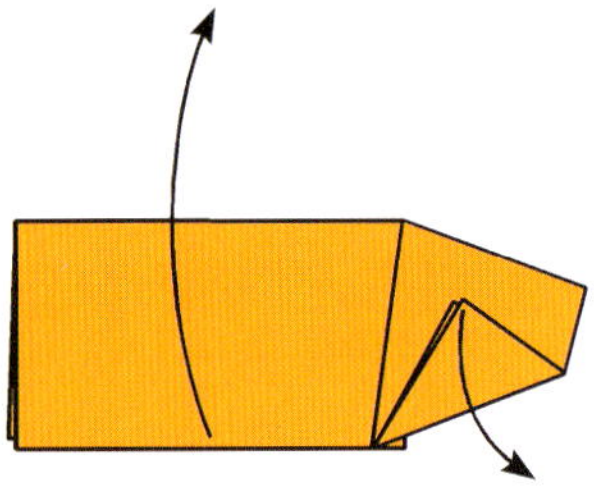

9 Unfold completely.

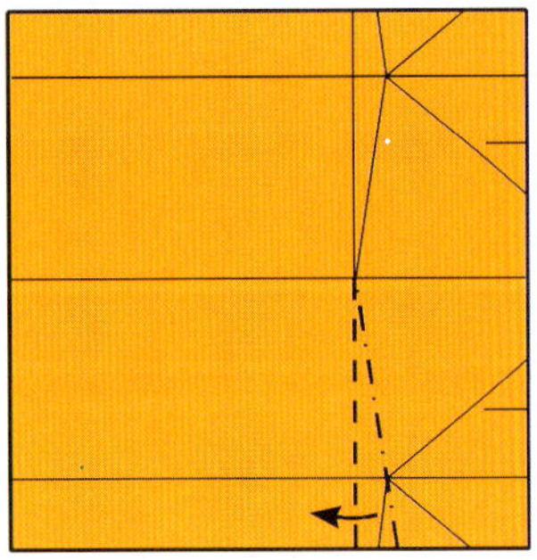

10 Make this fold using the lines of the existing creases. The right-hand crease will need to be extended downward slightly. The top half of the paper will not lie flat once this fold has been made.

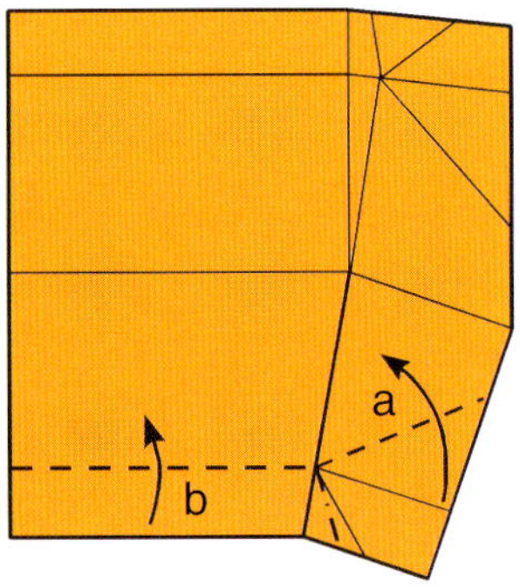

11 Make fold a then fold b using the existing creases. Only flatten the folds once fold b is made. A tiny new crease will form in between the other layers of paper as you do this. Picture 12 shows what the result should look like.

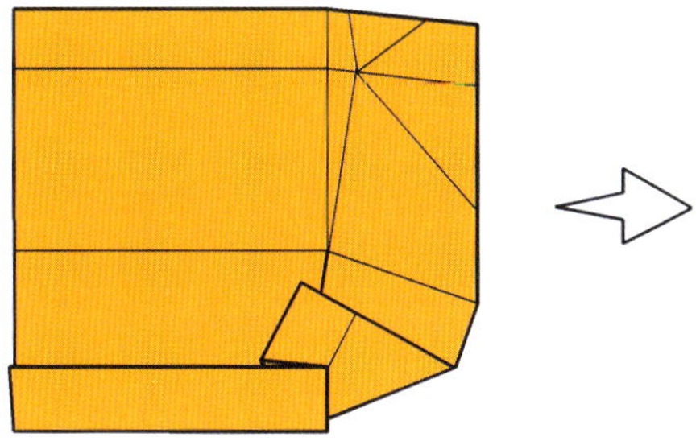

12 Repeat steps 10 and 11 on the top half of the paper. You will find this slightly more difficult because the direction of the creases will need to be reversed in order to make the folds. The design will not lie flat until step 13 is completed. The next picture has been drawn to a larger scale.

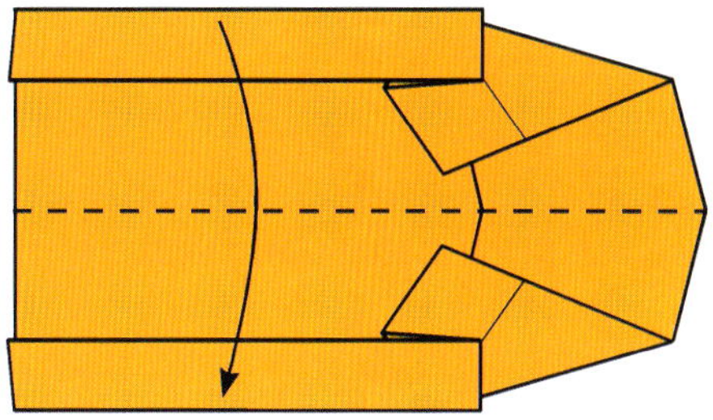

13 Fold in half to flatten.

14 Make this fold to create a simple tail.

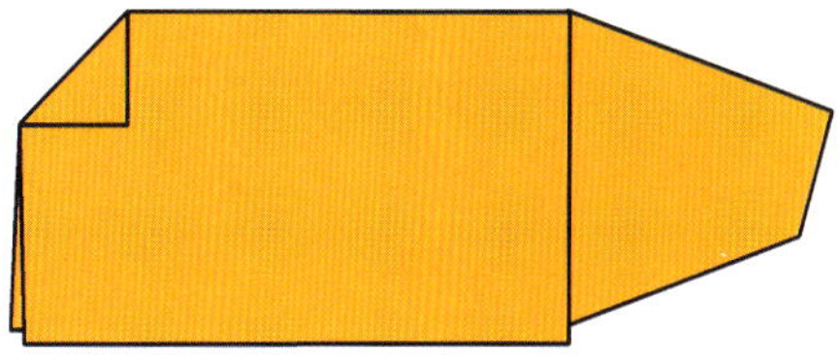

15 Hound is finished.

Pointer

Pointer is a development of the basic Hound design. The extra paper for the pointed tail is found by rotating the axis of the design so that the back of the dog now lies along the diagonal of the square. This also provides enough paper to create a slightly longer nose and a face that is further from the ground. If you experiment a little you will find that it is easy to vary the pose of the Pointer by adding extra folds to the tail and by varying the angle of the fold made in step 15.

Designed by David Mitchell.

Begin with your paper arranged in the way shown in picture 1.

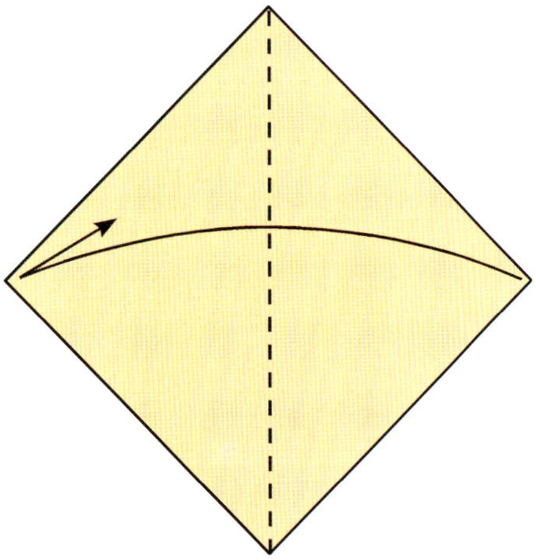

1 Fold in half from right to left, crease firmly, then unfold.

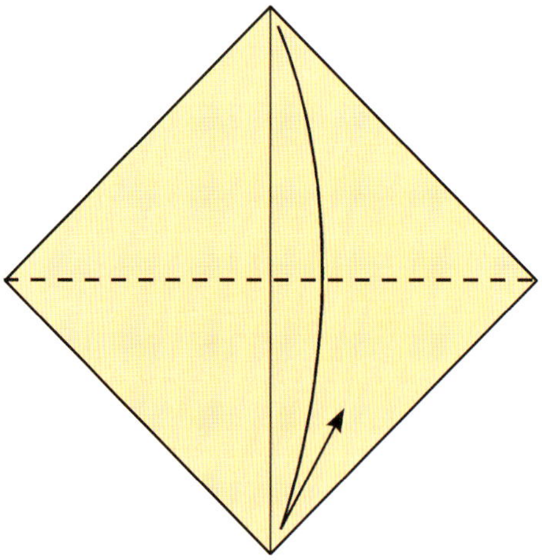

2 Fold in half from top to bottom, crease firmly, then unfold.

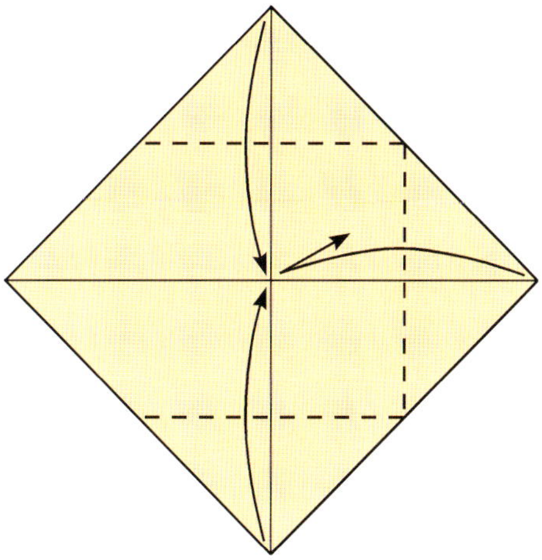

3 Fold three corners into the center as shown and crease firmly. Open out the right-hand corner only.

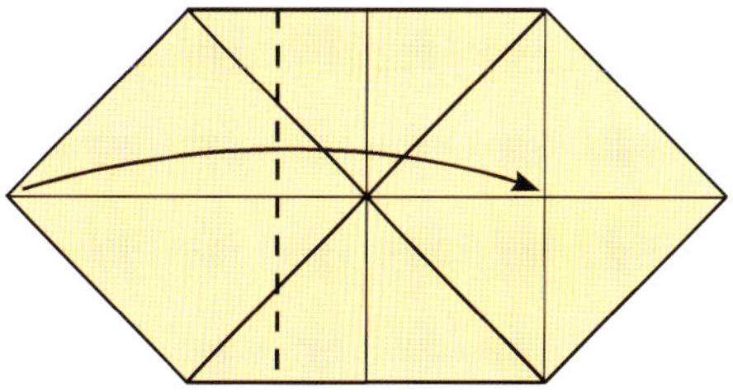

4 Fold the left-hand point across to the right as shown. This point will become the Pointer's tail.

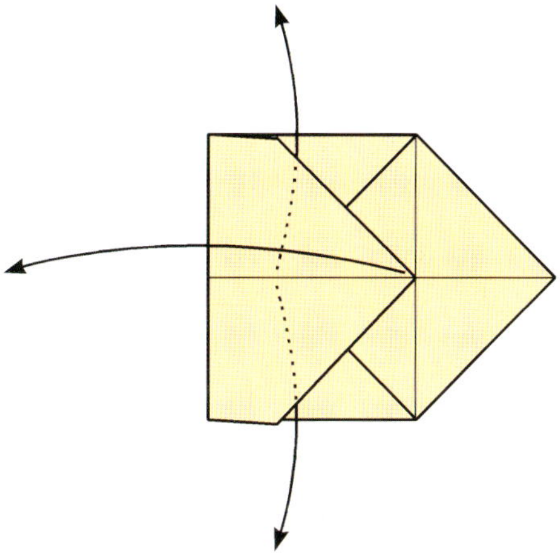

5 Unfold completely. Make sure you don't turn the paper over as you do this.

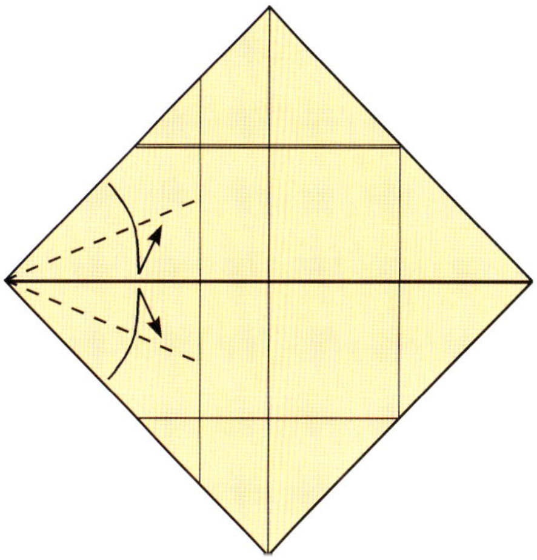

6 Fold both the sloping left-hand edges to the horizontal crease in turn, crease firmly, then unfold. Try to make sure your creases don't extend beyond the vertical crease you made in step 4.

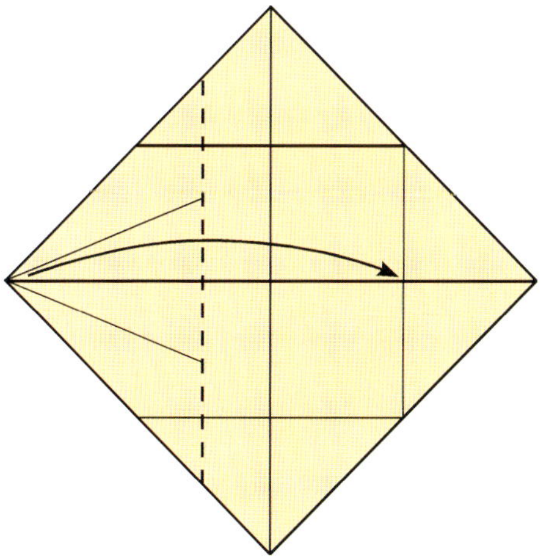

7 Fold the left-hand point across to the right using the crease made in step 4.

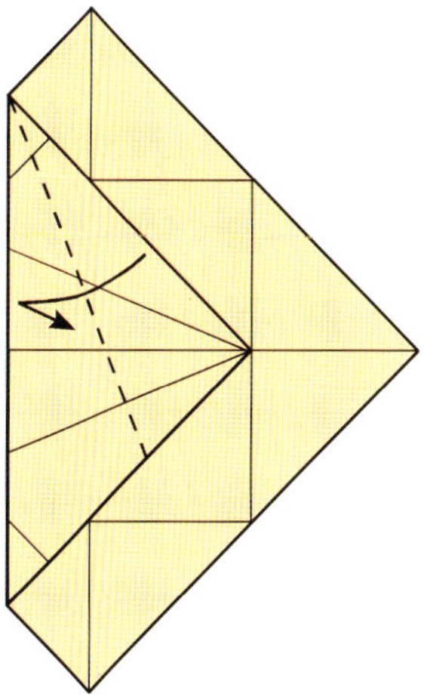

8 Fold the upper right-hand edge of the triangular flap onto the vertical edge, crease firmly, then unfold.

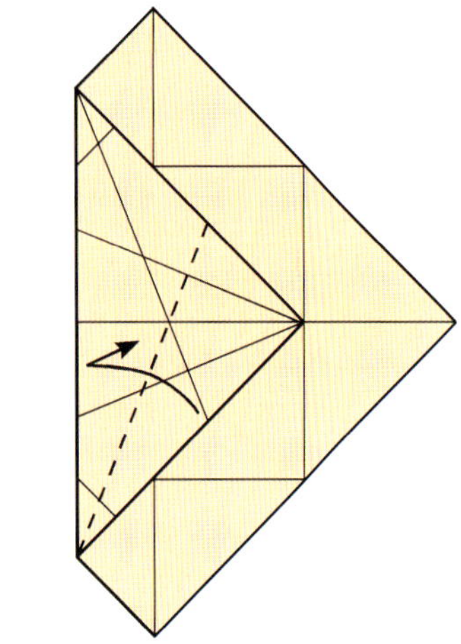

9 Repeat step 8 on the lower right-hand edge of the triangular flap.

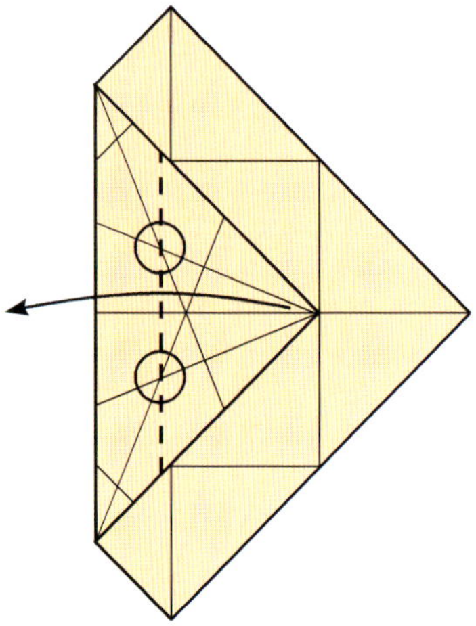

10 Fold the tail back out to the right as shown. The crease is vertical and runs through the two points where the creases made in step 6 and steps 8 and 9 intersect. Try to position this crease as accurately as possible.

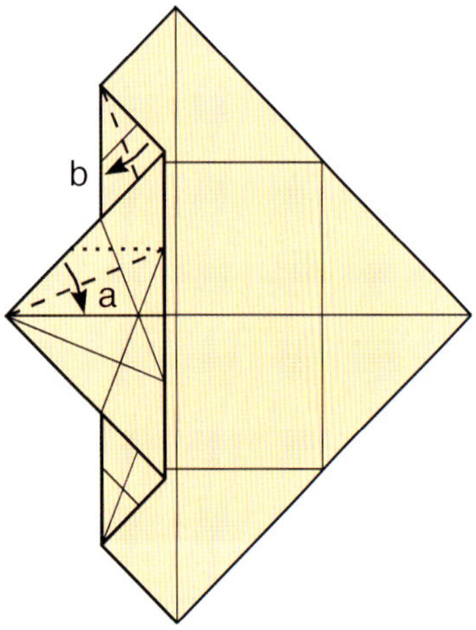

11 Make fold a by folding the upper left edge of the new triangular flap downward using the crease you made in step 6. As you do this fold b will happen automatically. As you flatten the fold a new crease will form. The position of this crease is shown by the dotted line. Picture 12 shows what the result should look like. In technical origami language this is called a swivel fold.

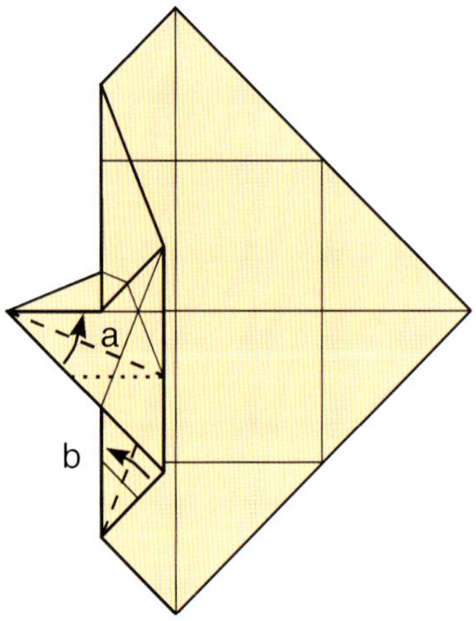

12 Repeat step 11 on the lower half of the tail.

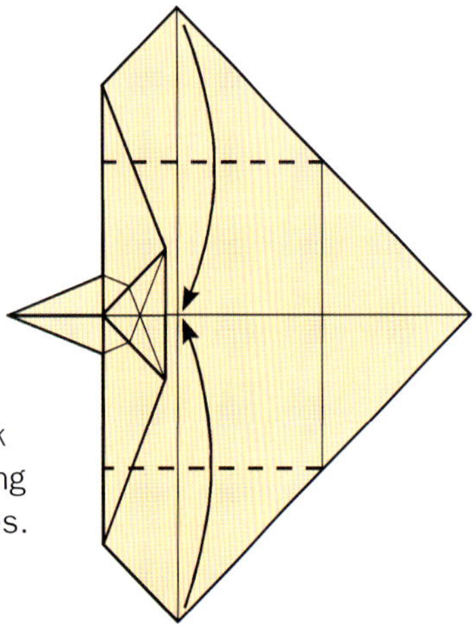

13 Fold the top and bottom points back into the center using the existing creases. Crease firmly.

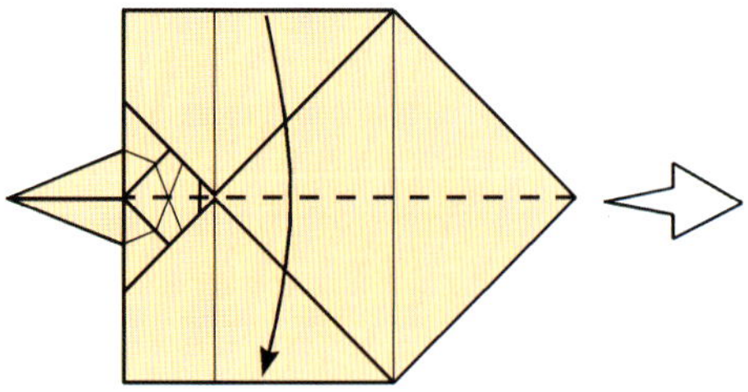

14 Fold in half from top to bottom. Crease firmly. The next picture has been drawn to a larger scale.

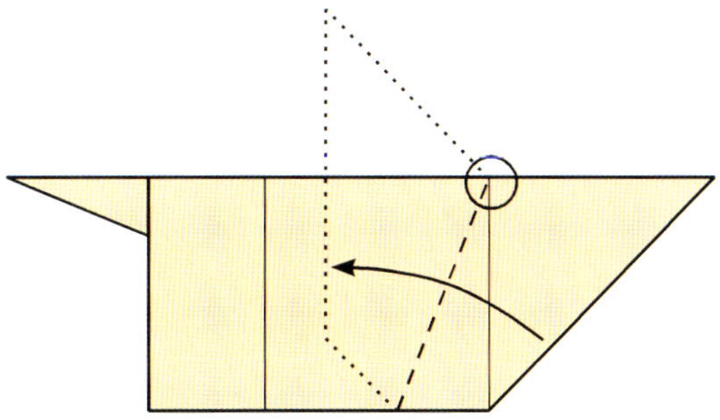

15 Begin to form the head by folding the right-hand point across to the left as shown. The dotted line shows where the paper should end up.

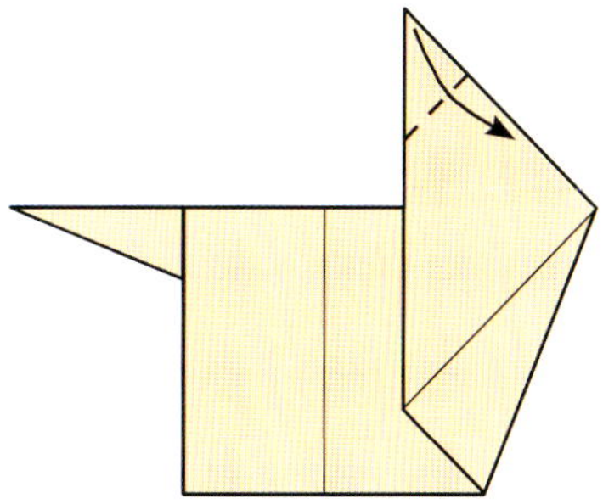

16 Fold the tip of the nose downward like this.

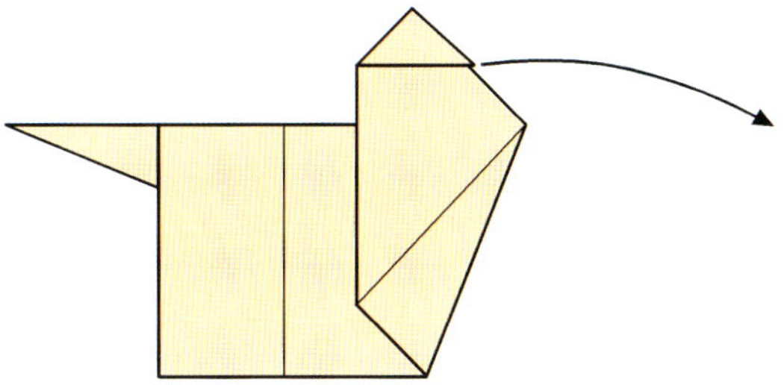

17 Pull the nose back across to the right to open out the folds made in the previous two steps.

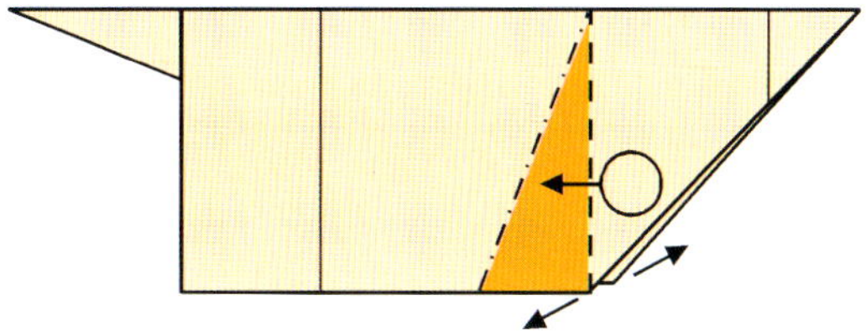

18 Separate the layers of the paper at the bottom of the design and hold them open with your left hand. With your right hand grip the paper firmly at the point marked by a circle and push gently in the direction of the arrow so that the area of the paper identified by the darker shading tucks away between the other layers. Picture 19 shows what the result should look like.

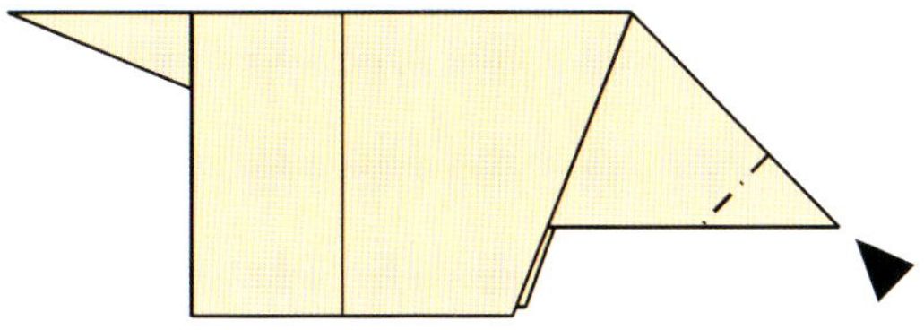

19 Finally turn the tip of the nose inside out using the creases you made in step 16.

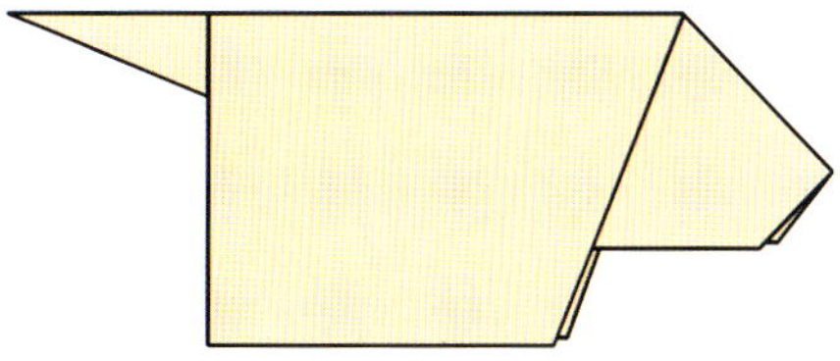

20 Pointer is finished.

Wolf Cub

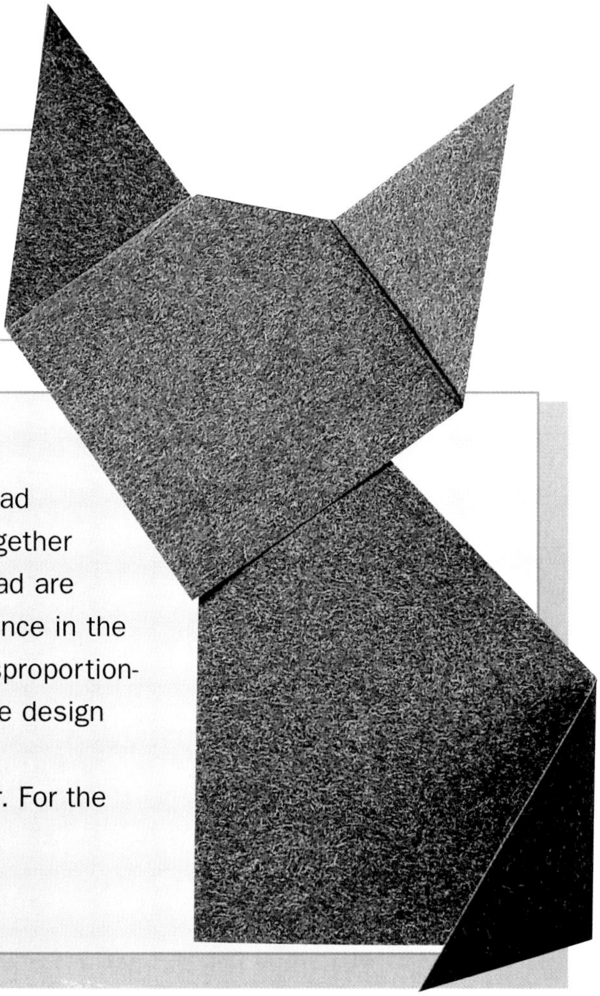

Wolf Cub is an extremely straightforward two-part design. The body is made from one square and the head from another, then the two parts are simply slotted together to achieve the final design. While the body and the head are both folded from squares of the same size, the difference in the folding sequences means that the head comes out disproportionately large. It is this disproportion in size that gives the design its cub-like appeal.

You will need two identical squares of gray paper. For the best result use fairly stiff paper.

Designed by David Mitchell.

Folding the Body

Begin with your first square arranged in the way shown in picture 1.

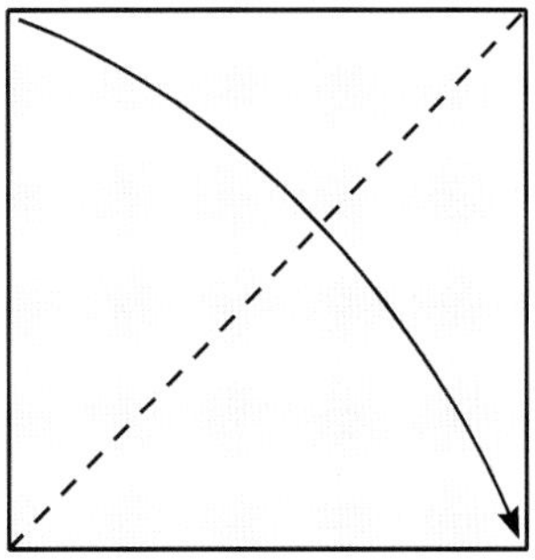

1 Fold in half diagonally.

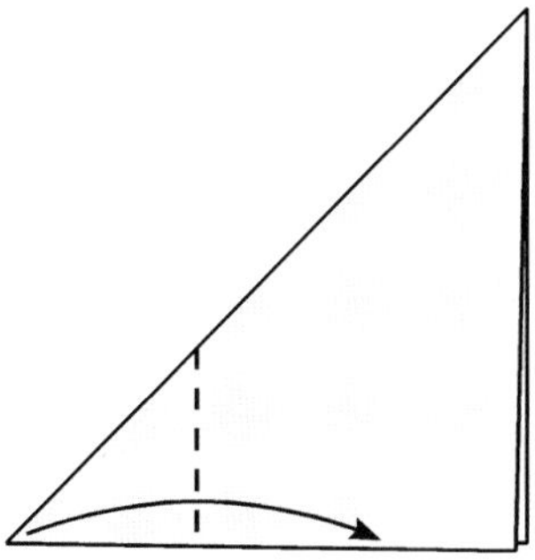

2 Fold the left-hand point across to the right as shown. Picture 3 shows what the result should look like.

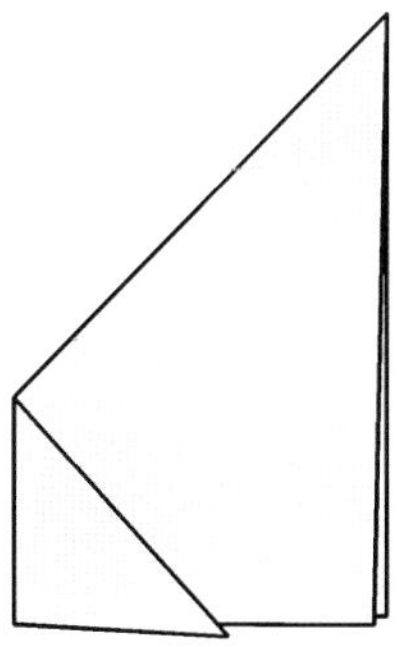

3 This is the result. Wolf Cub's body is finished.

Folding the Head

Begin with your second square arranged in the way shown in picture 4.

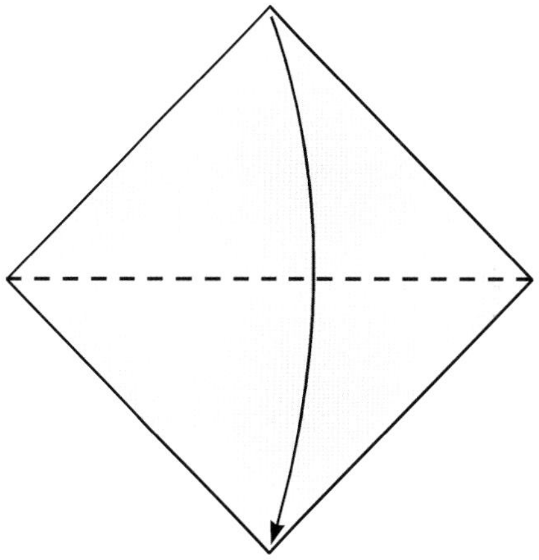

4 Fold in half diagonally from top to bottom.

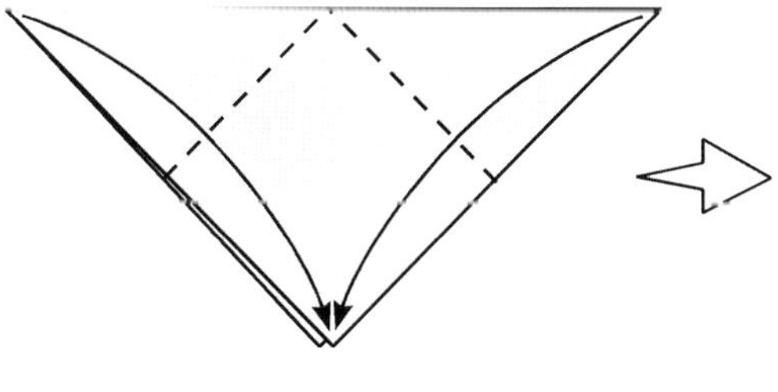

5 Fold both the top corners down to lie on top of the bottom corner. The next picture has been drawn to a larger scale.

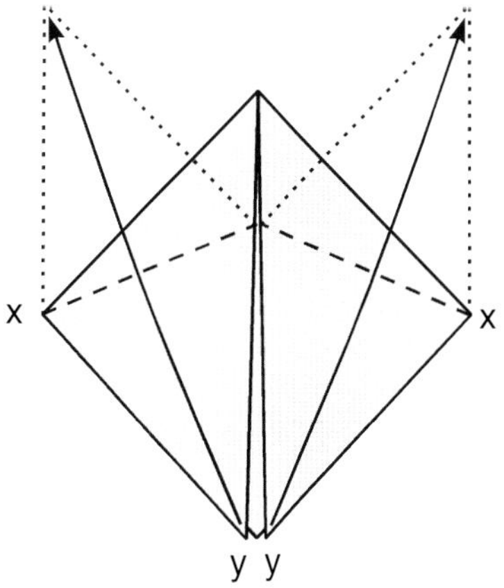

6 Fold the original top corners (both marked y) upwards as shown so that the edges lie vertically above the left and right-hand corners (both marked x). Picture 7 shows what the result should look like.

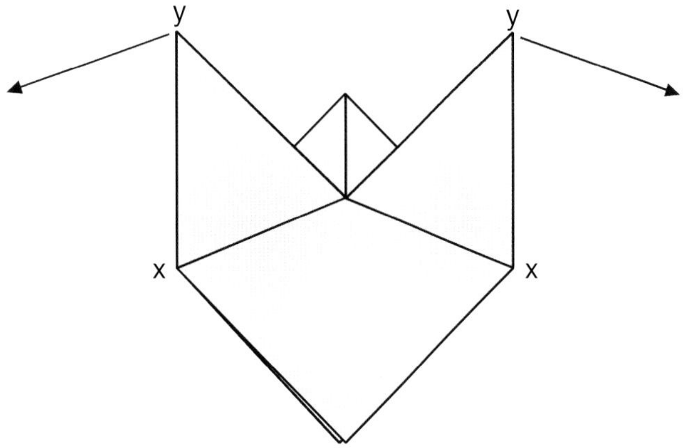

7 Pull the top corners outward to undo the folds made in steps 5 and 6.

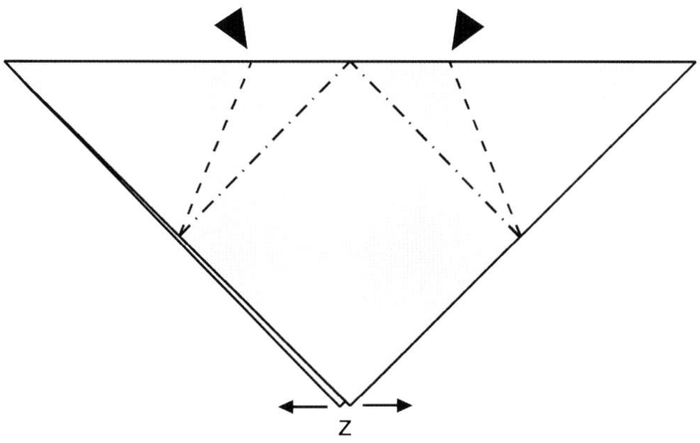

8 Separate the layers at point z and form the ears one by one by tucking the paper into a zigzag in between the layers of the head using the creases made in steps 5 and 6. Picture 9 shows what the result should look like.

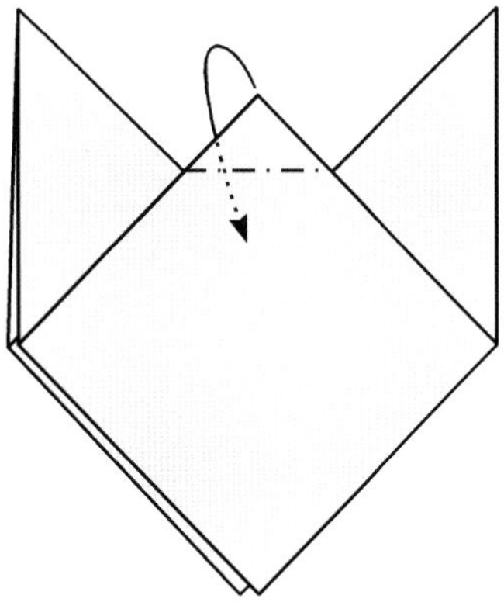

9 Fold the center top point backward to complete the head. Crease firmly.

Assembling Wolf Cub

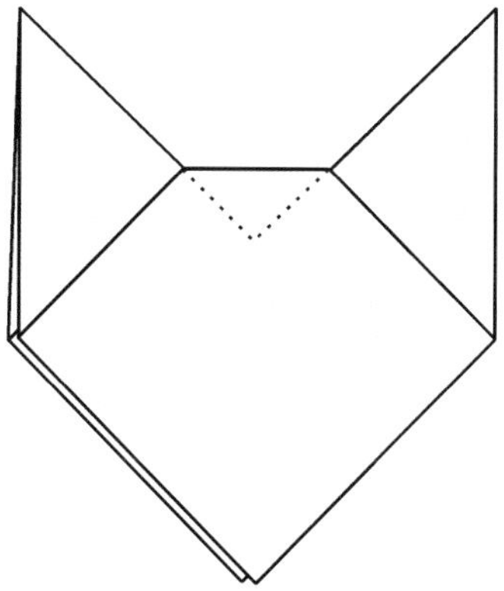

10 The dotted line shows the position of the original center top flap which is now hidden behind the other layers of the model. Wolf Cub's head is finished.

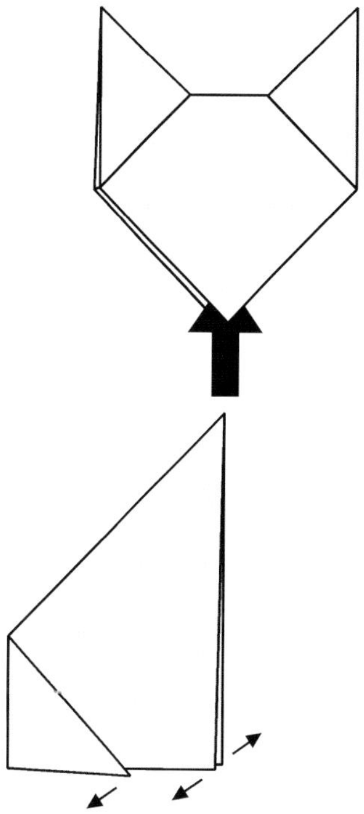

11 Slide the body inside the head. Sometimes the hidden layers of paper inside the head get in the way when you try to achieve this. If this happens open the head out slightly to help you sort things out. Picture 12 shows what the result should look like. Once the two parts are assembled open out the tail and the right-hand side of the body slightly so that Wolf Cub will stand.

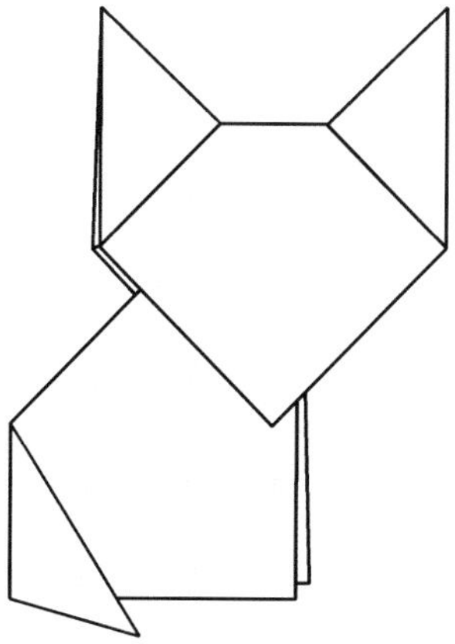

12 Wolf Cub is finished.

Pig

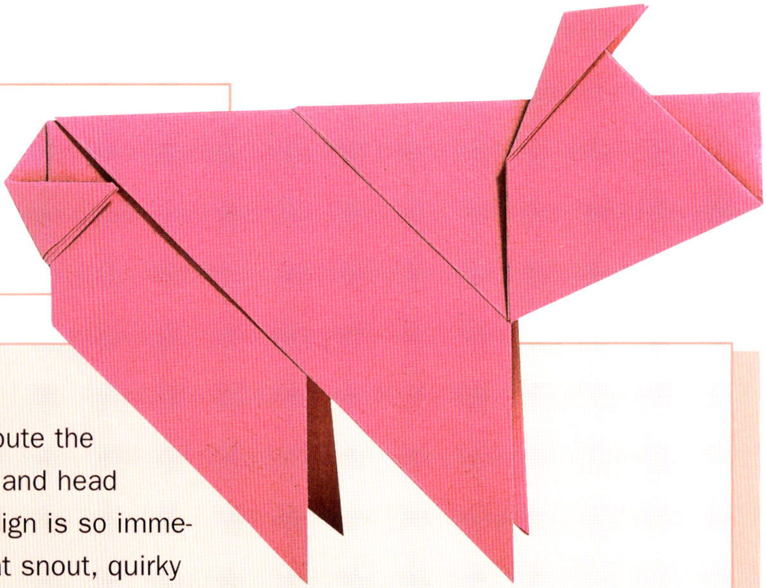

Pig is made in three parts which contribute the back legs and tail, front legs and body, and head and ears. It is easy to see why this design is so immediately recognisable as a pig with its flat snout, quirky ears, tapered legs and curly tail.

You will need three identical squares of pink or brown paper. The design works best from fairly stiff paper.

Designed by David Mitchell.

Begin with your first sheet of paper arranged in the way shown in picture 1. All three sheets are folded the same up to step 3.

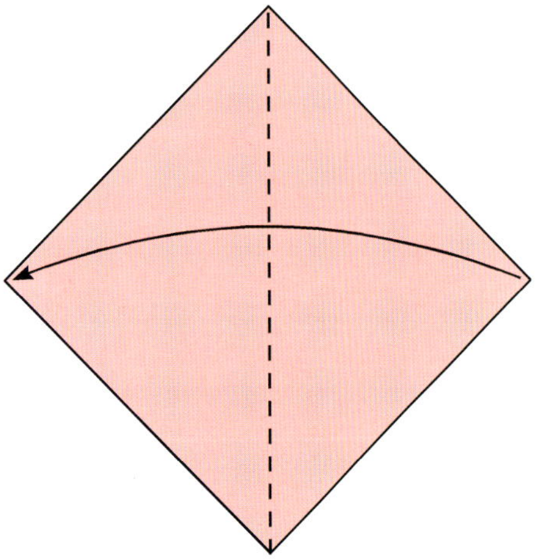

1 Fold in half from right to left as shown.

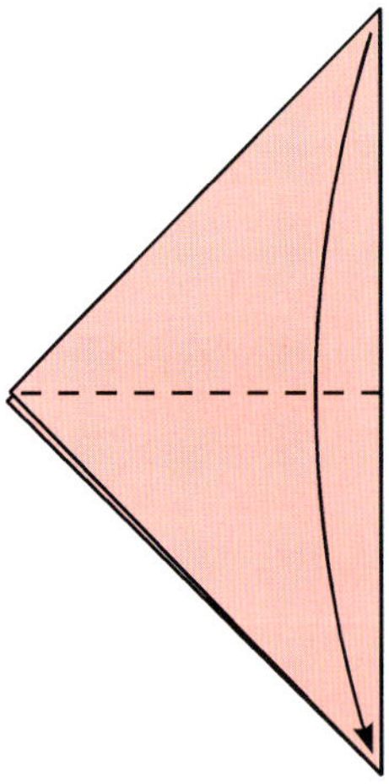

2 Fold in half again from top to bottom.

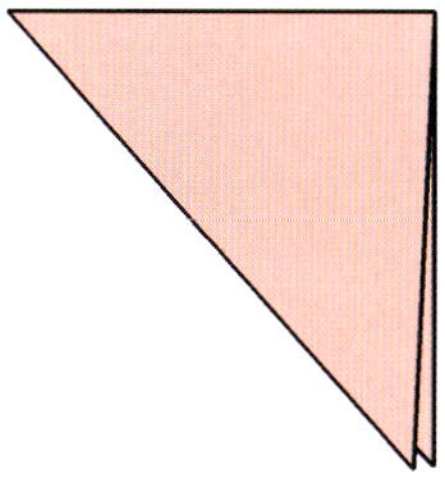

3 This is the result. Fold all three squares to this stage, then follow steps 4 through 9 to turn one square into the tail and hind legs. The next picture is drawn to a larger scale.

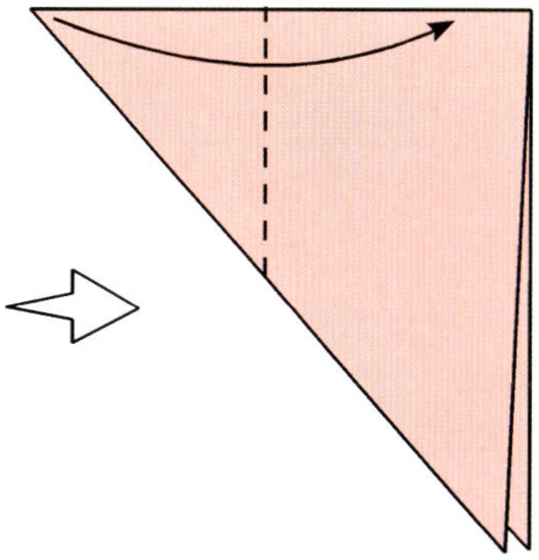

4 Begin to form the tail by folding the top left-hand corner across to the right as shown. There is no way of locating this fold exactly. Look at picture 5 to see what the result should look like.

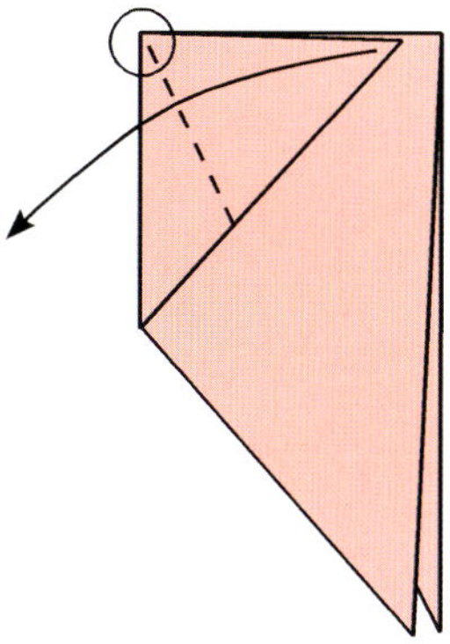

5 Now fold the tip of the tail back down to the right. Look at picture 6 to see what the result should look like.

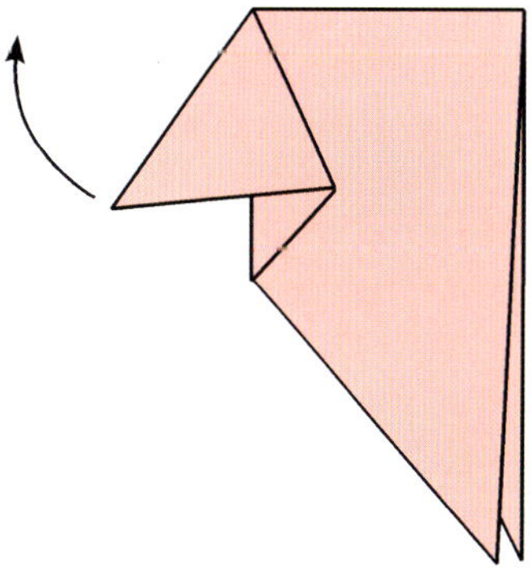

6 Once you are satisfied that your model looks something like this crease your folds firmly and pull the tail straight again.

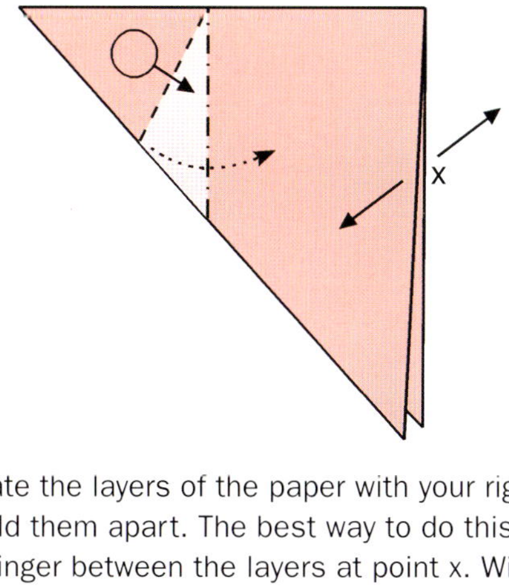

7 Separate the layers of the paper with your right hand and hold them apart. The best way to do this is to slip a finger between the layers at point x. With your left hand grip the paper firmly at the point marked by a circle and push gently in the direction of the arrow so that the area of the paper identified by the lighter shading tucks away between the other layers.

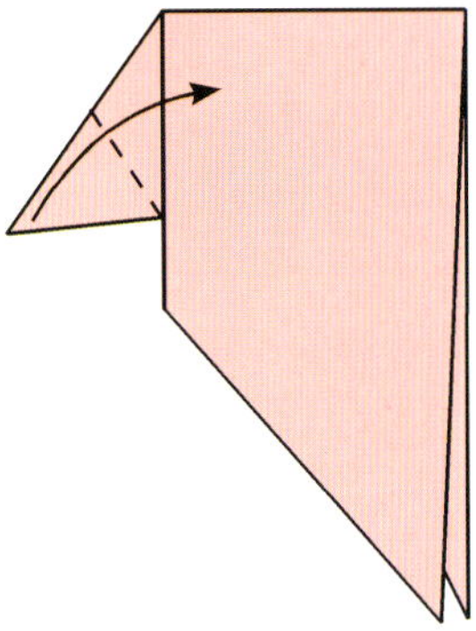

8 Complete the tail by folding the tip upward to the right in front of the body.

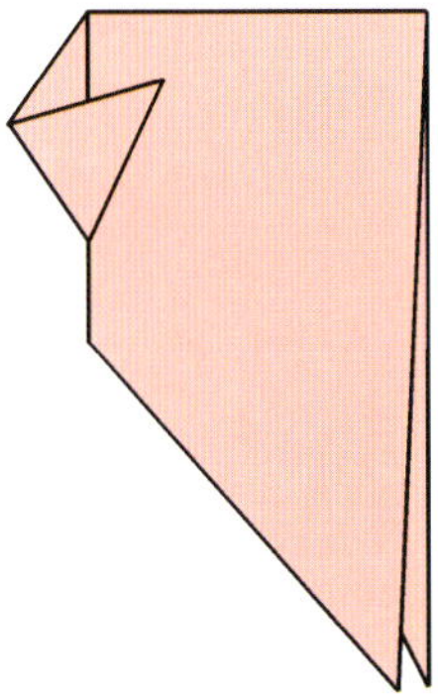

9 The tail and back legs are finished.

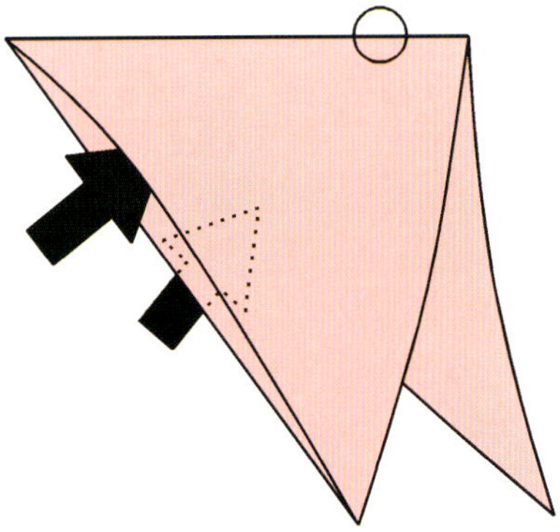

10 Take the second square and hold it loosely between the finger and thumb of your right hand at the point marked by a circle. Insert the finger and thumb of your left hand into the two pockets to the left and pull the inside flap slightly downward to separate the layers, then tighten the grip of your right hand to hold the layers apart.

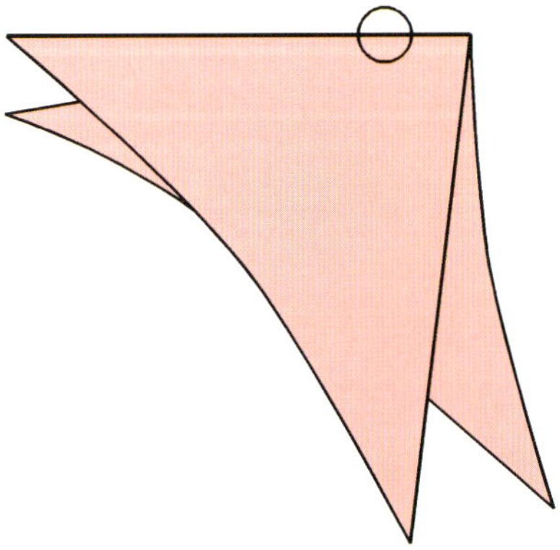

11 You should now be holding the paper in this position.

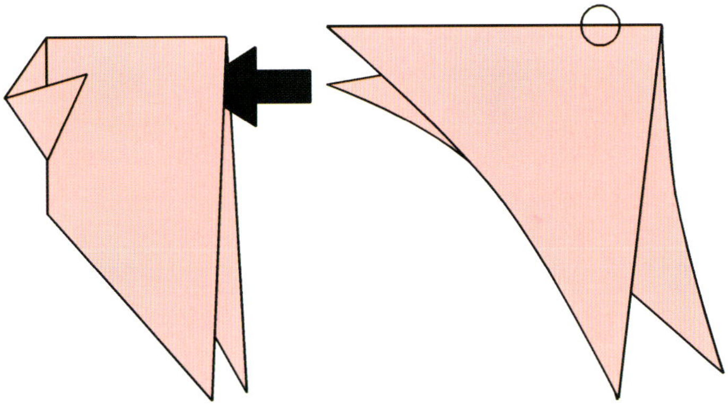

12 Still holding the layers of the center section apart slide the center section around the tail section to link them together. Picture 13 shows what the result should look like.

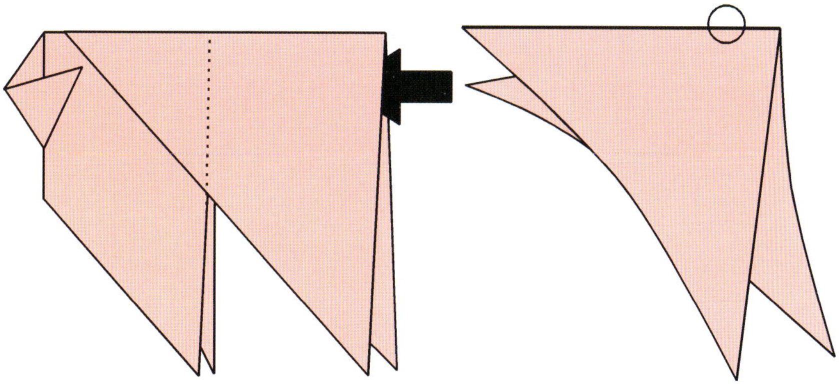

13 Add the front section in a similar way.

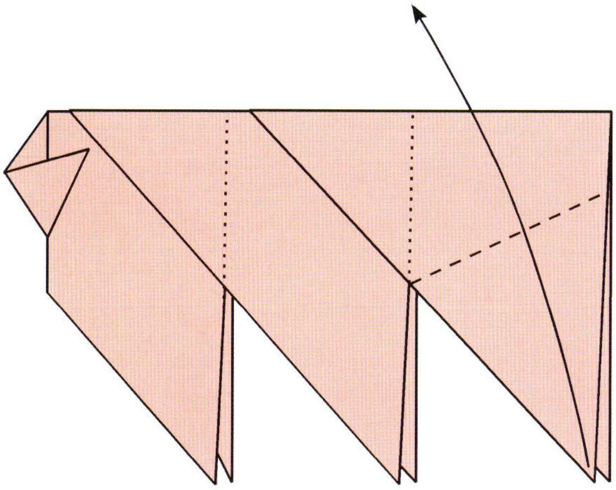

14 All three sections are now in place. Begin to form the head by folding the front bottom right-hand flap upward in the way shown. Picture 15 shows what the result should look like.

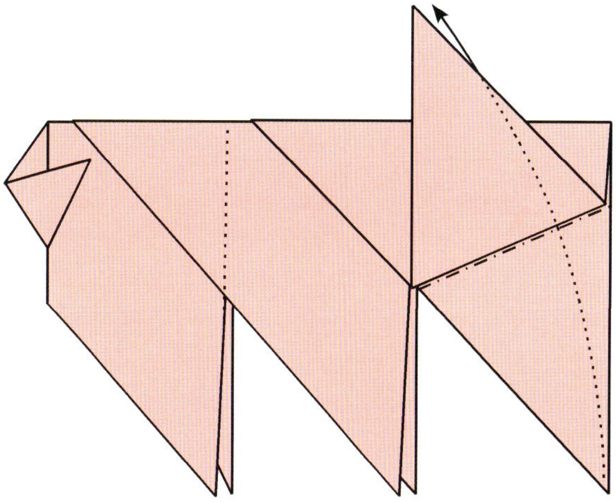

15 Fold the tip of the second flap upward behind the model in a similar way. Make sure that the edges and pointed tips of both flaps line up with each other as exactly as possible.

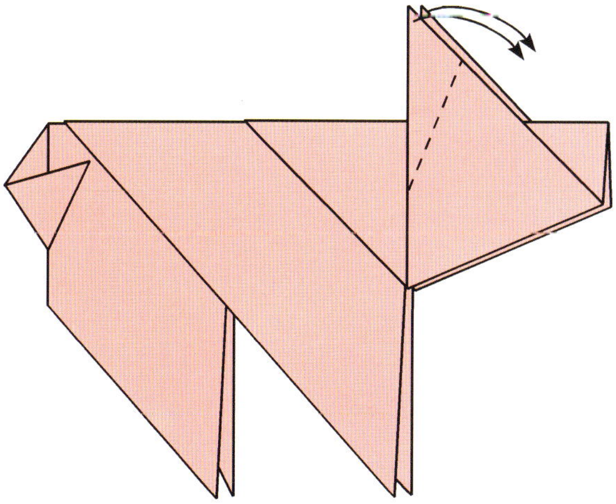

16 Fold the tips of both flaps forward to form the ears in the way shown here. Picture 17 shows what the result should look like.

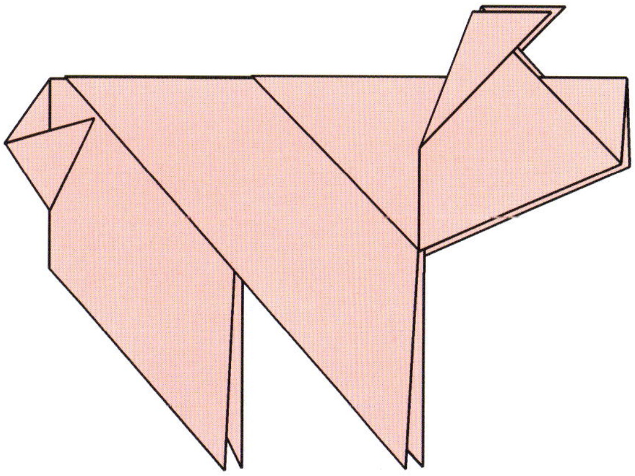

17 Pig is finished.

Horse

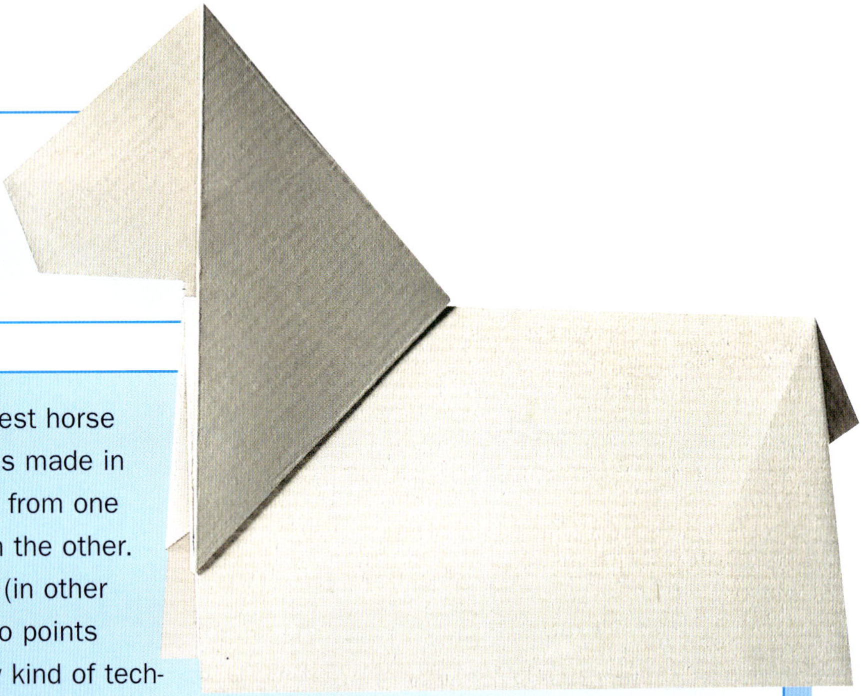

This design is undoubtedly the easiest horse in the animal origami repertoire. It is made in two parts, the body and tail coming from one square and the neck and head from the other. By a wonderful piece of serendipity (in other words a great piece of luck), the two points at the top of the head (which in any kind of technically decent design should not be there) act to suggest the pricked ears of a lively stallion.

You will need two identical squares of gray or black paper. For the best effect use fairly thin paper.

Designed by David Mitchell.

Folding the Body

Begin with the first square arranged in the way shown in picture 1.

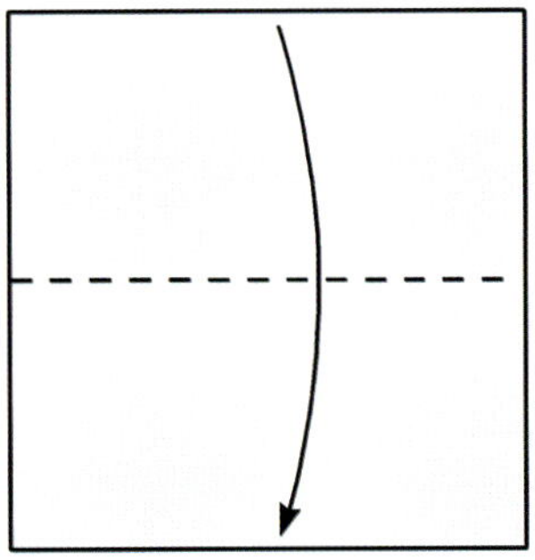

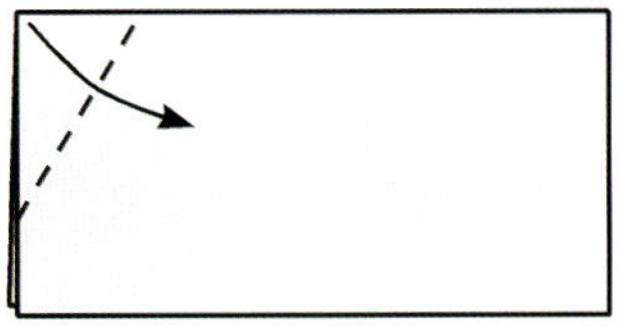

1 Fold in half from top to bottom.

2 Begin to form the tail by making the small fold shown here. Picture 3 shows what the result should look like. Crease firmly.

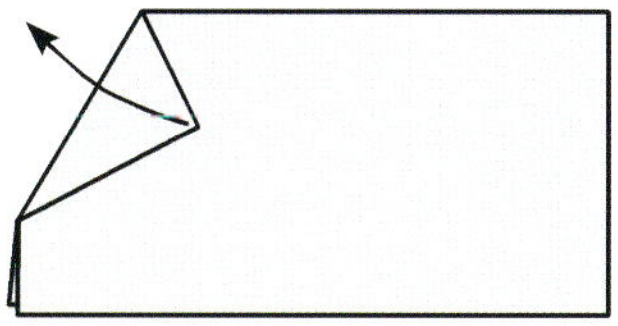

3 Open out the fold made in step 2.

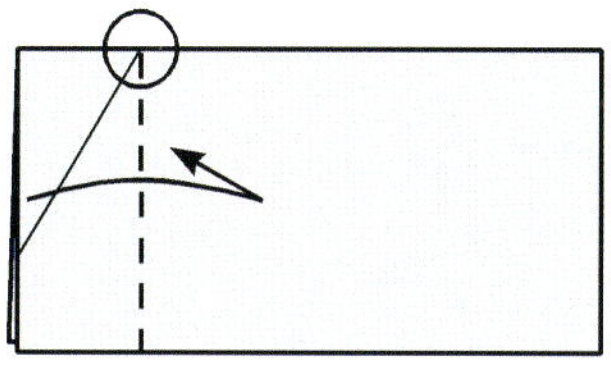

4 Use the point where the crease made in step 2 intersects the top edge (marked with a circle) to locate this fold. Fold, crease firmly, then unfold.

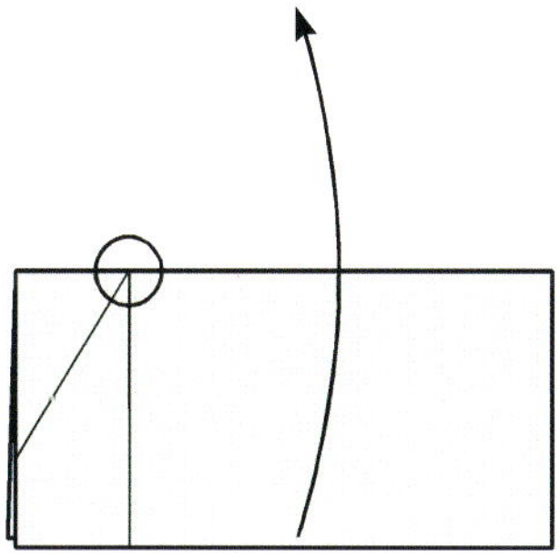

5 Open out the fold made in step 1.

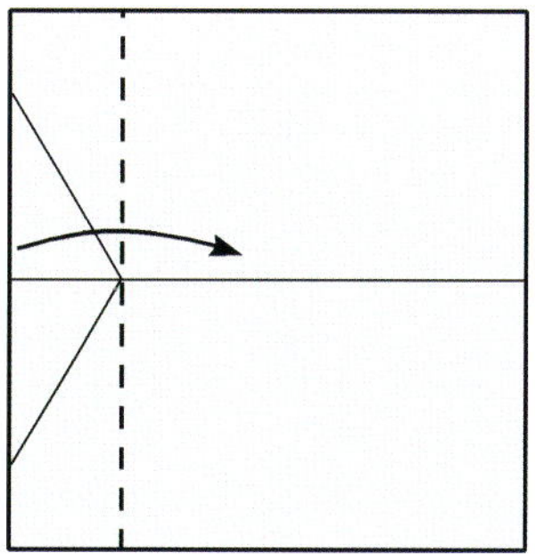

6 Make this fold using the crease made in step 4.

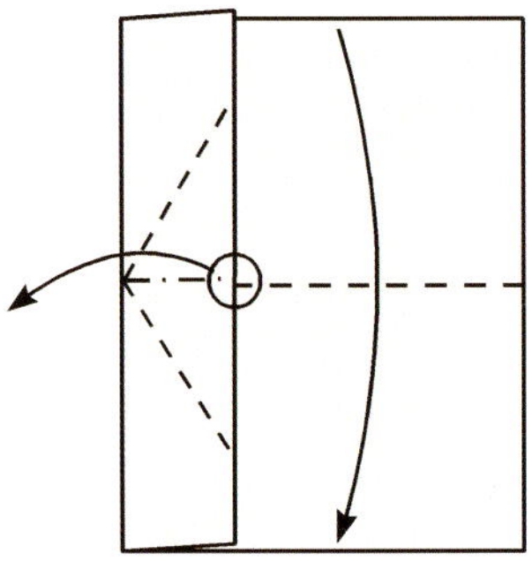

7 Fold the model in half from top to bottom while simultaneously pulling the tip of the tail across to the left. All the creases you need are already there. Picture 8 shows what the result should look like.

8 The body and tail are finished.

Folding the Head

Begin with the second square arranged in the way shown in picture 9.

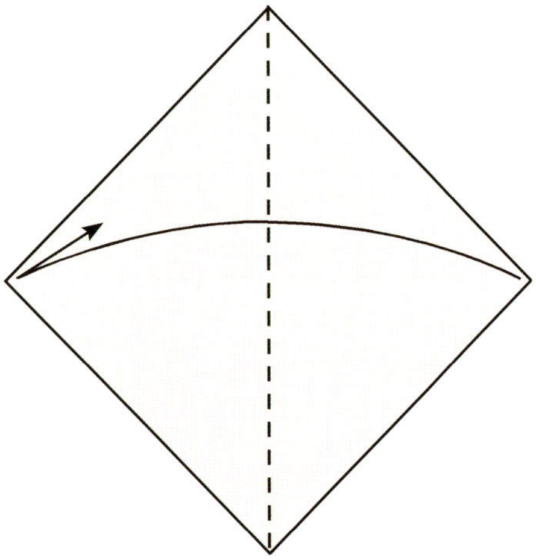

9 Fold in half from right to left, crease firmly, and then unfold.

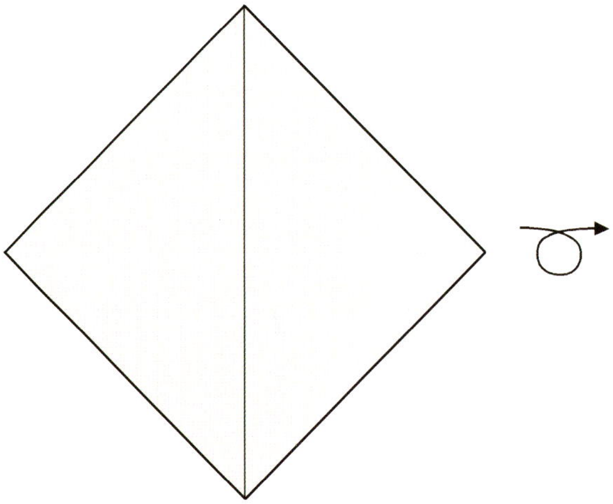

10 Turn over sideways.

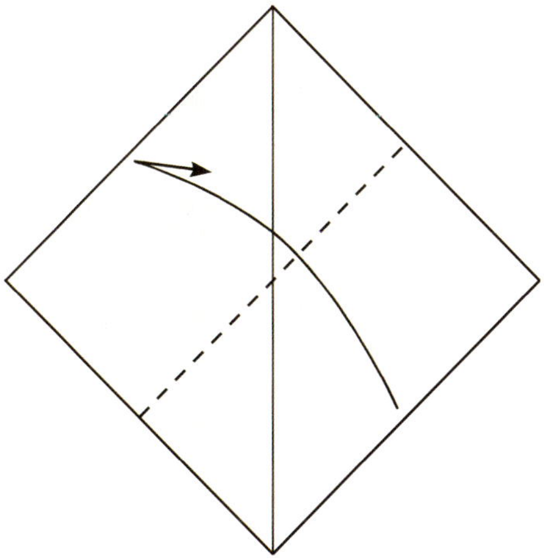

11 Fold in half as shown, crease firmly then unfold.

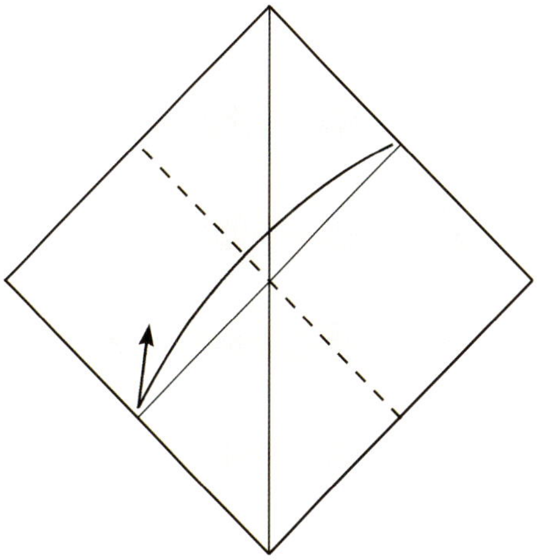

12 Fold in half as shown, crease firmly then unfold.

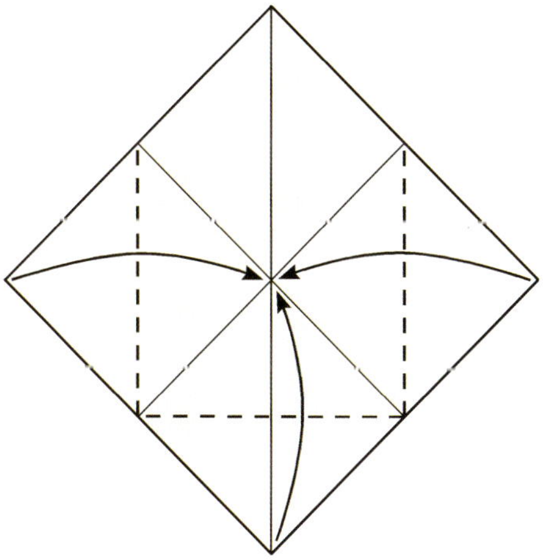

13 Fold three corners into the center as shown.

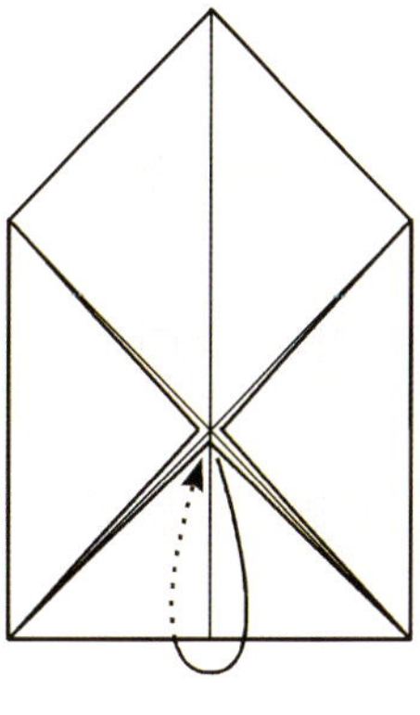

14 Swing the bottom flap out of sight behind the model.

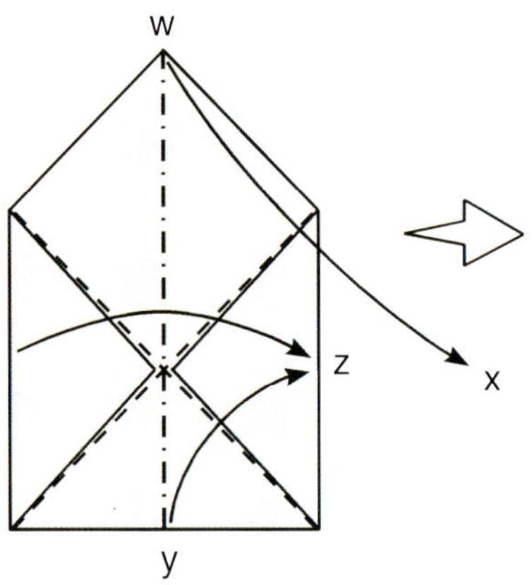

15 This is the crucial move. Fold in half from right to left while simultaneously allowing point w to collapse to point x and point y to z. If you have followed the instructions carefully to this stage the existing creases should allow this to happen quite naturally. The next picture has been drawn to a larger scale.

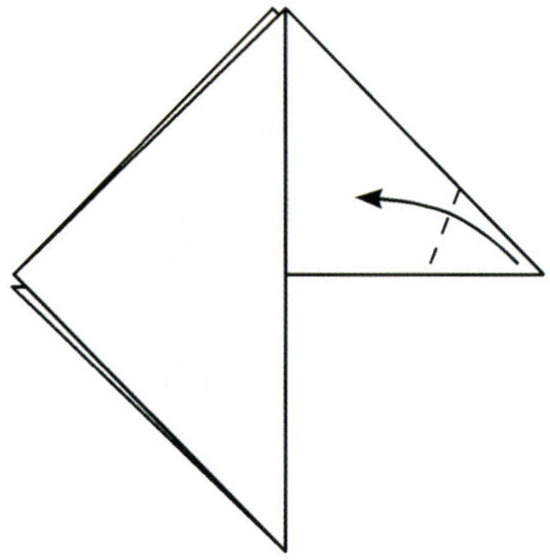

16 This is what the head should look like now. Fold the tip of the right-hand point inward to begin forming the nose.

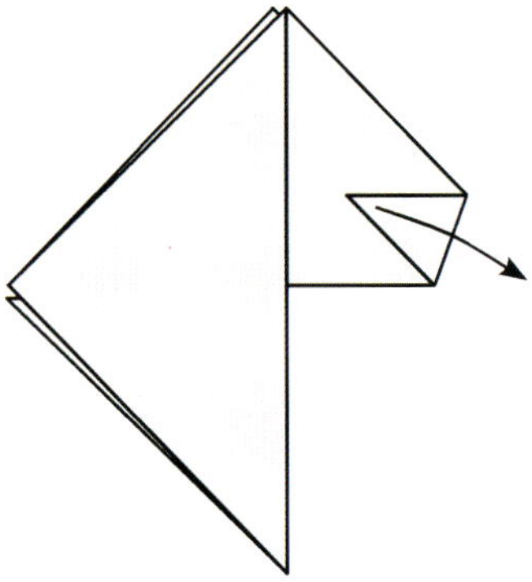

17 Undo the fold made in step 16.

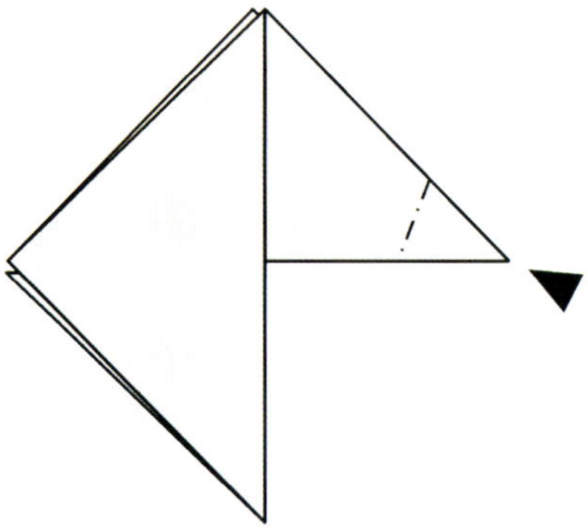

18 Push the tip of the right-hand point inside out in between the layers of the head using the creases made in step 17.

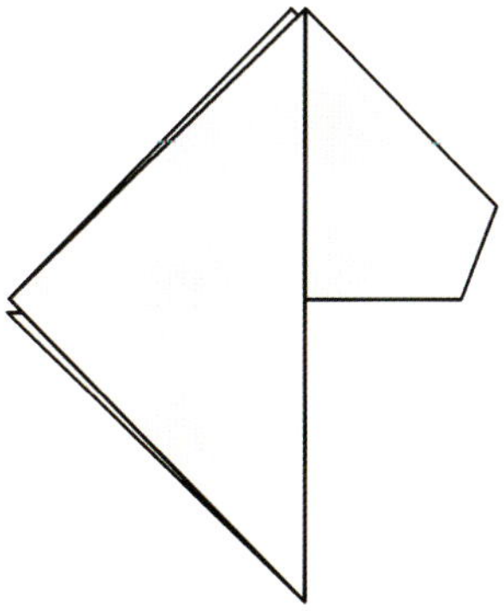

19 The head is finished.

Assembling Horse

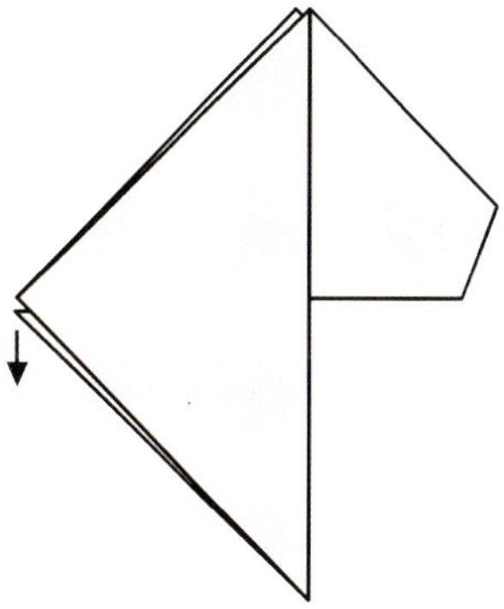

20 To begin assembling the Horse first pull the flap hidden inside the neck downward slightly.

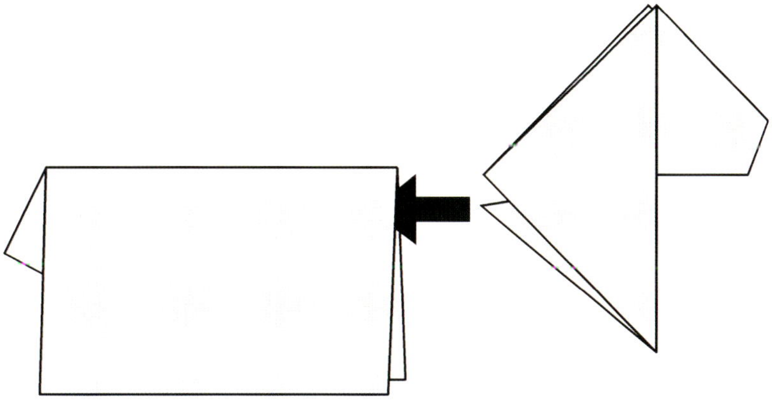

21 Slide the head onto the body like this. The flap inside the neck goes inside the body. The neck itself goes outside.

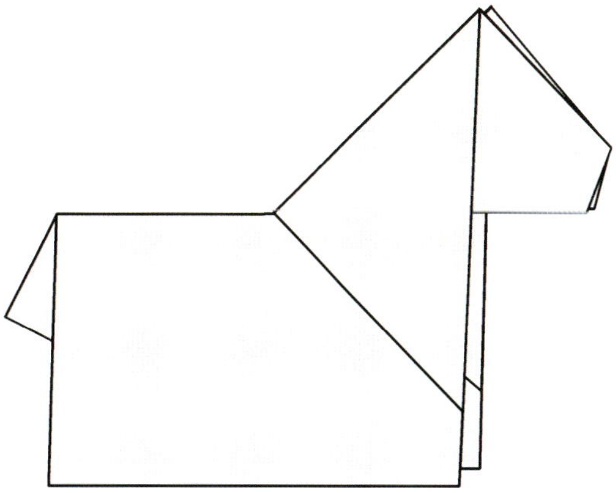

22 Horse is finished.

Fantasy Bat

Many animal origami designs are expressed in a style that is almost cartoon-like, in which the fundamental features that make an animal recognisable are exaggerated and distorted until virtually every element of realism is lost, yet the design remains recognisably what it is intended to be. The Fantasy Bat is a good example of this style. It is interesting to compare the fan-like spread of the wings with the real wing structure of a bat. The Fantasy Bat is also interesting because, for the sake of economy, it is folded from a triangle (created by cutting a square in half along one diagonal). The crucial crease, on which the geometry of the wings is based, is however established before the cut is made. You will need a square of black, gray, or brown paper for each Fantasy Bat. For the best result use fairly stiff paper.

Designed by David Mitchell.

Begin with your paper arranged in the way shown in picture 1.

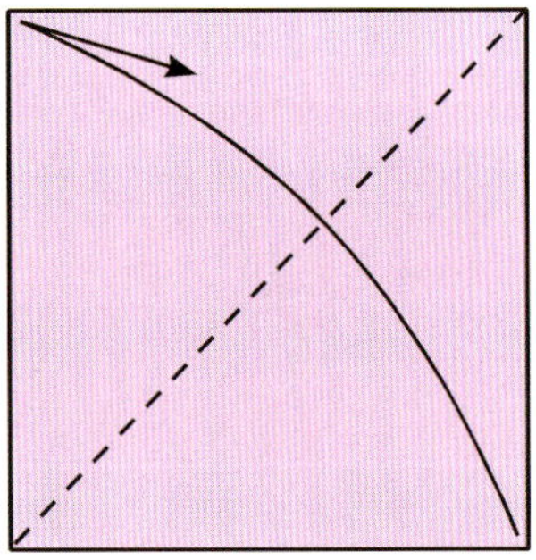

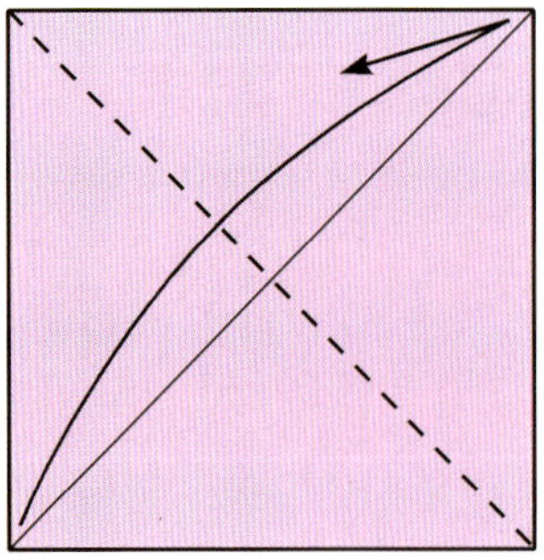

1 Fold in half diagonally as shown, crease firmly, then unfold.

2 Fold in half diagonally in the alternative direction, crease firmly, then unfold.

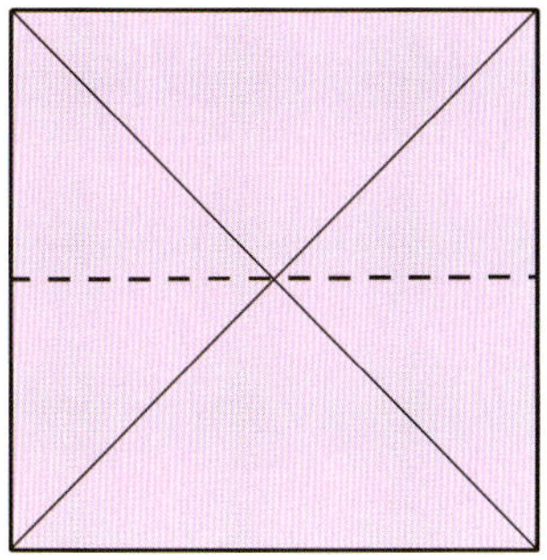

3 Fold in half from top to bottom.

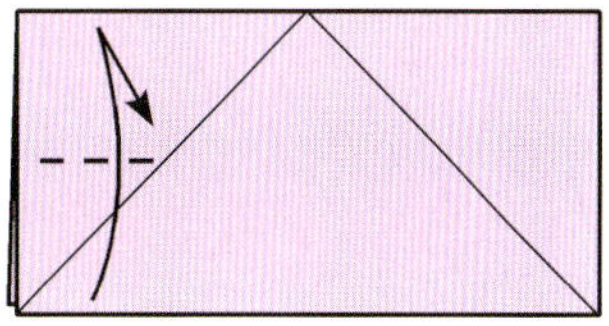

4 Fold the bottom edge onto the top edge, align carefully, make a small crease on the left hand side, then unfold.

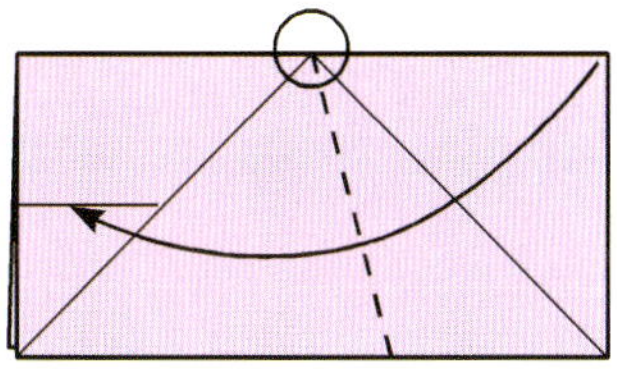

5 Fold the top right-hand corner across to lie on the crease you made in step 4 making sure that the crease passes through the point where the diagonal creases made in steps 1 and 2 intersect the top edge (marked with a circle).

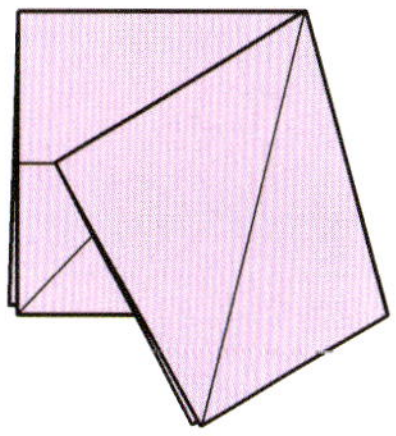

6 Open out completely by undoing the folds made in steps 3 and 5. Make sure you don't turn the paper over as you do this.

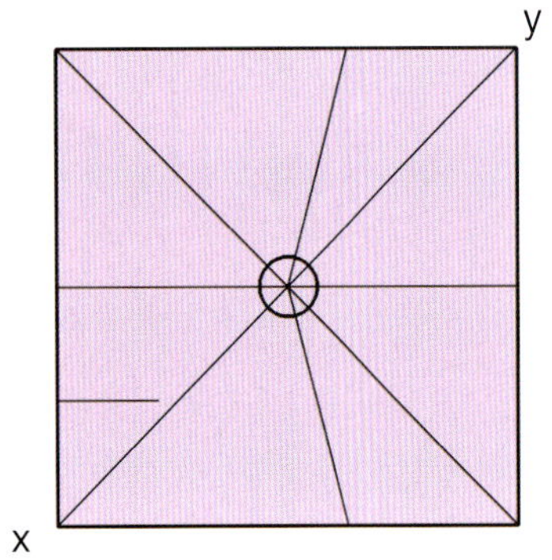

7 Make sure that the creases made in step 5 intersect the diagonal creases in the center of the square. If they don't go back and rework step 5. Once you are happy that your creases are accurate cut the square in half from corner to corner along crease xy. This will divide the square into two triangles. The one you need is the one on the lower right. Arrange this triangle in the way shown in picture 8.

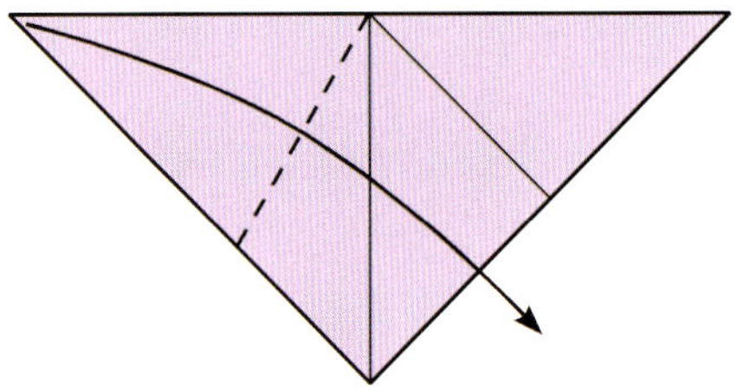

8 Use the crease made in step 5 to fold the left-hand point across to the right.

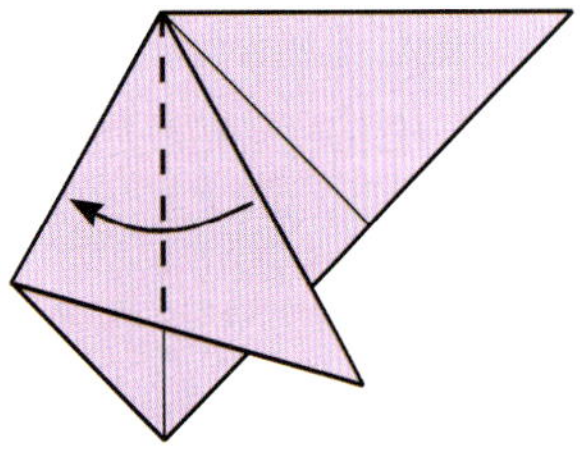

9 Fold the original left-hand point back to the left as shown.

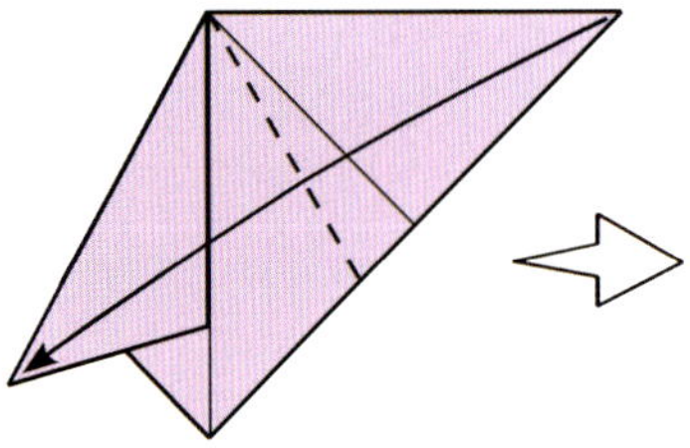

10 Fold the right-hand point onto the original left-hand point. The next picture has been drawn to a larger scale.

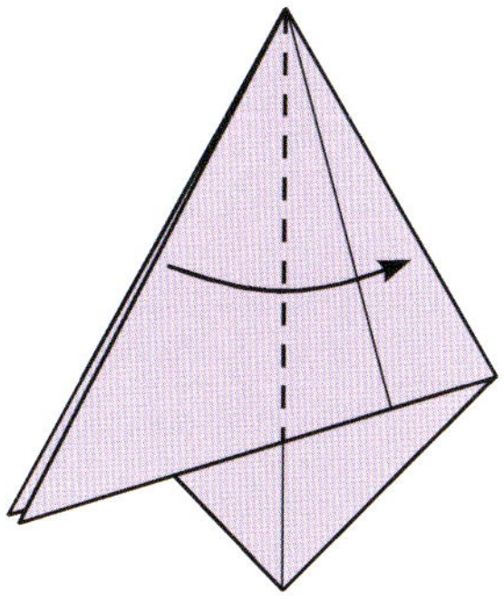

11 This is a repeat of step 9.

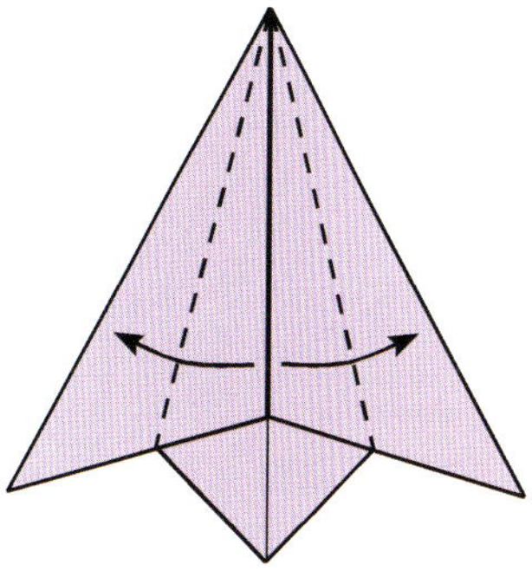

12 Fold the central vertical edges of both triangular flaps out to the sloping right and left-hand edges. Make sure the layers do not slip out of alignment as you make these folds.

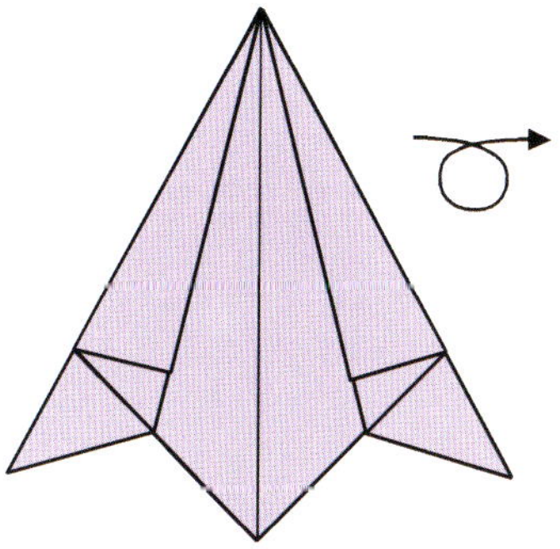

13 Turn over sideways.

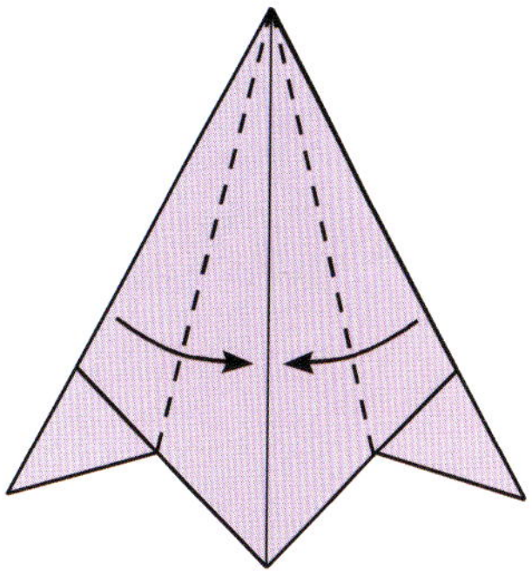

14 Fold the sloping left and right-hand edges to the center. Make these folds firmly through all the layers.

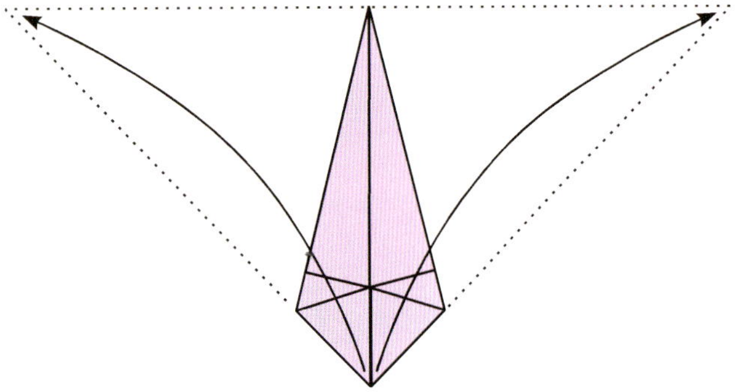

15 Open out completely by pulling the two points at the bottom outward and upward, then smooth out the creases so that the paper lies reasonably flat. Make sure you don't turn the paper over as you do this.

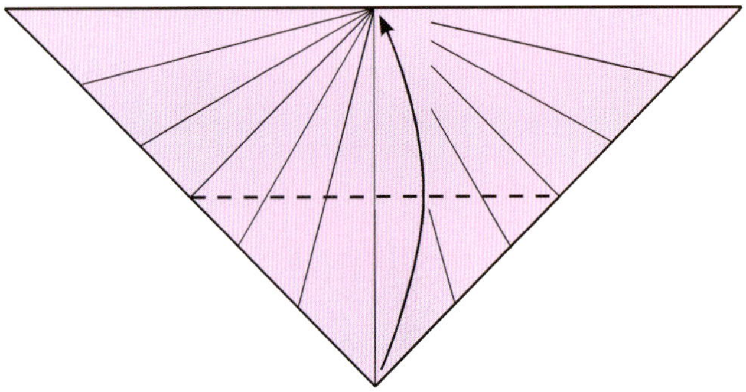

16 Fold the bottom point up to the center of the top edge. For the sake of clarity some parts of some of the creases have been omitted from this drawing.

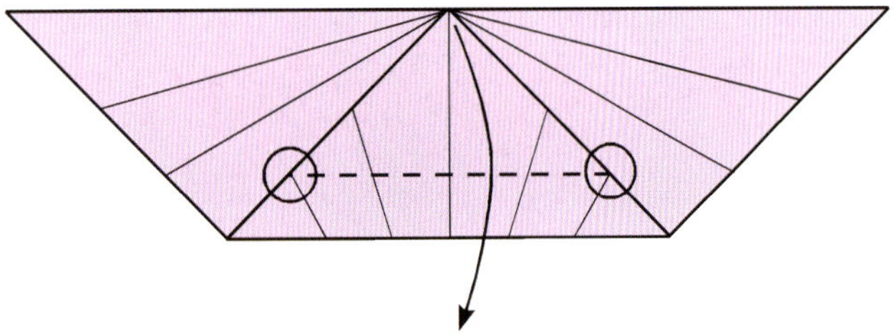

17 Fold the same point downward again in the way shown here, using the intersections of creases and edges marked with circles as location points.

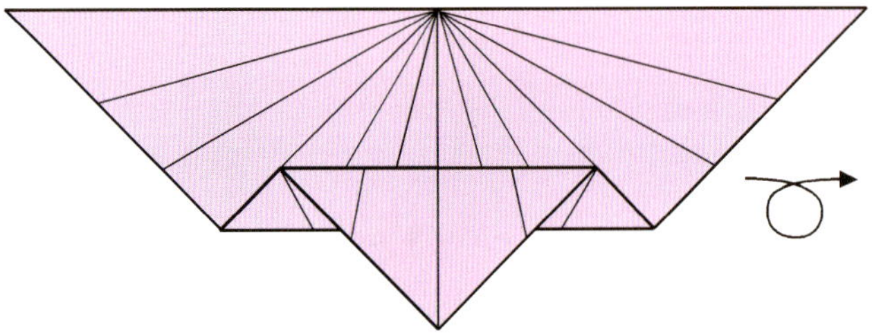

18 Turn over forward.

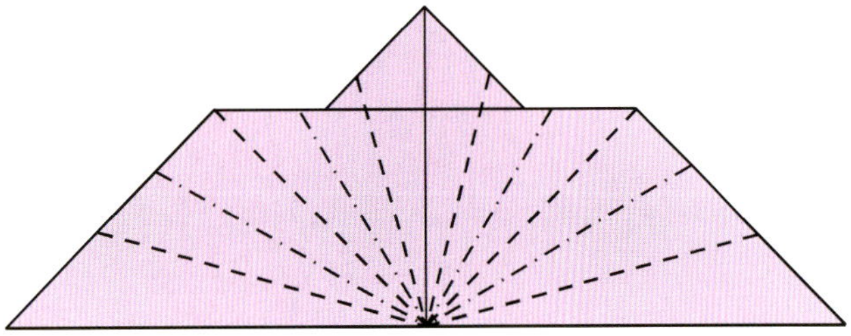

19 Fold the wings up like fans. All the creases you need are already there although you will need to make some of them through new layers of paper and reverse the direction of others.

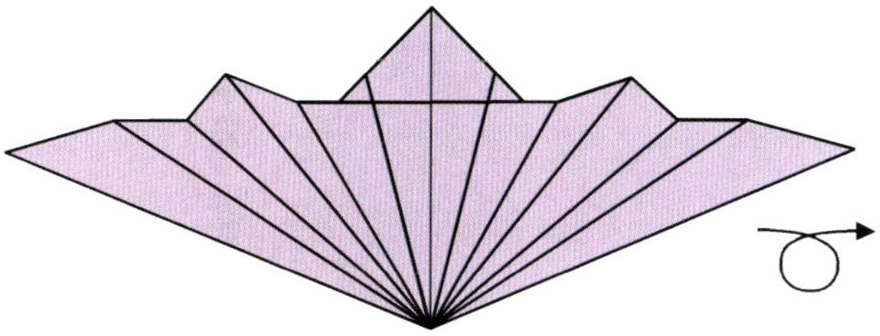

20 Turn over sideways.

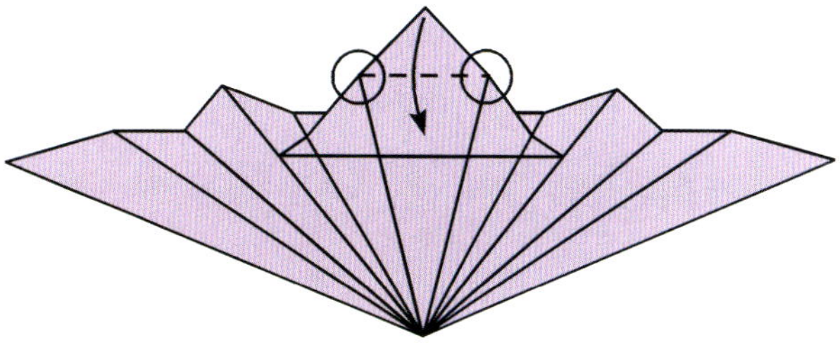

21 Fold the top point downward to form the face.

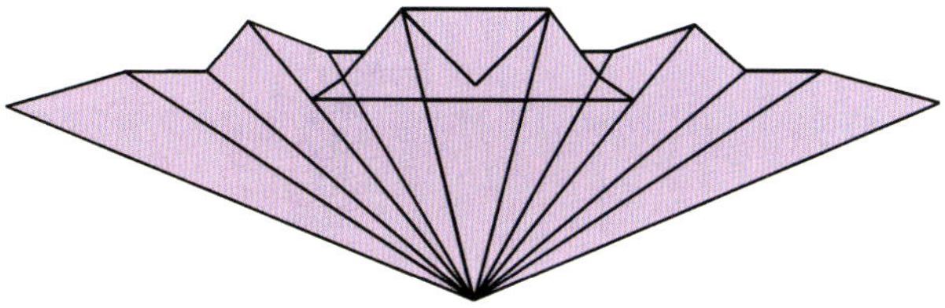

22 This is the result. There are just three tiny finishing folds to make.

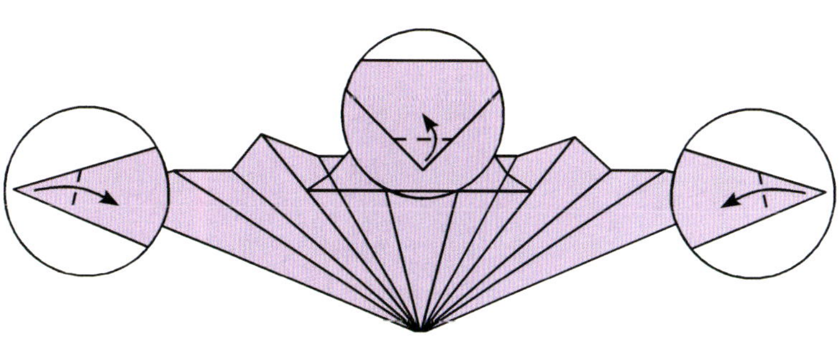

23 Fold up the tip of the nose and fold both wing tips inward. Finally pose the wings to taste.

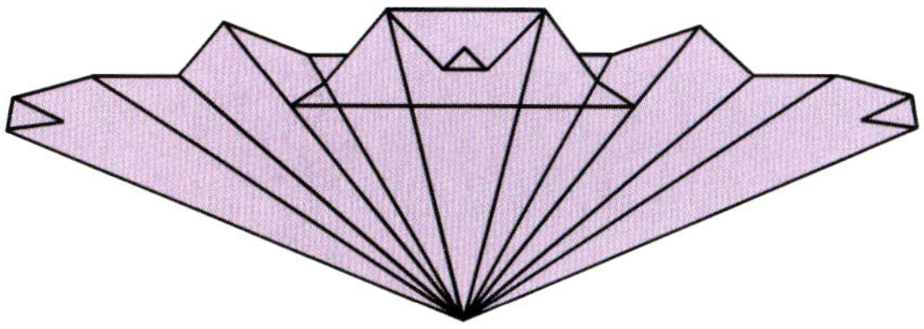

24 The Fantasy Bat is finished.

Grazing Buffalo

The Grazing Buffalo is one of the very few simple animal designs which represent the subject in a naturalistic pose. The Grazing Buffalo is designed with its nose to the ground, clearly grazing in fact. Apart from the horns, which can be curled and twisted in many different ways, the overall impression of the design is one of power and bulk. It is very square-cornered until the final three small shaping folds have been made.

This design features a move known to paperfolders as a closed sink (you will find it in step 20. It's the middle fold of the three). Closed sinks are a notoriously difficult type of fold but fortunately this particular one is easy.

You will need a square of brown paper for each Grazing Buffalo. For the best result use fairly thin paper.

Designed by David Mitchell.

Begin with your paper arranged in the way shown in picture 1.

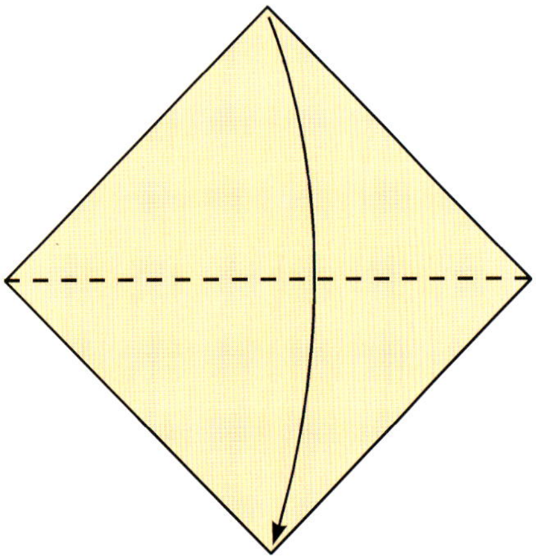

1 Fold in half diagonally from top to bottom.

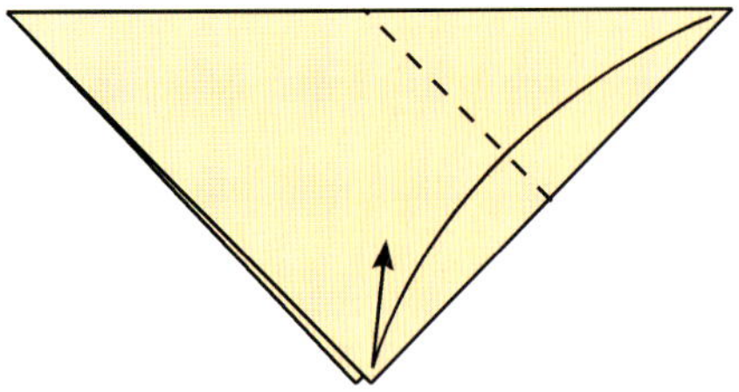

2 Fold the right-hand corner down to lie on top of the bottom corner, crease firmly, then unfold.

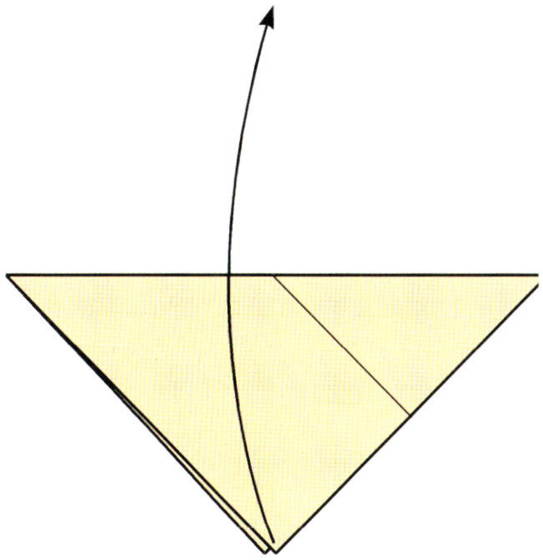

3 Open out the fold made in step 1.

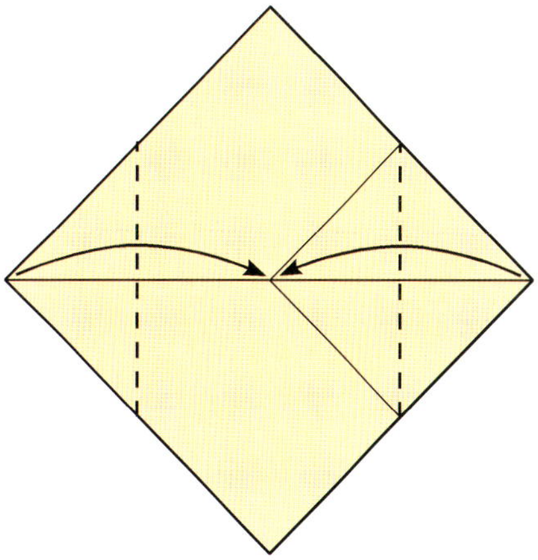

4 Fold the left and right-hand corner into the center.

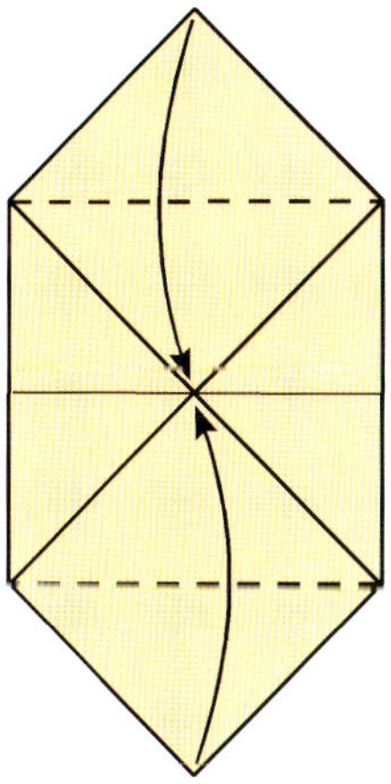

5 Fold the top and bottom corners into the center.

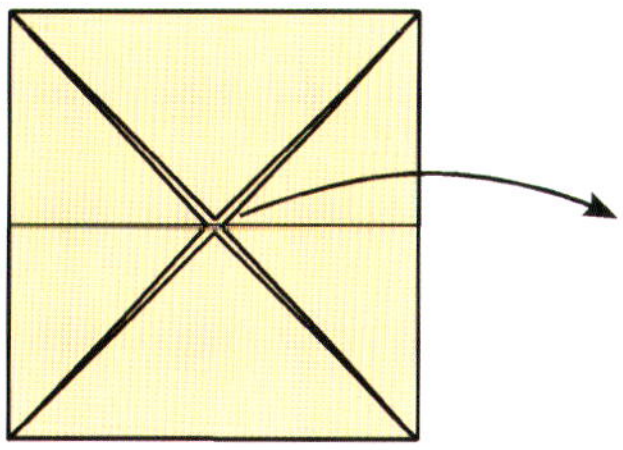

6 In technical origami language this is known as a blintzed square. Open out the right-hand blintz.

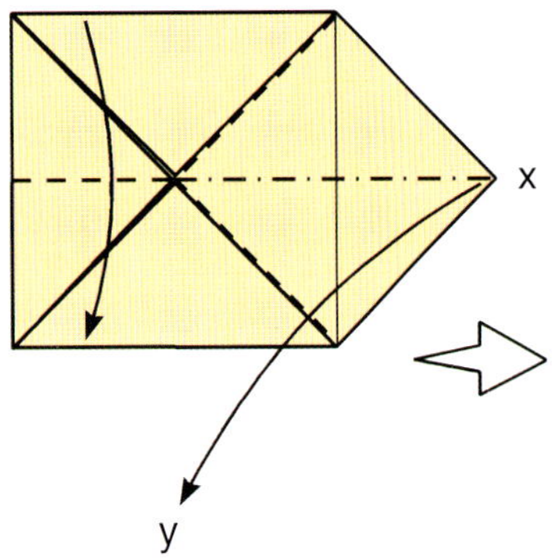

7 Fold in half top to bottom while simultaneously folding point x to y. All the creases you need are already there. Picture 8 shows what the result should look like.

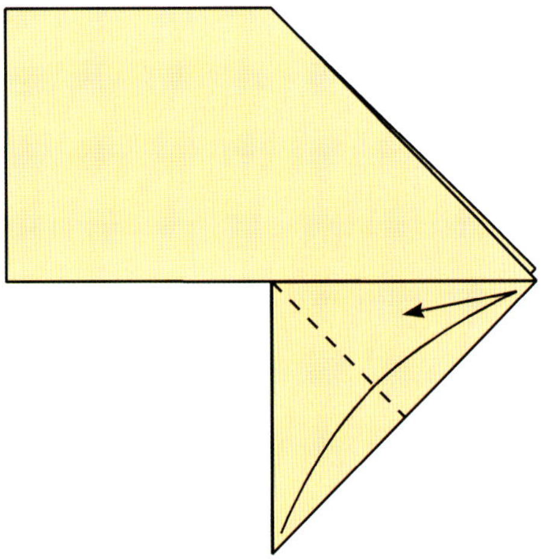

8 This picture is drawn on a larger scale. Fold the triangular flap in half as shown, crease firmly, then unfold.

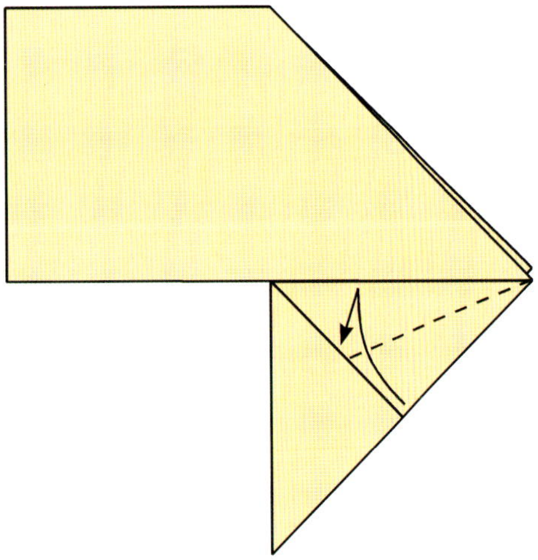

9 Fold, crease firmly, then unfold as shown. Try not to allow this new crease to cross the line of the existing crease made in step 8.

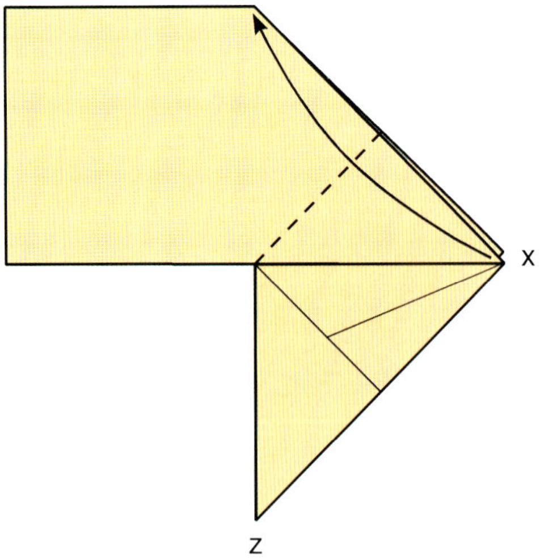

10 This fold is only made in the top layer of the paper. As you flatten the paper after making the fold point z will end up at point x. Crease firmly.

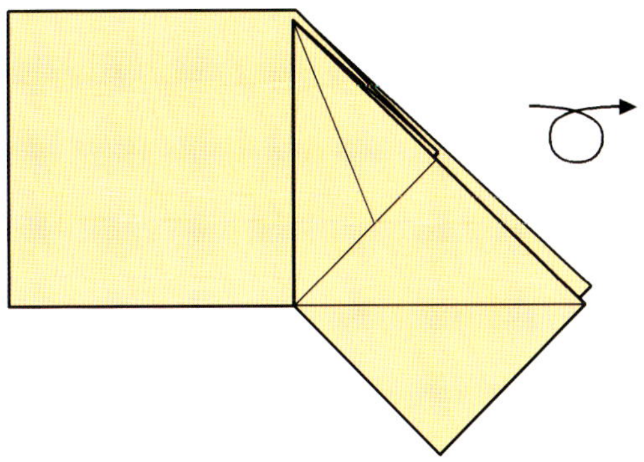

11 Turn over sideways.

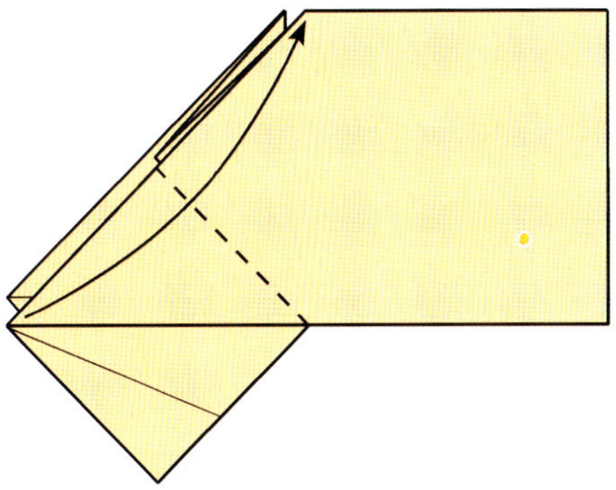

12 Repeat step 10 on this side of the design. Picture 13 shows what the result should look like.

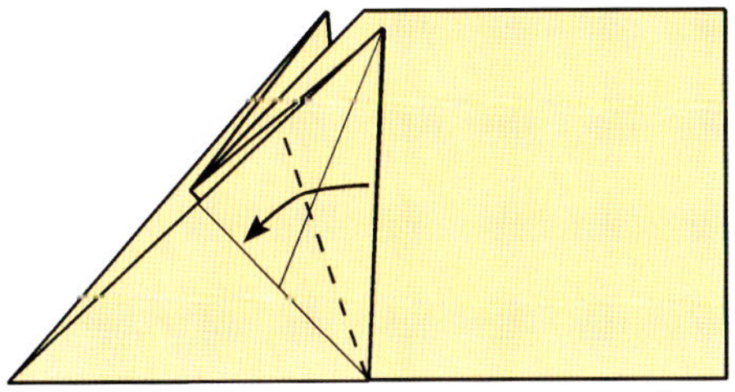

13 Fold the right-hand edge of the triangular flap across to lie on top of the diagonal crease. Crease firmly.

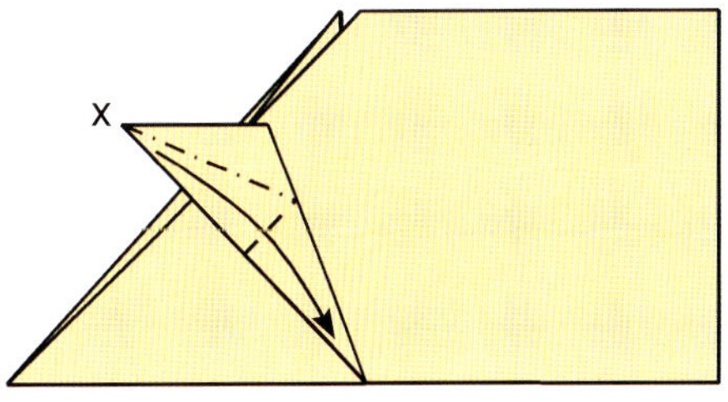

14 Fold point x to point y, flatten, and crease firmly. Picture 15 shows what the result should look like. In technical origami language this procedure is known as forming a Rabbit's Ear.

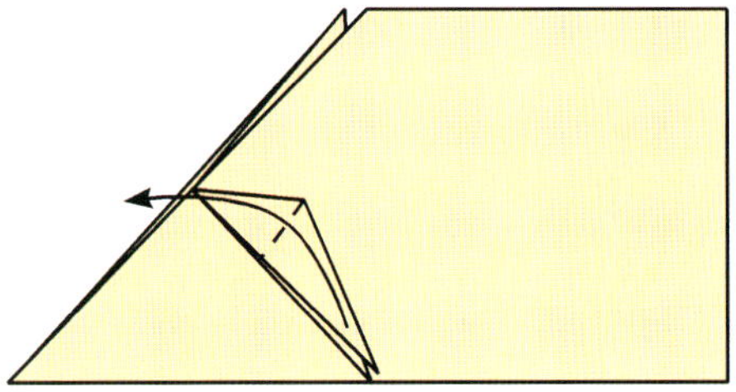

15 Fold the tip of the horn forward as shown. Picture 16 shows what the result should look like.

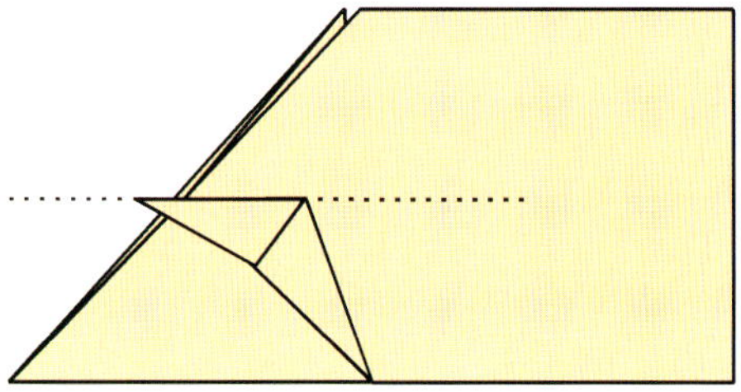

16 Try to make sure the top edge of the horn is roughly parallel to the bottom edge of the design. Crease firmly, then turn over sideways.

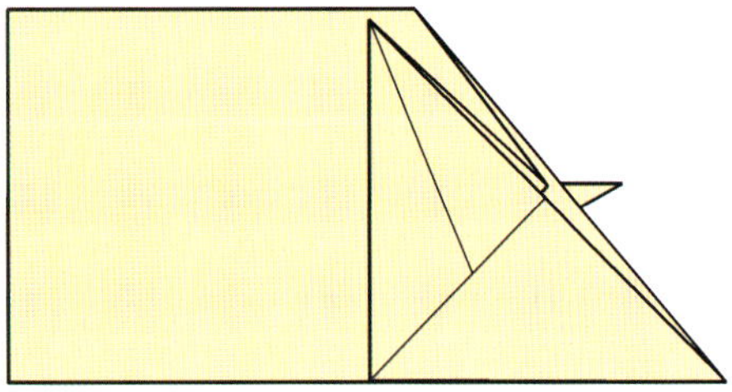

17 Repeat steps 13 through 15 on this side of the design to form the second horn.

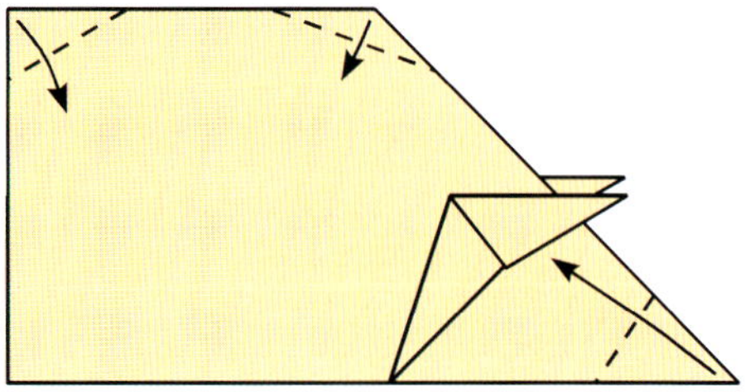

18 Make these three small shaping folds as shown.

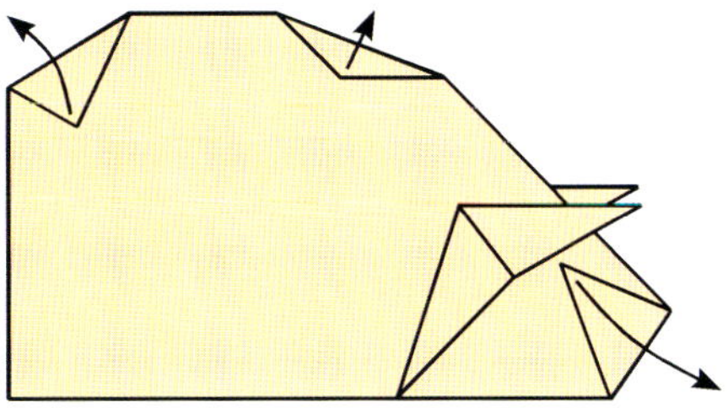

19 Open out the folds made in step 18.

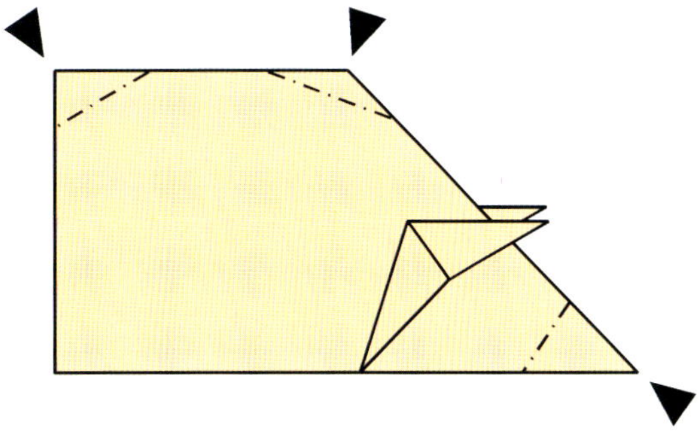

20 Turn these three points inside out in between the layers of the body and head using the creases made in step 18. You will find that in order to turn the crease that shapes the shoulders inside out you will need to push a finger up inside the design to spread the layers apart.

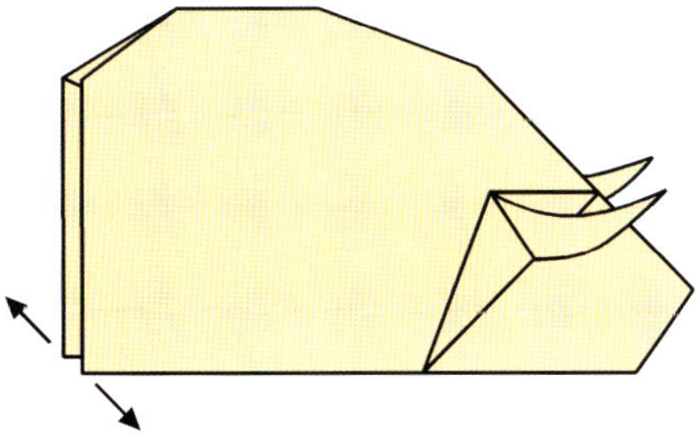

21 Curl and twist the horns to taste and spread the back of the design slightly so that it will stand. The Grazing Buffalo is complete.

Mouse

The Mouse is essentially a very similar design to the Grazing Buffalo, though it looks very different because the elements are developed in different ways. The horns are replaced by ears, the flap hidden inside the body (unused in the Grazing Buffalo design) is developed into a tail, and the small fold that blunts the nose is omitted entirely.

From a paperfolding connoisseurs point of view however the most interesting aspect of the design is the final subtle rearrangement of folds that locks the layers together at the top of the head. You will have fun with this!

You will need a square of black, gray, or brown paper for each Mouse. For the best result use fairly thin paper.

Designed by David Mitchell.

Begin with your paper arranged in the way shown in picture 1.

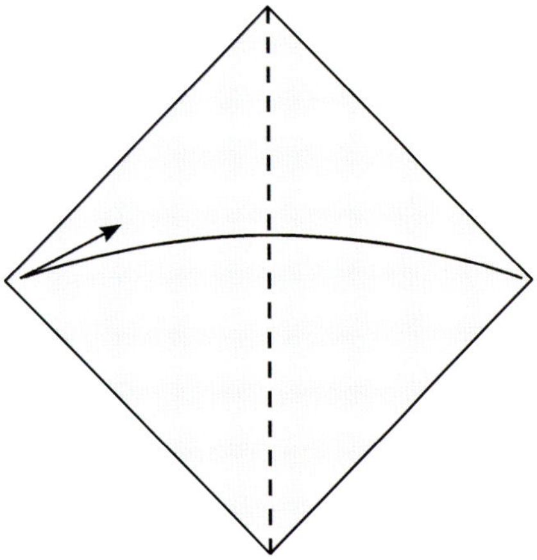

1 Fold in half from right to left, crease firmly, then unfold.

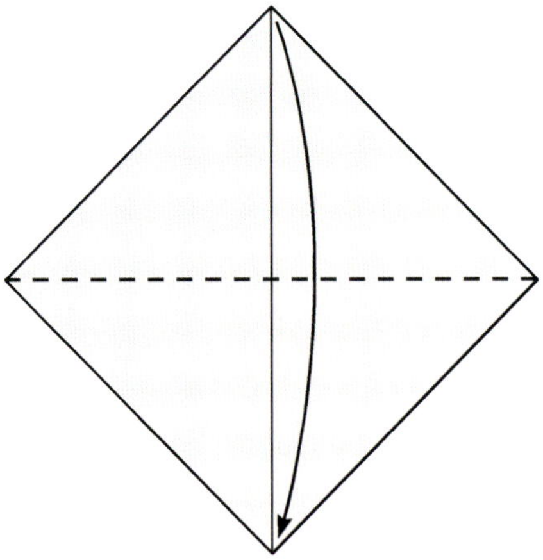

2 Fold in half from top to bottom. Crease firmly.

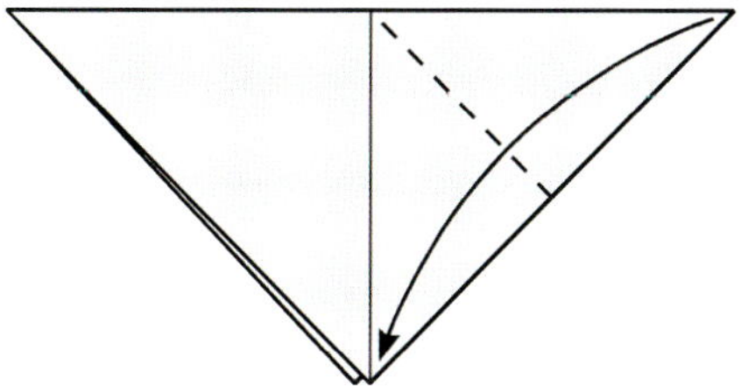

3 Fold the right-hand corner down to lie on top of the bottom corner.

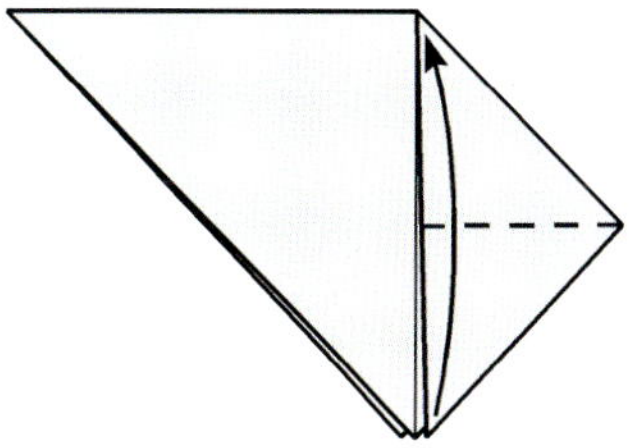

4 Fold the triangular flap in half upward.

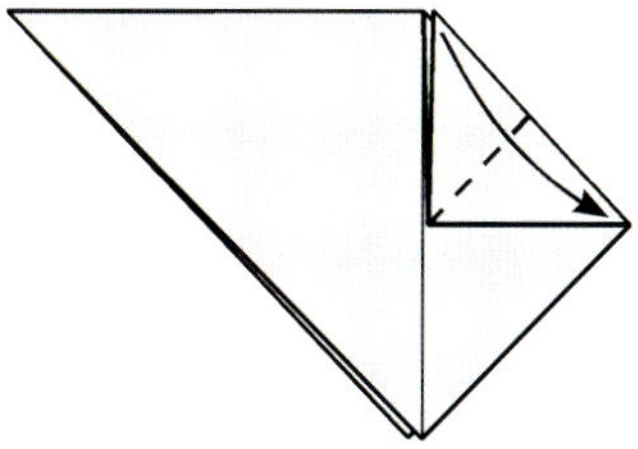

5 Fold this new triangular flap in half as well.

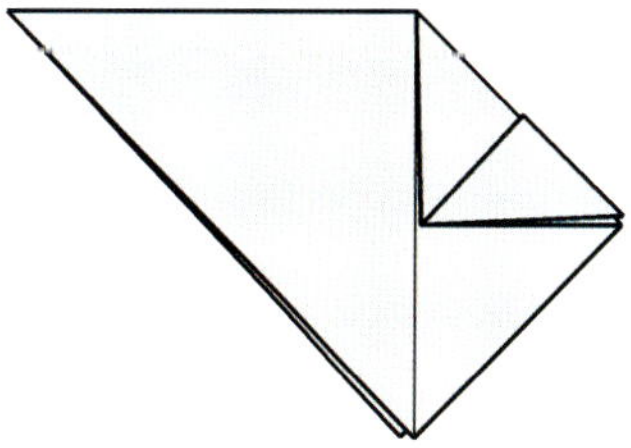

6 Make sure all the creases made in steps 3 through 5 are really sharp, then unfold completely, making sure you don't turn the paper over as you do so.

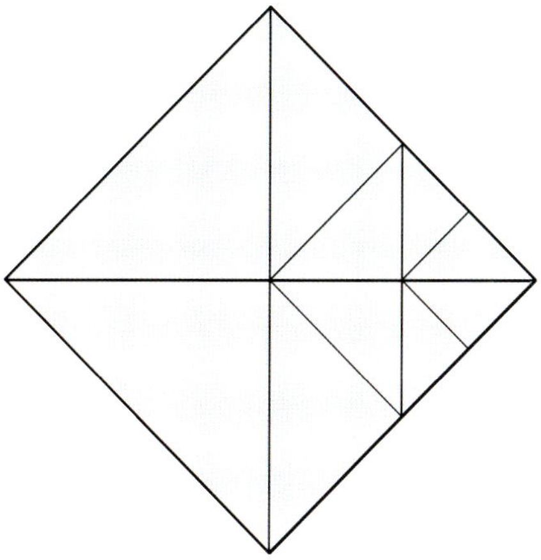

7 Before moving on to step 8 check that you have made all the creases shown here.

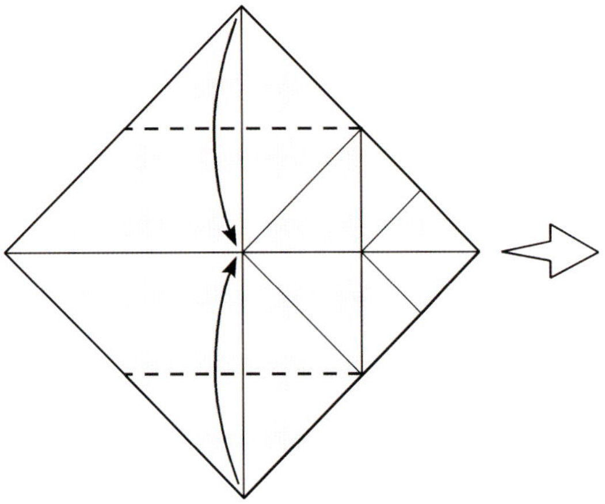

8 Fold the top and bottom corners into the center of the design. The next picture has been drawn to a larger scale.

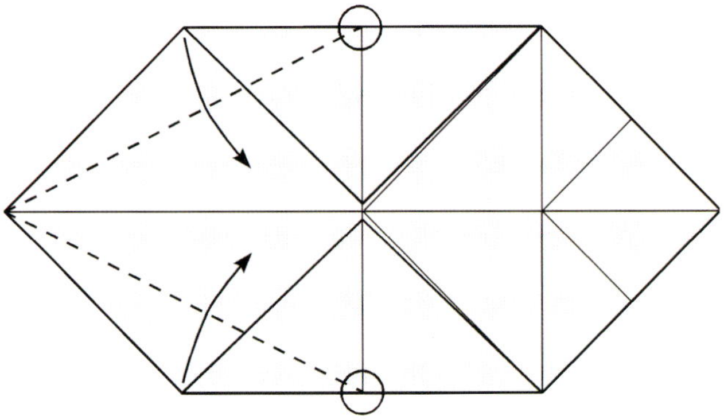

9 Begin to form the tail by making these two folds. Note that the creases should run from the tip of the right-hand point of the design to the intersections of the vertical crease made in step 1 with the edges of the paper (marked with circles). It is very important to make these folds as accurately as possible.

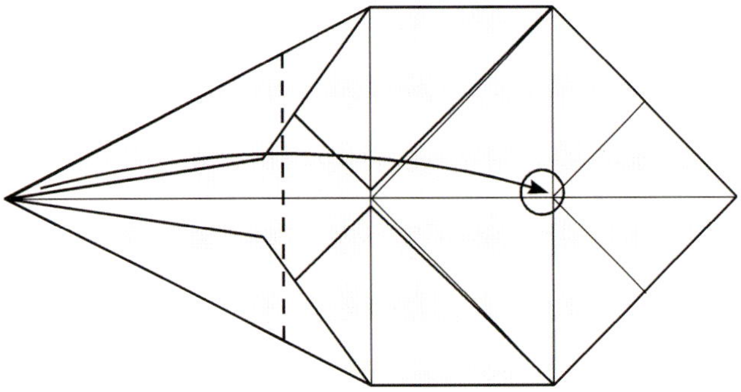

10 Fold the tip of the tail across to the left as shown. Picture 11 shows what the result should look like.

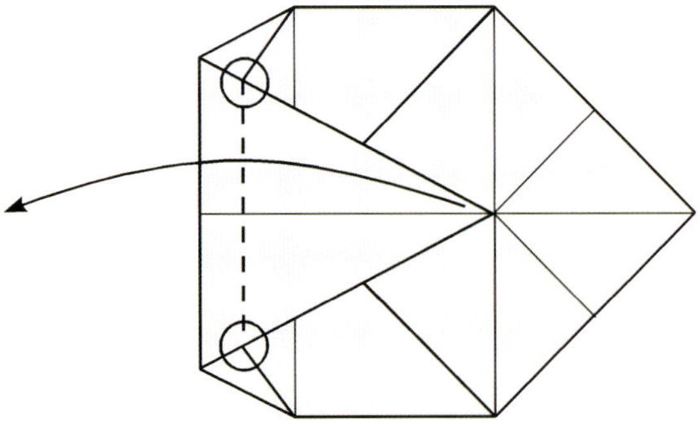

11 Fold the tip of the tail back out to the right. The circles show how the crease is located. Picture 12 shows what the result should look like.

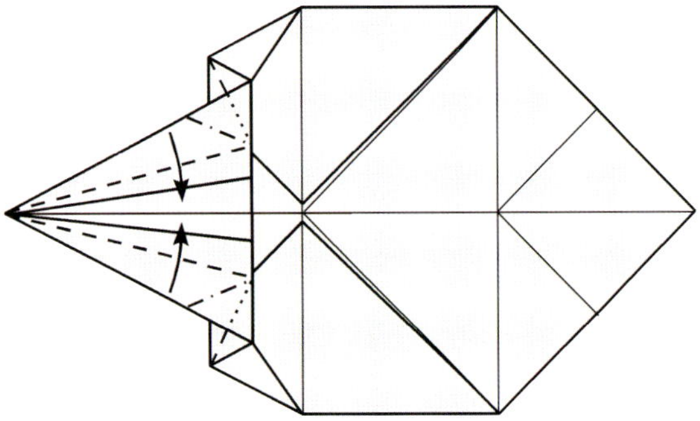

12 Narrow the tail by folding both edges to the horizontal crease in turn. You will find that in order to flatten the paper you need to make two more tiny folds at the base of the tail. Picture 13 shows how these folds should be arranged.

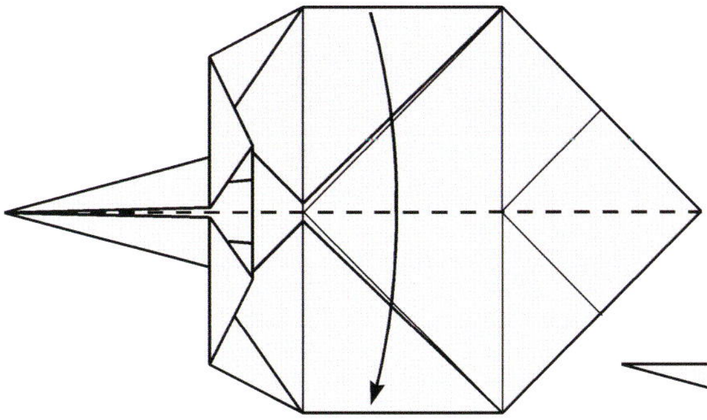

13 The tail is finished. Fold in half from top to bottom.

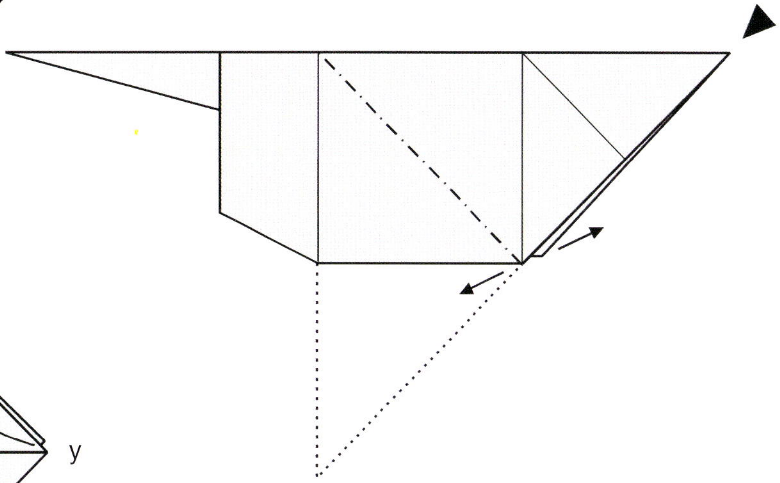

14 Turn the left-hand point inside out between the layers of the design using the crease made in step 3. The dotted line shows where the point should end up.

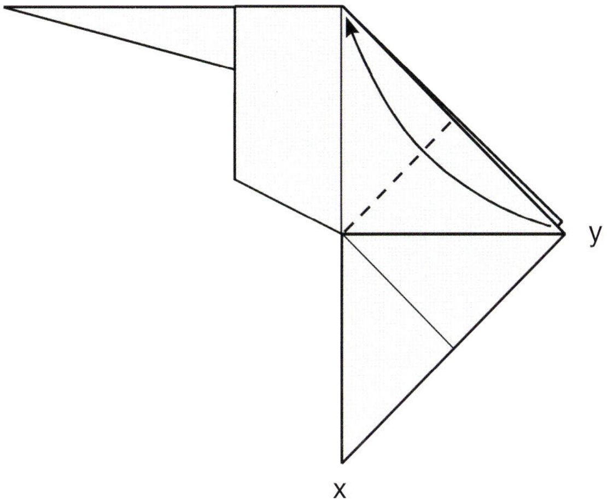

15 This fold is only made in the top layers of the paper. As you flatten the paper after making the fold point x will end up at point y. Crease firmly.

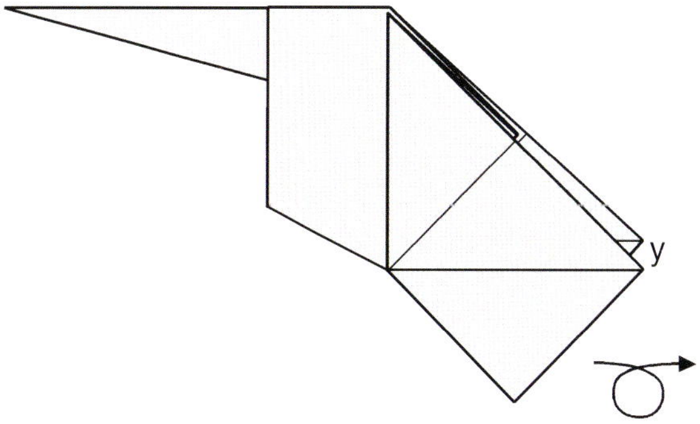

16 Turn over sideways.

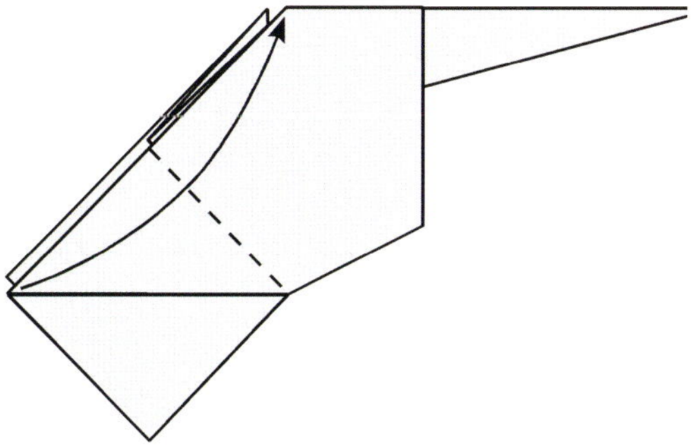

17 Repeat step 15 on this side of the design. Picture 18 shows what the result should look like.

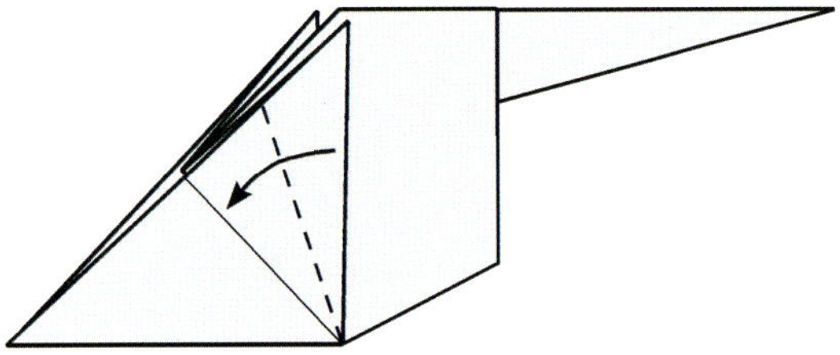

18 Form the first ear by folding the right-hand edge of the triangular flap across to lie on top of the diagonal crease. Crease firmly.

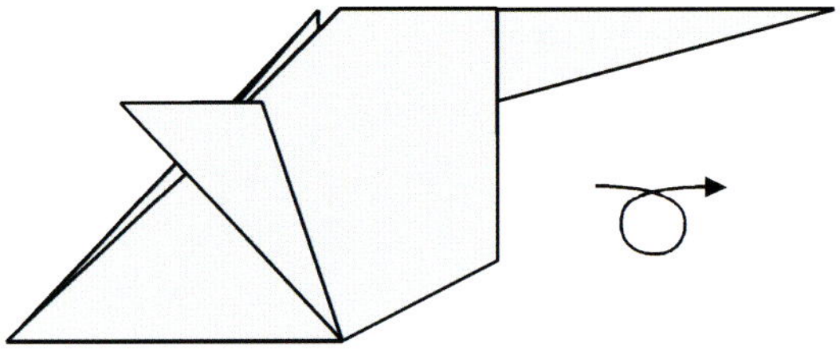

19 Turn over sideways.

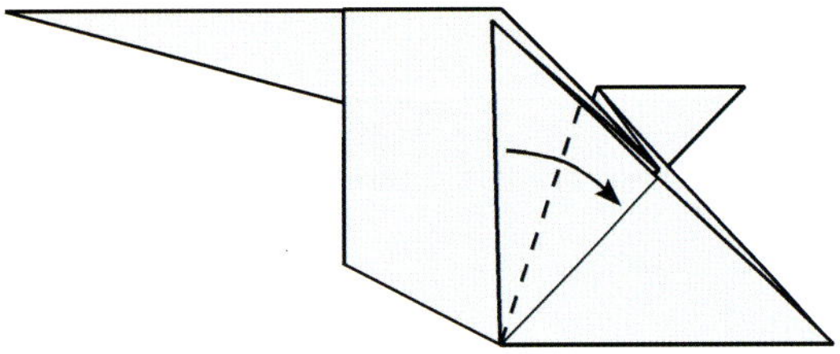

20 Repeat step 18 on this side of the paper.

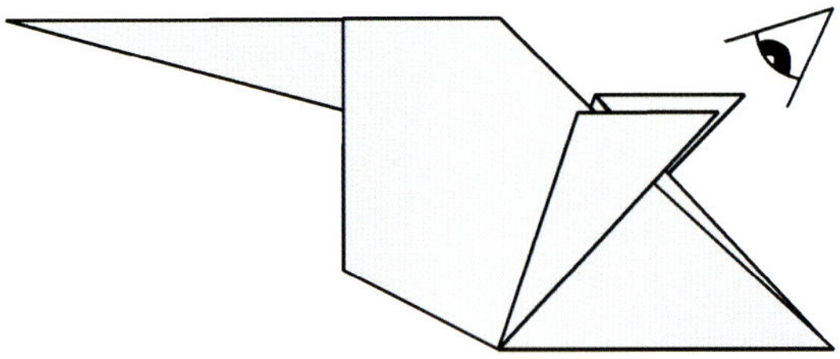

21 The next picture shows the view from above the ears.

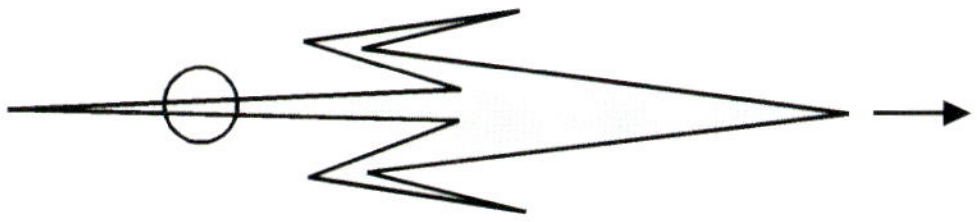

22 Hold the top of the body in the place marked with a circle and pull gently on the nose. The layers inside the ears will pull out.

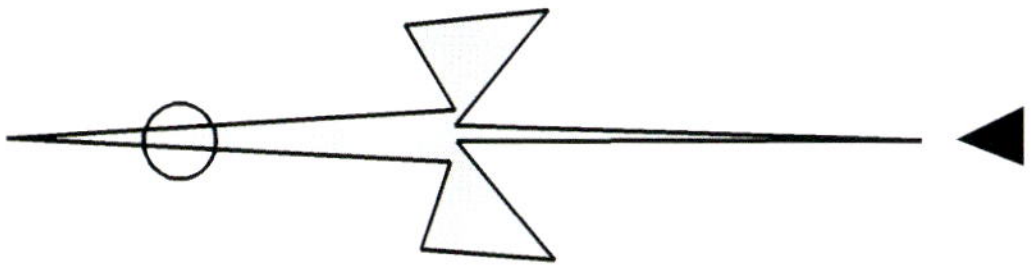

23 Now push the nose gently back into position making sure that the inner layers of the ears go in between the layers of the body.

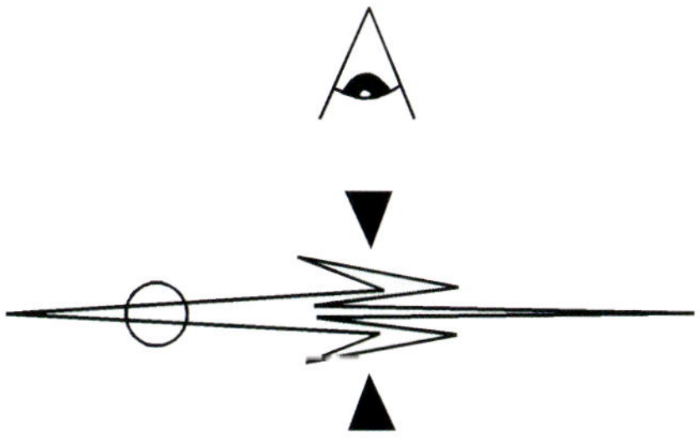

24 This is the result. Gently squash flat. The tension in the creases will hold the two sides of the head together.

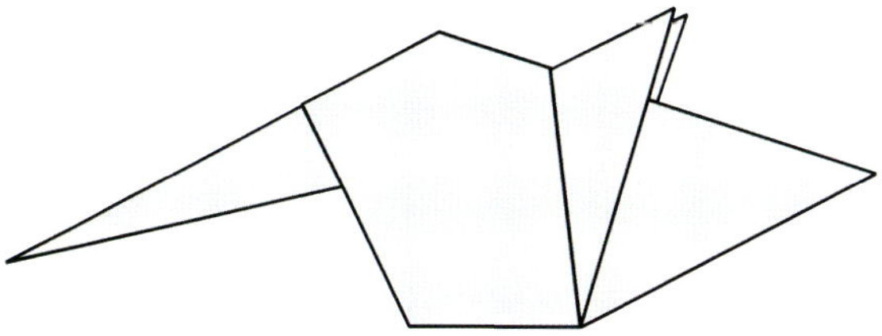

25 Mouse is finished.

Bull's Head

The Bull's Head is included to show you what can be achieved using white paper that has been overprinted with a single plain color on just one side. Much commercial origami paper is of this kind. The advantage of using this kind of paper is that the contrast between the two sides can be used to draw a picture (or, in more complex designs, to realistically model the color pattern of an animal like a Panda or Zebra).

The Bull's Head is a very simple fold of this kind, but it is an attractive one since, as the instructions show, it can be folded front side down so that the picture is not revealed until the design is turned over at the end.

You will need a square of differentiated paper, white on one side and black or brown on the other. Paper of this kind is normally fairly thin.

Designed by David Mitchell.

Begin with the paper white side up and arranged in the way shown in picture 1.

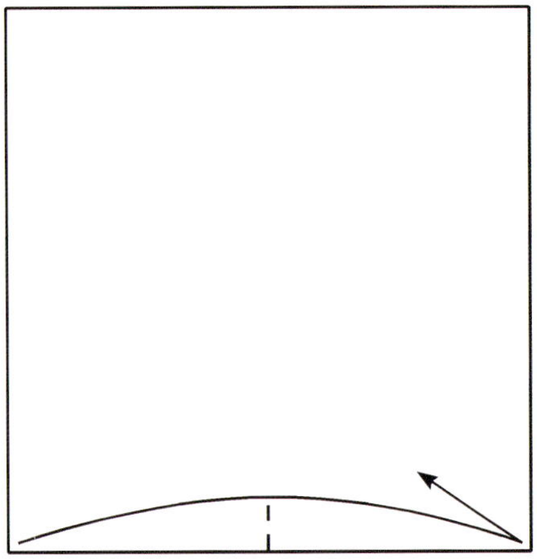

1 Gently pinch in the half-way point. (This step may be omitted for a cleaner result.)

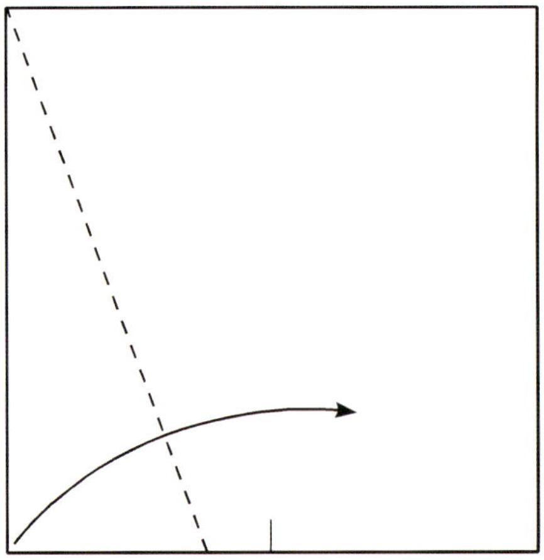

2 Fold the bottom right-hand corner across as shown. If you have made the pinch in step 1 you can use it to help you position folds 2 and 3 symmetrically.

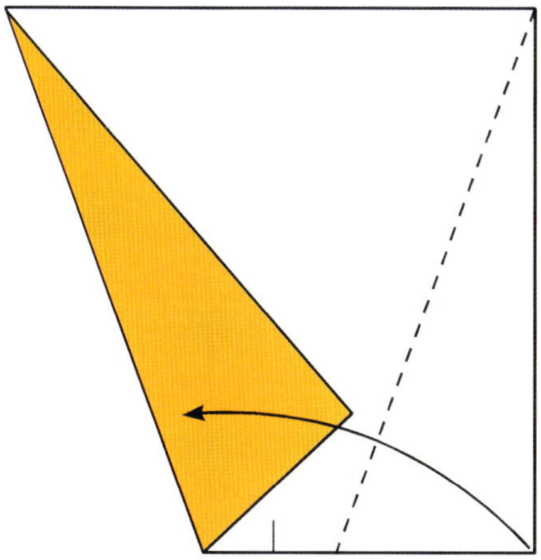

3 This fold should be made as a mirror image of the fold you made in step 2.

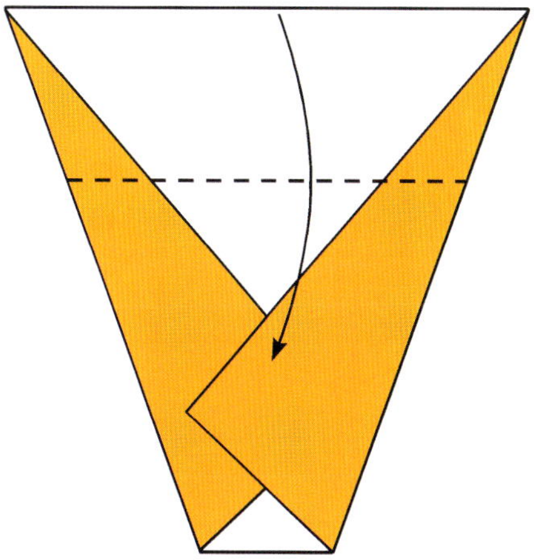

4 Fold the top edge downward as shown. Picture 5 shows what the result should look like.

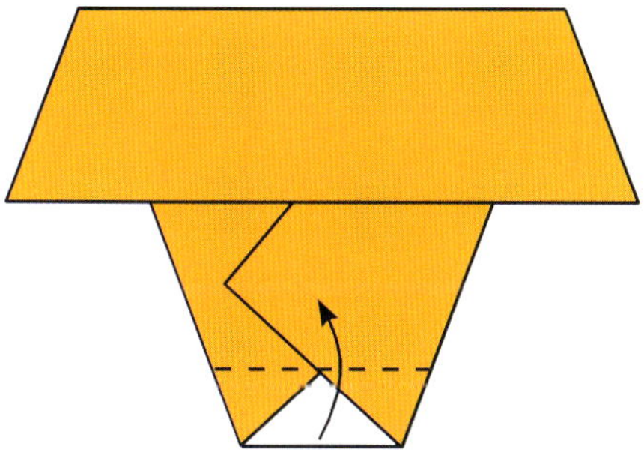

5 Fold the bottom edge upward. This fold is made just fractionally above the point of the white triangle.

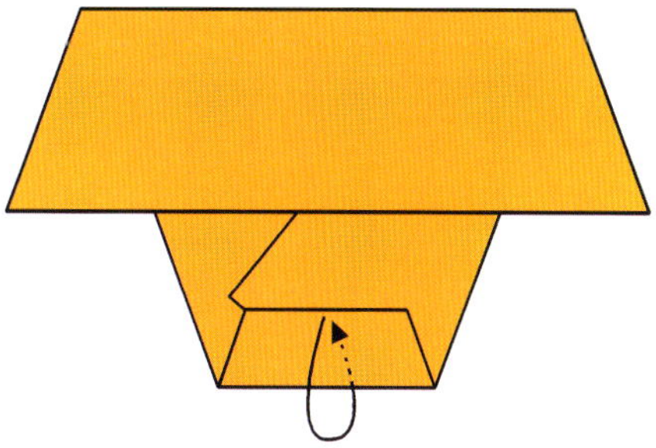

6 Swing the bottom flap out of sight using the crease made in step 5 as a hinge. Crease firmly then turn over sideways.

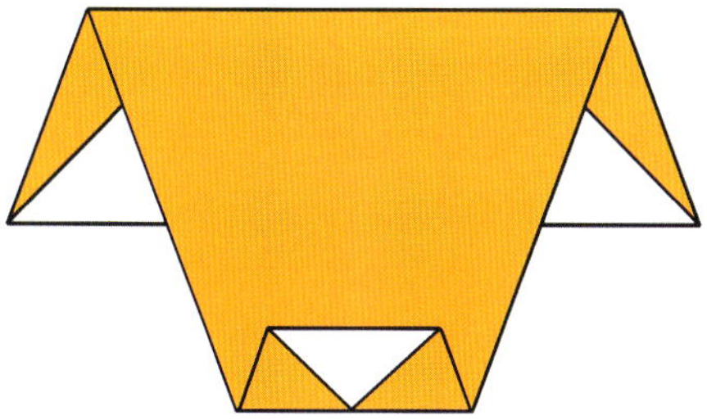

7 The Bull's Head is finished.

Acknowledgments

Paperfolding designers stand firmly on each others shoulders. The author is particularly indebted to all those anonymous and unsung paperfolders whose memorial is the portfolio of traditional origami designs that continue to bring so much pleasure to so many people every year. Such a debt can scarcely be acknowledged let alone repaid.

The author is also particularly indebted to:

David Brill, Wayne Brown, Nick Robinson and Paul Jackson (who taught me to value simplicity).

Akira Yoshizawa (for the inspiration of his compound animal designs).

Tung Ken Lam (for finding the Rooster).

Michael Shall (who was the first to praise the pig).

Picture Acknowledgments
All photographs © Chrysalis Image Library/Simon Clay with the exception of the following: © Chrysalis Image Library / Eddie MacDonald 40, 46, 76.

All illustrations © Chrysalis Image Library / David Mitchell.